The Faith of Israel
Its Expression in the Books of the Old Testament

William J. Dumbrell

BAKER BOOK HOUSE
Grand Rapids, Michigan 49516

Library of Congress Cataloging-in-Publication Data

Dumbrell, William J.
    The faith of Israel.

    Bibliography: p.
    1. Bible.   O.T.—Theology.   I. Title.
BS1192.5.D86   1988   221.6   88–22312
ISBN 0–8010–2976–7

The Faith of Israel

Contents

Abbreviations

ABR	*Australian Biblical Review*
Bib	*Biblica*
BibSac	*Bibliotheca Sacra*
CBQ	*Catholic Biblical Quarterly*
ConBibOT	Coniectanea Biblica, Old Testament Series
EJ	*Encyclopaedia Judaica*
HTR	*Harvard Theological Review*
HUCA	*Hebrew Union College Annual*
IDBSup	Supplementary volume to *Interpreter's Dictionary of the Bible*
IEJ	*Israel Exploration Journal*
Int	*Interpretation*
JAAR	*Journal of the American Academy of Religion*
JBL	*Journal of Biblical Literature*
JJS	*Journal of Jewish Studies*

JSOT	Journal for the Study of the Old Testament
JSS	Journal of Semitic Studies
JTS	Journal of Theological Studies
NICOT	New International Commentary on the Old Testament
OTWSA	Die Ou-Testamentiese Werkgemeenskap in Suid-Afrika
RB	Revue biblique
RTR	Reformed Theological Review
SEÅ	Svensk exegetisk årsbok
TynB	Tyndale Bulletin
VT	Vetus Testamentum
VTSup	VT Supplement
ZAW	Zeitschrift für die alttestamentliche Wissenschaft

Introduction

In writing this introduction to the Old Testament, I endeavor particularly to bring the theological purpose of the respective Old Testament books into clear focus. The authors of the biblical materials had defined objectives in mind. The present work seeks to come to terms with such objectives and to present the theology underlying them. In the case of some books, such as Exodus or Kings on the one hand, and Isaiah or Ezekiel on the other, the purpose of the writer is not difficult to present. Both Exodus, with its movement from slavery to worship, and Kings, with its review of the monarchical period from Solomon to the fall of the Davidic dynasty, offer a theological assessment of a period in Israel's history. Isaiah with its Jerusalem emphasis, and Ezekiel with its concern for the temple, both offer a prophetic reaction to one of Israel's important symbols. When such overmastering concepts of purpose may be clearly discerned, the task of the reader is to bear these in mind as the respective books are being studied. In the case of other books, such as Deuteronomy (which draws the themes of the Pentateuch together), Psalms, or the wisdom literature, anthological interests account for the content. Themes, rather than a consistent single emphasis, need thus to be presented.

Israel's confessional faith came to her progressively and through history. Seminal for the introduction of theological concepts in the Old Testament are the five books of the Pentateuch and the works that are our canonical Former Prophets (Joshua to 2 Kings). These books provide the basis of Israel's faith, particularly her covenantal understanding of her relationship with Yahweh. The prophetic books are an attempt to turn refractory Israel back to the basis of her faith. Speaking generally, the prophetic books interpret and apply theological truth to their own age but do not in the main add to Israel's theological understanding. The same may be said of Psalms and the wisdom literature.

The account of the faith of Israel begins with the fact of creation itself and with a description of divine intention for the world. Israel's covenant experience therefore operates within this broader understanding of more comprehensive divine purpose. Israel wrote her confessional faith this way to indicate that the redemptive emphasis of her special relationship with Yahweh had wider ends in mind, namely, the achievement of Yahweh's saving purposes for the world at large. In this wider concept of purpose Israel was to be Yahweh's special witness. Of course the Christology of the New Testament explains more particularly the manner in which the divine purpose, made clear in Genesis 1–2 for the world, will be achieved. With the expectation of the advent of the new creation, the New Testament ends (Rev. 21–22).

The Old Testament ends with the expectation of a new covenant to be erected. Malachi, which concludes the Greek Old Testament, anticipates the return of Elijah, a major covenantal figure. Chronicles, which ends the Hebrew canon, finishes with the decree of Cyrus the Persian by which the Babylonian exile was ended and Israel returned to her land. By this concluding emphasis Chronicles raises hopes of the fulfilment of the expectations generated by Isaiah 40–66: a return to the Promised Land, which will usher in a new covenant and then a new creation. Both the Greek and Hebrew canons thus end with material which draws striking attention to covenantal expectations. The Old Testament as a whole is a record of how Israel's thinking advanced from creation to covenant at Sinai to a new covenant calculated to lead to a new creation. We must be aware of this theological progression and the reasons for it as we read the literature.

It may be objected that, in such a review, Israel's faith has been substituted for Israel's history and thus for reality. Chronologically, it is often suggested that a belief in creation is a late item, stemming in fact from the experience of the Babylonian exile. Such an assertion is open to argument, but the point of the Old Testament canonical presentation remains the same. Israel's covenant at Sinai has to be finally understood by the logical and theological precedence of creation. Exodus, in short, must be preceded by Genesis. Yet this precedence given to creation is a faith assertion, since the major Old Testament presentation of Israel's history insists and underscores that Israel's role and experience can be understood only against the background of the Sinai experience.

In the final analysis, any theology of the Old Testament had best adhere to the Hebrew canonical sequence of Law, Prophets, and Writings, since this is the manner in which Israel presented her faith. Much attention has been given in recent years to the question of a center for Old Testament theology. In view of the canonical (and, I would argue, the historical) unfolding of Israel's faith, such a search for a center becomes illusory and unnecessary. To be rejected also, in view of this final canonical redaction, is the idea of inconsistent, differing theologies, often claimed for different Old Testament traditions (e.g., J vs. P).

Of course, it is undeniable that sources in some form or other preceded the canonical material we now have. But it cannot be emphasized too strongly that we must interpret what we have. The identification of sources becomes a very subjective process and is always subject to dispute. There are no assured results of literary criticism, while the question of the relationship of Israel's faith to Israel's history is a vexed one which is usually addressed presuppositionally. Moreover, the more modern disciplines of rhetorical criticism and structural analysis have tended to diminish the importance ascribed twenty years ago to form criticism.

Within the broader concept of the theology underlying the canon as a whole, therefore, I attempt to present the theological movement of each book, endeavoring, where possible, to indicate how the flow of content in each book contributes to the concept of that book's purpose. I interact also with materials from contemporary scholarship. Unless noted otherwise, scriptural quotations are from the Revised Standard Version, copyright 1946, 1952, 1971, and 1973 by the Division of Christian Education of the National Council of the Churches of Christ in the United States of America. The other versions cited are the King James Version (KJV) and the New International Version (NIV).

Part 1

The Books of the Law

1

Genesis

The Book of Genesis is structured by a recurring formula, "these are the generations of," set before each of ten sections to which it refers. It appears at 2:4; 6:9; 11:27; 25:19; 37:2, which begin major sections, and at 5:1; 10:1; 11:10; 25:12; 36:1, where it introduces minor sections within the larger units. Additionally, other genealogical notations demarcate sections (see 4:17–24). Genesis 1–11 presents the account of creation (1:1–2:4) and then moves from Adam to Noah (the tenth from Adam) by interconnecting genealogies, and then from Noah to Abraham (the tenth from Noah), again with interspersed genealogical connections. Chapters 12–50 present a narrative history of the patriarchal period. We may thus outline Genesis as follows:

1–2   Creation and its implications
3   The fall
4–11   The effects of the fall
12–36 The patriarchs
37–50 Joseph

Genesis opens with an account of creation, consisting of eight acts in six days. The divine work of creation reaches its climax on the seventh day; the division between chapters 1 and 2 emphasizes this climax of the seventh day. The implications of this activity for human beings and their work are then drawn out (chap. 2) before the narrative continues with the fall of humankind (chap. 3). Next, the spread of sin in the world is documented, closing with what amounts to the fall of society, narrated in the Babel episode. Having sketched the problems that the fall created for human life and society, the narrator begins the biblical account of redemption, effected through the call of Abram (12:1–3). The patriarchal narratives which follow recount the fortunes of Abraham, Isaac, and Jacob, particularly in relationship to the land of Canaan. Finally, the book closes with the Joseph narratives, which concern Israel's preservation in Egypt. The books from Exodus to Deuteronomy then take up the matter of Israel's entry into the land of Canaan. Deuteronomy details the manner of life which must be displayed within the covenant framework if Israel is to retain the land.

Creation and Its Implications (Gen. 1–2)

Genesis 1:1 functions as a heading for the Book of Genesis itself, if not for the Old Testament as a whole. This role is suggested by (1) the elaborate alliteration (in the Hebrew), (2) the reference to the creation of "the heavens and the earth," or the totality of creation, and (3) the lofty theological tone which is struck. Whatever the possibilities of translation may be, the context demands that this verse indicates an absolute beginning. The effortless way in which the world is brought into being by divine command goes beyond what may be parallels in the Babylonian or Egyptian creation accounts. Indeed, it is possible that such accounts were in the author's mind and that Genesis 1 serves as a polemic against them. If verse 1 is a summary introduction, then it seems best to take verse 3 as referring to the commencement of the work of creation. Verse 2 would then be dependent upon verse 3 and describes the process by which the world was brought into its present state of order.

On any view, the account of creation presents difficulties. The so-called gap theory, however (which views v. 2 as indicating the recovery process by which the formless darkness and chaos into which the world had fallen between 1:1 and 1:2 were dispelled), is not tenable, given the Hebrew syntax, which very clearly separates verse 2 from verse 1. Taking the words "without form and void" of verse 2 as our cue, we have the eight creative acts of the first chapter distributed into a sequence of form and use (see fig. 1).

While we should apparently take the days chronologically, note that

Figure 1 **Form and Use of the Creative Acts**

Form		Use	
Day 1	Light	**Day 4**	Luminaries
2	Water and sky	**5**	Fish and birds
3	Land and vegetation	**6**	Beasts and human beings

the Hebrew word for "day" is used in three senses between Genesis 1:1 and 2:4: for evening and morning taken together (e.g., v. 5), for light as opposed to darkness (v. 5), and in the broader sense of "when" (2:4). The special subject of Genesis 1 is man. His creation is the result of particular divine deliberation. (Most likely the "let us" of 1:26 refers to deliberation within the Godhead, though the matter is debated. Jewish expositors have generally understood the "let us" as an address to the angels. Certainly, the Spirit is the agent of creation in Job 33:4; Ps. 104:30; Ezek. 37:14. While Gen. 1:26 prepares the way for the later doctrine of the Trinity, we cannot read a trinitarianism into it.) The Hebrew for the phrase "in our image" is perhaps better translated "as our image," that is, man is created to function as the image. This rendering would make the understanding of the term *image* relational and revelational rather than primarily ontological (the word includes the notion of concreteness and visibility). "Image" in this view concerns relational function in the world rather than merely an ontological property belonging to human beings, such as rationality.

Given the nature of man as described in the Old Testament, "image" in 1:26 refers to the whole person, but with the major emphasis falling upon function. In Psalm 8, with clear reference to Genesis 1, humankind is depicted in royal terms. (Note that in Ps. 8:5 man is crowned with "glory and honor"; elsewhere these are divine attributes—see Ps. 29:1, 4; 90:16; 104:1; 111:3; 145:5; Job 40:10.) The allusion in Psalm 8:6 to all things being put under the feet of created man is an ancient Near Eastern symbol of submission to authority (cf. Josh. 10:24; 1 Kings 5:3; Ps. 110:1). Finally, "have dominion" in Genesis 1:28 has reference elsewhere in the Old Testament to the exercise of kingly functions (cf. 1 Kings 4:24; Ps. 72:8; 110:2; Isa. 14:6; Ezek. 34:4). The notion of image as referring to royal authority is attested in both Mesopotamia and Egypt (Schmidt 1973, 137–48).

The creation of man in Genesis 1 thus climaxes in his presentation as vice-regent set over creation. The account stresses the essential dignity of the image, a dignity which is not lost as a result of the fall (9:6). Man and woman are created to be rulers in their domain and, in view of their role in the garden in chapter 2, to be priests, as we shall see. Human rule is also clear from the later meditation of Psalm 8 as well as from the language of Genesis 1:26–28 ("have dominion" and "subdue"). If the fall robbed human beings of this function, we would expect the biblical doctrine of redemption to restore it. The presentation of Jesus in the New Testament both as the image of God and as true man points to what individuals in Christ will become. Finally, it may be noted that the sexual distinctions referred to in 1:27 are not necessarily a component of what is conveyed by creation in the image: verse 27b may be more than simply a repetition of verse 27a and may anticipate the blessing conferred in verse 28 (Bird 1981, 134).

Genesis 1 stresses the sovereignty of God exhibited in his effortless superintendence of the work of creation. He stands outside of the historical process, and all within it is under his total control. The writer assumes God's presence, which alone makes sense of our whole world. Thus, the Bible never attempts to prove God's existence but rather offers a world view which accounts for the reality we experience. Such an attitude may be termed fideistic, but we are called upon to share it as we join the ranks of the circle of faith.

This first chapter also portrays the power of God. We stand in awe as we read this remarkable account of how our world began. We recognize that the very heavens declare the glory of God (Ps. 19:1). In addition, the emphasis of Genesis 1:31 that what was made was declared to be "very good" reminds us that creation perfectly corresponded to the divine intention. This need not mean that an absolutely perfect world stemmed from the actions of Genesis 1. It is possible that the world outside of the garden setting of chapter 2, a setting which seems to be so distinct, needed to be brought completely under human control, since it may have contained all the difficulties which we experience in our natural world today. This suggestion raises difficulties, but the direction of biblical eschatology as well as the facts of human experience points toward a consummation of history which is more than a mere return to the beginning.

The account of creation finds its conclusion and its climax in the activity of the seventh day (Gen. 2:1–4a). God declares his work complete and, by implication, invites human beings to enter into the special situation of rest which the seventh day has brought into being. We are left with the distinct impression that the account of the seventh day leaves the continuity of Genesis 1 and enters a more open-ended situation. The seventh day is not an ordinary day. Unlike the other days, no mention is made of a morning or an evening. Though the noun *Sabbath* does not occur in this section, the verb from which it is derived occurs twice, and

Exodus 20:8–11 points to the creation account as the warrant for Sabbath observance. God blesses the day (i.e., endows it with the potential to be the day which God had intended for human experience) and then hallows it (i.e., makes it his own day). The links that Exodus 20:8–11 forges encourage us to see in the episode of the seventh day in Genesis 2 a model of what the later Sabbath was to represent. Humankind in direct fellowship with God in an unbroken relationship, living in harmony with the earth from which they were drawn and with the animate world with which they are placed in direct relationship, is the message of Genesis 2.

The particular implications of creation for man are drawn out in Genesis 2:4b–25. The account appears to be an expansion and not simply a repetition of some of the material of chapter 1. Created as part of his world, the man is then, somewhat paradoxically in view of the mandate to exercise dominion over the world, withdrawn from it (vv. 7–8). He is placed in the garden which God had made, and in this setting God is experienced directly. It seems to follow that humans will exercise dominion and authority over their world only when they are directly and centrally related to God. The first man is appointed to "till" and to "keep" the garden (v. 15). The verb *till* later occurs frequently in the technical sense of worship. This usage, together with the priestly and royal allusions to original man in Ezekiel 28:11–19, encourages us to see man in the garden as a royal figure exercising also a priestly function. This dual and interconnected role strikingly anticipates the call offered to all Israel in Exodus 19:3–6. It also implies that the garden is a world sanctuary. Indeed, the presence of God there in the manner depicted in the account would make it so. The notion of a world center from which all revelation emanates and to which all the world defers is a concept running through the fabric of the whole Bible. It plays a prominent role in Israel's prophetic hopes concerning Jerusalem and is the theme upon which the Bible concludes (see Rev. 21:9–22:5, the so-called Jerusalem appendix).

Two trees in the garden are singled out for special mention. The fruit of the tree of the knowledge of good and evil may not be eaten (Gen. 2:17). This prohibition assumes human freedom to choose and thus an inherent moral capacity. In the center of the garden, and thus in some sense controlling it, is the tree of life—the tree which enhances life (cf. Prov. 11:30; 13:12; 15:4). No prohibition against eating of this tree is placed upon the man and woman before the fall. Only after the fall is access forbidden (Gen. 3:22), and then apparently in the interests of Adam and Eve themselves, lest they live forever in a fallen state. The remainder of the account in 2:18–25 establishes an order: God, the man, the woman, and the animal world (Walsh 1977, 174). The chapter concludes with an aside by the author indicating that it is within the marriage relationship that the expectation of fellowship between man and woman is supremely met and experienced (vv. 24–25).

The Fall (Gen. 3)

The fall narrative of Genesis 3 is presented as a direct reversal of the order carefully established in chapter 2 (Walsh 1977, 174–77). Now the animal world, in the person of the serpent, seizes the initiative. In turn, the woman is deceived and assumes a position of prominence which is not given to her in chapter 2. At this point we must remember the ideal meaning of the word *dominion* in the Bible. It means protecting the relationship for which one is responsible; it is to serve others and to seek their good (see Matt. 20:25–28). The man is then enticed, and finally God pronounces judgment upon the whole scene. He assigns appropriate punishments, which strike the serpent, woman, and man in the very nature of their roles within creation. This reversal of order suggests that sin represents an attack upon the harmony of the created order and not merely a moral lapse.

What did it mean to eat the fruit of the tree of the knowledge of good and evil? Many suggestions have been offered, including acquiring total knowledge ("good and evil" taken as expressing totality), moral knowledge, and sexual experience. But all of these founder either upon the serpent's claim and God's acknowledgment that eating would make the person "like God" (3:5, 22) or upon the facts of human experience. Neither the addition of moral knowledge or sexual experience would make a person like God, and we do not see human beings in our world as the possessors of total knowledge. It is therefore better to take the term "knowledge of good and evil" as expressing moral discernment, moral autonomy, and the ability to be self-legislating (Clark 1969, 277). Only God ultimately possesses knowledge of this character. Humankind is thus presented in the narrative as the usurper of the divine prerogatives and snatching at divinity, a situation which the second Adam was to reverse (see Phil. 2:6). The results of the fall find the man and woman possessed of this knowledge, that is, self-legislating and morally autonomous. They are able to make the necessary choices but will always remain uncertain as to whether their choices are wise or right or whether the means they devise to reach correct goals are valid.

The Effects of the Fall (Gen. 4–11)

The effects of the fall are traced in the subsequent narratives, ending with Genesis 11:1–9. The fall, the account of Cain and Abel, the epi-

sodes of the sons of God (6:1–4) and the flood, as well as the Babel narrative, all have common elements. Each of them deals with sin, divine
confrontation which announces an appropriate punishment, some
amelioration of that punishment, and then the imposition of the punishment. Unlike the other narratives, Babel contains apparently no
movement of divine grace toward the offenders. It would thus seem that
Babel offers us a point of transition in the narratives, and so it proves to
be. After Babel, the Bible strikes out in an entirely new direction.

Clearly, the midpoint of Genesis 1–11 is the narrative concerning the
flood. It is immediately preceded by the strange account of the intermarriage of the sons of God (preflood kings?) and the daughters of
men, an account which seems to characterize the preflood age. By the
flood, creation is destroyed (7:11–24). After it, the creation mandate to
human beings is renewed (cf. 1:28 with 9:1–7). It is sometimes suggested
that a new beginning occurs with the divine commitment to refrain
from direct action in the future and not again to curse the ground
(8:21–22). But these verses merely establish the bounds within which
the lot of human beings will continue in a disordered world. Nothing is
said about the removal of curses already pronounced upon humankind
generally as a result of the fall (e.g., childbearing, which in 3:16 came
under the curse of the fall).

After the flood, the effects of sin are seen continued in Noah's family,
until we reach the most blatant assertion so far of human authority, in
Genesis 11:1–9. Before we take up that account, we must mention the
covenant to which God refers in dialog with Noah in 6:18. God declared
to Noah that, notwithstanding the flood, he would "establish" his covenant. This is the first mention of a covenant which, in fact, receives no
detailed treatment until chapter 9. It is therefore customary to suggest
that 6:18 is an anticipation of 9:8–17. But there are good reasons to think
otherwise. First, the verb translated "establish" in 6:18 means, in its sustained use in the covenant contexts of the Old Testament, to confirm
what already exists. Second, when used in the divine and secular covenant contexts of the Old Testament, the word *covenant*, whatever its basic meaning may be, gives quasi-legal backing to a relationship already
existing. It is never used in the sense of initiating a relationship. Third,
when a covenant arrangement is initiated that confirms an already existing relationship, the terminology invariably used is the phrase "cut a
covenant." It is sometimes suggested that the peculiar language of 6:18
reflects a particular literary source, namely, the P, or Priestly, document.
(P, a strand of supposedly priestly interests, is one of the three sources
thought to underlie the present Genesis narrative. The other two proposed are the Yahweh [J] and Elohistic [E] sources, so labeled because of
their respective preference for using the divine names Yahweh or

Elohim.) The use of the expression "cut a covenant," however, is too widely distributed in the Old Testament to argue this way.

The emphasis upon "my" covenant and the use of "establish" suggest that the reference in Genesis 6:18 is to something which is unilaterally already in existence. The absence of the normal initiatory terminology by which covenant parties are bound ("cut a covenant") suggests this conclusion. The term *cut* is used in all divine covenants imposed upon individuals (Abraham) or nations (Israel) where two parties to the covenant exist. God is declaring here his willingness to continue what has been already set up. In spite of human failure and independent of human participation, whatever arrangement God is referring to here will be continued. Not all are agreed that "covenant" is the best or an adequate translation, but it is generally conceded that the word has the note of obligation in it. The commitment of God to the total created order therefore seems highlighted here.

The details of this arrangement are given in Genesis 9:8–17. It was to be established with Noah, but it includes Noah's descendants (v. 9), every living creature (v. 10; i.e., all animate beings), and indeed the whole earth (v. 13). God promises never again to bring a threat like the flood, but providentially to sustain the order of creation. We may suggest, then, that the covenant referred to in 6:18 came into existence in 1:1–2:3 by virtue of God's act of creation itself. Such an act established an enduring relationship between God and the world. He pledged to sustain it. His pledge at 6:18 was directed toward the part of creation that was threatened by the catastrophe of the flood and reassured humankind of the providential continuance of the created order. The sign of the rainbow in 9:14–16 is a reminder to God of his promise to continue the general conditions of the universe whereby human beings may exercise their allotted role in the created order.

Genesis 11:1–9 concludes the narratives of the spread of sin and disorder. Humankind, who possess a broad set of unities (common language, common ethnic framework, and, if we take Gen. 10 logically to follow chap. 11, a common social basis), congregate at Babel to preserve these unities. They propose to build a city and a tower, the top of which is to be "in the heavens." Since the word *tower* refers commonly in the Old Testament to a fortress tower, some fanciful lines of exegesis have seen in this proposal a human assault upon heaven or a human observation post erected to ward off a threat from heaven directed against their independent social advance. The detail in verse 4 about the tower, however, refers simply to its impressive size. The divine reaction to this human initiative is to scatter the people and to confuse their language—that is, frustrate their ability to communicate. Thus begin the social, linguistic, ethnic, and cultural distinctions which have frustrated all efforts at interhuman cooperation since Babel. Why was the divine action taken? No reasons are directly advanced by the narrative, but the implication is that the problem attacked by God was the problem of the misplaced center. Human beings regarded themselves as the measure of all things, able to control the course of their world, able to build better worlds! Of course, by such an endeavor the naked meaning of sin is exposed. Such human attempts, then and since, which leave God out of consideration are sin in its baldest and most blatant form. Note that, unlike the age of Noah, there is no godly remnant at Babel. The immediacy of the divine reaction and its nature are therefore understandable.

The Call of Abraham (Gen. 12:1–3)

Though no interpretation is offered by the divine writer for the Babel episode, the ensuing narratives provide clues. The genealogy of Shem which follows in the account (Gen. 11:10–32) leads us to Abram, for whom God will provide what the boastful builders at Babel sought: a great name (12:2; cf. 11:4). Unlike the other narratives of Genesis 4–11, which record the spread of sin, no movement of divine grace appears in 11:1–9. The call of Abram, however, displays God's grace, for with him God will begin again. Chapters 1–11 are critical for the development of a biblical world view and thus a biblical theology. We began in Genesis 1–2 with the description of an ideal world in which human potential could be expressed and developed. Yet such a possibility was frustrated at once by the fall, and the remaining chapters of 1–11 tell us why we fail as we do, alienated in our world from each other and from the natural order itself. These chapters therefore formulate a perceptive analysis of the human predicament. What God will do in response to this situation is now unfolded in the patriarchal narratives, preeminently in the call of Abram from Ur of the Chaldeans.

Genesis 12:1–3 thus offers the divine counter to the effects of the fall. It is noteworthy that the account begins with somewhat the same formulation as we see in 1:3, namely, a divine speech followed by a virtual command (actual in 12:1). In substance, 12:1–3 provides details of what will become known as the Abrahamic covenant. Although the term *covenant* is not used of the arrangement with Abram until 15:18, the detail of chapter 15 clearly confirms an already existing relationship. Progeny and land, the promises offered in 12:1–3, are guaranteed by the divine oath of chapter 15. Genesis 12:1–3 thus appears to be basic for the later narratives.

After the introductory verse 1, verses 2–3 present a structure of five subordinate clauses followed by the final principal clause. After the initial command of verse 1, the sequence is divided by a further command ("be a blessing"), which ends verse 2 and completes the primary reference to Abram. Verse 2 is probably best translated as comprising two clauses only ("I will make of you a great nation" and "I will bless you by making your name great"). The extensive reference to Abram's influence then follows in verse 3 and comprises two subordinate clauses relating the world to Abram in terms of either blessing or curse. The whole section is rounded off by the principal clause that ends verse 3, upon which the main weight of 12:1–3 rests: "in you shall all the families of the earth win for themselves a blessing" (my translation).

We have noted that the material of verses 2–3 differs in emphasis. Verse 2 has the future of the Abrahamic descendants in view, while the next verse concerns the relationship of the wider world community to Abram. Abram's descendants are to become "a great nation" (v. 2), foreshadowing immediately the political future of Israel. The word *nation* is interesting. When used of Israel in the Old Testament, it is normally used derogatively, in condemnation (Deut. 32:28; Isa. 1:4; Jer. 5:9, etc.). The word normally used of Israel in relationship to Yahweh is "people," a family term which expresses the closeness of the election relationship. "Nation" is a political term, normally applied to an ethnic unity that is geographically delineated and bound together by social and cultural factors. Perhaps the political term is used here in contrast to the term *families* (v. 3), which characterizes the remainder of the world. Perhaps the point is that only in connection with Abram can a true governmental relationship among people be established. All other associations which may be formed are dismissed in 12:3 as "families" (or "clans"). We bear in mind that 12:1–3 involves the recovery of the ultimate divine purpose, which takes us back to the divine intention for the world expressed in chapters 1 and 2, namely, a kingdom of God which establishes God's rule in the world and which would have united human beings with their world.

The choice of the word *nation* here for Abram's descendants may thus have been studied and deliberate. It may initially have had Israel in view, but Israel as representative of the wider saved community which was to stem from her witness. The centrality of purpose which the Babel builders had vainly sought may therefore be supplied by this call of Genesis 12:1–3. No final political structure, no system of world rule will prevail outside of the framework established here in 12:1–3. Perhaps, the "great nation" of this passage is to be taken eschatologically to mean the company of the redeemed who will finally represent the fulfilment of the call to Abram (cf. Rev. 5:11). We may therefore look to the New Testament to provide the fulfilment of the concept of Israel, which failed to be realized in the Old Testament.

In Genesis 12:1–3 we need also to note the five occurrences of the word *bless(ing)* and thus its decided emphasis. Some have contrasted the use of "bless(ing)" in this section with the fivefold occurrence of the word *curse* in chapters 3–11 (3:14, 17; 4:11; 5:29; 9:25). In short, the call of Abram redresses the curse incurred by the fall. Human alienation, the flight from God, and the bondage to slavery which the curse of chapters 3–11 envisages are all potentially reversed in 12:1–3.

We may say a further word about Israel and its mission in the Old Testament from the detail of Genesis 12:3b. Much depends here upon the translation of the verb *bless* in this clause. Most modern translations have taken this verb as suggesting the world's invoking Abram's blessing upon themselves (e.g., "by you all the families of the earth shall bless themselves"). But while the content of 12:1–3 appears to be climactic, such a translation appears to be somewhat anticlimactic and somewhat lame as a final item. The rendering "win for themselves a blessing," which also imparts the reflexive sense of the Hebrew verb, seems preferable. This translation echoes the struggle for identification with Abram's God and the blessing to which the world is called. Additionally, the prepositional phrase of verse 3b seems best rendered "in you." The somewhat parallel context of 21:12 supports this translation, as does Galatians 3:28–29. Such a translation leaves open the question of how the Abrahamic blessing is to be transferred, since the possibility of subsequent outreach by Israel is not raised. The presumption is, rather, that the nations will come in. The Old Testament views the role of Israel in this light. She is to be the rallying point to which nations will come, and Jerusalem is to be the divine center.

The Patriarchal Narratives (Gen. 12:4–36:43)

The content of the Abrahamic promises concerned land and progeny, and these two concerns are taken up in reverse order in the patriarchal narratives. The main emphasis is upon progeny. The Abrahamic narratives see the promises maintained but virtually end with the emphasis upon Abraham as a stranger and pilgrim in the land (Gen. 23). An heir for Abraham is provided in the form of Isaac, to whom the Abrahamic promises are repeated (26:4). Isaac, to judge from the degree of attention paid to him in the narrative, is somewhat of a lesser figure, though his neighbors in the wider world notice that the blessing of God is with him (see v. 28). The Jacob narratives (25:19–35:29) take up the questions of progeny and land much more thoroughly. The theological importance of the Jacob narratives lies in their indication of the manner in which the Abrahamic promises are to be worked out in Israel's future.

Blessing, inheritance, and possession of the land are the issues which the Jacob narratives address. Much attention is paid within them to progeny, stemming primarily from Rebekah and Rachel, and then from Leah. Rebekah and Rachel (as well as Sarah before them) are both initially barren, and blessing comes only—as it always must—by divine intervention. God alone will bring into being the people of the promise! The conflict narratives between Ishmael and Isaac, Esau and Jacob, and then between Jacob and Laban arise from these birth narratives, and thus the ground is laid for the later Old Testament hostility between Israel and the Transjordanian peoples.

Of particular importance is the question of the occupancy of the Promised Land. It is significant that this question is raised in the Bethel narrative (Gen. 28:10–22) immediately before Jacob leaves Canaan, and again in chapter 32 immediately before he returns to the Promised Land, blessed with a numerous family acquired in Haran and with considerable substance. The detail of chapter 32 is particularly important for the history of later Israel. Jacob halts at Mahanaim on the border of the Promised Land. The name *Mahanaim* ("double camps") points to the conflict which is to be resolved within the chapter. Jacob cannot reenter Canaan until he is changed by struggle and, in the rite-of-passage narrative of this chapter, receives the new name *Israel* (which probably means "God strives"). As one with whom, all his life, God has striven, Jacob can now be said to prevail over himself; as a changed man he is now able to meet and be reconciled with his brother Esau (Fokkelman 1975, 197–222).

These details foreshadow the later history of Israel. They point to the difficulty which the twelve tribes will have in occupying the land and suggest that the land will come to Israel only when she too has learned the meaning of full submission. The Jacob cycle pivots on Genesis 30 (Fishbane 1975, 20), in which the barren Rachel is now fertile in Haran and Jacob's substance is also established. Up to that point the narratives present themes of family alienation, strife, infertility, and bitterness. From that point onward there is a change, and the tone becomes one of return, reconciliation, abounding fertility, and blessing. In sum, the Jacob cycle underscores the prospect of blessing for Israel as national fertility and substance within the Promised Land, yet acquired only by discipline outside of the land and by due recognition of the source from which the gift of the land must come.

The Joseph Narratives (Gen. 37–50)

The long and very distinct Joseph narratives close the Book of Genesis and add their own emphasis. Their theme is Israel's remarkable preservation outside of the Promised Land, just as the theme in the Jacob cycle was the establishment of the twelve tribes of Israel. As such, the Joseph account functions as a bridge between the patriarchal narratives and the Book of Exodus, tying together the promises to the fathers with the pending occupation of the land. Joseph is presented as the preserver not only of Israel's traditions but of Israel herself. Life at this stage for Israel is to be had in Egypt (Gen. 42:2), and Joseph is there at the source of life, having been placed there providentially by God after being callously abandoned by his brothers. He is there as a pledge of Israel's future (Brueggemann 1972, 100).

The turning point of the Joseph narrative is the recognition scene of Genesis 45:4–8a, where Joseph reveals himself to his brothers and thereby breaks the cycle of famine, estrangement, and death as dominant issues. From this point onward in the account, there come family reconciliation, healing, abundance, and blessing. Israel's future is clearly under God's providential care. The brothers had meant Joseph's sale into slavery for evil, but God meant it for good (50:20). God put him where he was so that "many people should be kept alive."

The Book of Genesis concludes with one aspect of the Abrahamic promise actualized. A great nation from Abraham is about to emerge on the political horizon. What must be added to this people, now so numerous as to pose a threat to the Egyptians, is the land which they will occupy. The Book of Exodus will show us how the land is to be added to this already existent people. It will not be added by the mere fact of historical occupancy, but God will give it as the climax of the great redemption of the exodus.

The narratives of Genesis 12–50 have insisted that God's hand now lies upon the history of Israel. Chapter 1 began with the grand design for this world. Chapter 11 ended with society alienated from the promise. In Genesis 12 the divine attack upon this problem commenced. All the nations of the world, scattered as a result of Babel, would find their center in Abraham. His descendants would in turn find their habitat in a land whose center God would form. By the end of the Book of Genesis, the promise of the land is sure, but the fulfilment will come in God's good time. A viable and populous people of God has been developed, and the redemption of the exodus will bring together the two Abrahamic themes of land and people. The remaining content of the first five books of the Bible (the Pentateuch) will focus on a theology of prospect for the people of God, showing the manner in which the situation of Eden will potentially be realized in and through Israel, the Old Testament people of God.

2

Exodus

As Exodus begins, Israel is enslaved, helpless, and weak. She will often be reminded of this position when she in turn, by governmental neglect, becomes the oppressor of the weak and the poor in her own community. But nothing seems a less likely prospect for Israel as we approach the narratives at the beginning of the Book of Exodus. The redemption which is to follow is engineered by God through the man Moses, a mode in the history of salvation that we have come already to expect. Before we consider the significance of the Mosaic period, however, it will be well to remind ourselves of the direction of the Book of Exodus.

The book commences with Israel's great need and concludes with the nation about to embark upon the march to the Promised Land, led by the manifested presence of God. Actually, the book ends with a discussion of the community at worship. We need to remind ourselves as we are considering the theological contribution of this book that more than one third of it (Exod. 25–31, 35–40) is devoted to the establishment of Israel's cultic framework, in particular to the erection of, and the regulations for the use of, Israel's tabernacle. This is no meaningless cultic digression, but is designed to emphasize the importance of a response of worship in Israel's continuing covenantal relationship.

For the moment, however, we simply note that the general contours of the Book of Exodus are erected around the movement from the opening scene of slavery to the concluding picture of worship. This movement echoes the experience of every Christian life and, as it were, offers an ongoing analogy to the people of God in every age. Even more pertinent to personal and corporate experience is the fact that the transition from slavery to worship is accomplished by means of a very great redemption effected at the center of the book itself. Basic to all Israel's later theology is the redemption of the exodus. Centering on this theme, the book can be outlined as follows:

1–4	Birth and call of Moses
5:1–15:21	The liberation of Israel
15:22–19:2	Murmuring in the wilderness; the journey to Sinai
19:3–24:18	Covenant and covenant ratification
25–31	Blueprint for the tabernacle
32–34	Golden calf and covenant renewal
35–40	Tabernacle erection and dedication

The Birth and Call of Moses (Exod. 1–4)

The narrative of the birth and call of Moses occupies our attention in Exodus 1–4. Since Moses' experience virtually anticipates Israel's, many of the episodes in these four chapters point forward to parallel events in chapters 5–14, as Israel seeks to extract herself from Egypt. The background circumstances to Moses' birth are described in Exodus 1. After the reference in verses 1–7 to tribal Israel as now numerous, the account details the rigor with which Egypt dealt with Israel (vv. 8–14; note the similar pattern of hard labor imposed on a populous Israel in 5:5–19). Egyptian attempts to curb the Israelite population increase by drowning Israelite children (1:15–22) somewhat parallel the drowning of the Egyptians which concludes the account of the flight of Israel from Egypt in chapter 14 (Fishbane 1979, 73–76).

Exodus 2 presents Moses' birth, flight, and sojourn in Midian. Exodus 3, with its account of Moses and the burning "bush" (sĕneh; note the similarity to sînay, or Sinai) on Horeb, "the mountain of God," where the character of Yahweh is revealed, strikingly anticipates Israel's experience at Sinai, "the mountain of God" (24:13), where the law is revealed. Moses' own experience at Horeb is thus a mirror image of Israel's. Circumstances thrust him out of Egypt, and at Sinai (the Horeb of 3:1) he finds the true significance of what his life is to be. His own experience at Horeb, his perception of the divine holiness, and his understanding of the divine name and thus of the divine character anticipate Israel's later Sinai covenant experience, though Moses' steadfast obedience stands in strong contrast to Israel's later rebellion.

Whether the new divine name ("Yahweh") which God himself reveals to Moses at the burning bush is new in the absolute sense is a question which need not detain us for any length of time. Some of the Israelite personal names (e.g., Jochebed, Moses' mother, and Joshua) suggest that the name Yahweh is older than the event, and Egyptian inscriptional material has provided evidence of the probable occurrence of the divine name at about 1500 B.C. as a geographical term denoting the area contiguous to Edom (de Vaux 1970, 55–56). It is probable, therefore, that Moses asks at 3:13–15, not for the name itself, but for the significance of the name (cf. 6:3). To the mind of the ancient Near Eastern person, the name of the deity opened up the possibility of a relationship. Once given the name, the worshiper could "call upon the name" in prayer. The revelation of the name was an assurance of commitment by the deity whose character was therein disclosed. Although the exact meaning of the name *Yahweh* is still uncertain, it includes some component of the verb "to be." Two translations are possible: (1) he causes to be or will cause to be (i.e., creates), and (2) he is or he will be. The majority opinion and the context of chapter 3 favor the latter possibility; the meaning of the somewhat enigmatic verse 14 ("I am who I am") may thus be "I am he who is."

Whatever the precise nuances of the name may be (and clearly they were finally unimportant, since no real play is later made upon its meaning), the general intent of the episode in Exodus 3 is to assure Moses and Israel of Yahweh's presence with her in her developing history. God would be known by his future acts, by the unfolding of his character by both deed and word. We should note also that verses 13–15 link this new revelation to the patriarchal period. Moses is to tell the Israelites that the God who has sent him is "the God of your fathers" (v. 15). This type of expression, which in the singular form (God of your [my, our] father) is prominent in the Book of Genesis, appears in the early chapters of Exodus but is absent thereafter. This peculiar usage is amplified by particular appellations (Shield of Abraham, Fear/Kinsman of Isaac, Mighty One of Jacob) in the patriarchal narratives. On the other hand, the Book of Genesis contains more precise descriptions such as El Roi, El Olam, El Bethel, and El Elohe Israel (Gen. 16:13; 21:33; 31:13; 33:20), in which El, the common Semitic term for deity, is found in compound with descriptive elements derived from the place or the circumstances concerned. This has led to the suggestion that two strands of religious thought are present in the patriarchal narratives. The older, "God of your father" type of terminology (e.g., Shield of Abraham) was brought into Palestine by immigrants who encountered the El names from Canaanite contact. Certainly the occurrence of these two sets of names in Genesis and, in particular, the occurrence of the "God of your father" type calls for explanation. El names, however, are hardly Canaanite borrowings, since (1) the term *El* is generally Semitic, (2) the lofty monotheistic tone of Genesis, which is almost unparalleled in the Old Testament, tells against this hypothesis, and (3) the patriarchs largely avoided direct contact with the urban culture of the period. Finally, a neat separation between these two types of names is to be avoided, since mixing of types occurs in Genesis and Exodus (see Gen. 46:3; Exod. 3:6). Nevertheless, it is clear that the revelation of the name *Yahweh* in Exodus 3 is in some way a distinct advance associated with Israel's salvation history.

While Moses' origins are priestly (of the tribe of Levi; see Exod. 2:1), his call is clearly prophetic in Exodus 3, consisting of divine confrontation (vv. 1–4a), introductory divine word (vv. 4b–9), commission (v. 10), typical objections (v. 11), divine reassurance (v. 12a), and the promise of a sign (v. 12b). Covenant continuance is stressed in 3:13–15, for prophet and covenant are interrelated Old Testament figures (for the Old Testament prophetic office as modeled upon Moses, see Deut. 18:15–22). The subsequent narratives typically present Moses as the protector or deliverer of Israel, in the manner of the heroic figures of the Book of Judges. But as the divine messenger whose function was to proclaim God's will to Israel and to keep them within the covenant, his ministry was undoubtedly prophetic. And as the initiator of Israel's cultic institutions, the ministry of Moses was also priestly.

To reassure Moses and to authenticate his ministry, God gives him three signs (4:1–9) culminating in a fourth (vv. 24–26) in which blood is the dominant factor and to which the death of Pharaoh's firstborn (v. 23) stands in some relationship. Such an arrangement, as has been pointed out, broadly parallels the ten plagues of chapters 7–11, which form a scheme of three triplets and a final plague in which blood and the fate of the firstborn are the significant factors (Fishbane 1979, 70). There follows in 4:10–17 a further call of Moses, this time in specific terms. Aaron's role as spokesman is one to which later chapters also refer (cf. 6:12, 30; 7:1–6).

Chapters 5–15 narrate the liberation of Israel from Egypt. Exodus 5:1–6:1 sets the scene for what is essentially in these chapters a conflict between Pharaoh (who is presented as a threat reminiscent of primeval chaos; cf. Ezek. 32:2) and Yahweh; 6:2–9 places a revelation of the divine name in this context of persecution and supplication by Israel (cf. the revelation in 3:1–15, which had been associated with Israel's oppression in Egypt). Yahweh will now respond to Israel's situation in fulfilment of

the promise to Israel's forefathers (6:8). Exodus 6:10–7:7 brings Moses
and Aaron into close relationship before the onset of the plagues
(cf. 4:10–17, 27–31, where the relationship had begun).

The Plagues (Exod. 7:8–11:10)

Exodus 7:8–11:10 presents the narratives of the plagues, which occur
in triplets of three to which is added a final plague which clearly stands
outside of the total sequence (Greenberg 1972, 606–7). In each triplet
Moses is first required to present himself before Pharaoh in the morning
by the Nile to warn him of what will come (7:15; 8:20; 9:13). He is then
sent to Pharaoh's palace (8:1; 9:1; 10:1). In each third plague, God commands Moses (and Aaron) to commence the plague without warning
(8:16; 9:8; 10:21).

The initial plague of each triplet suggests the distinct motif of each
sequence. In the first triplet (blood, frogs, lice), the note is the superi-
ority of God and his agents over the magicians of the court (7:12). In
the second sequence (insects, pestilence, boils), God's presence in Egypt
and thus his control are signaled by the separation made between Israel
and Egypt (8:18–24; 9:4–7). The third triplet (hail, locusts, darkness) emphasizes the incomparability of Yahweh (see 9:14 and the unique character of the plagues, noted in 9:18, 24; 10:6, 14). Pharaoh's unreasonable-
ness must give way before Yahweh's manifested power. Israel needs to
learn the effectiveness of its Deity, his creative power, and his ability to
save.

The tenth plague is set off from the rest of the series. It is announced
before Passover but takes place during the celebration. The final two
verses of chapter 11 present a theological justification of the plagues
which counterbalances the one which occurs at the beginning of the account (7:1–5). The continuing and culminating purpose of the episodes
is to compel Pharaoh to recognize Yahweh's power. Judgment after
Yahweh's merciful longsuffering is a concurrent theme.

Passover and Exodus (Exod. 12:1–15:21)

By the tenth plague we are prepared for the Passover (12:1–13:16),
which is both a supreme act of judgment and yet a great act of deliverance. The New Testament presentation of the death of Christ builds
upon this duality. We leave aside the details of this section and the physical deliverance recorded in chapter 14 to dwell upon the theological interpretation of the exodus and its prospects, offered in the Song of
Miriam (15:1–18). The poem is divided into an introduction (vv. 1–6),

an initial strophe (vv. 7–10), a refrain or chorus (v. 11), a second strophe or verse (vv. 12–16a), another refrain (v. 16b), and then a conclusion (vv. 17–18).

The introduction describes the manner of Yahweh's victory over Egypt in the military coloring of the late Bronze Age. The picture of Yahweh as a warrior who fights for Israel introduces us to one of the most impressive presentations of Deity in the Old Testament. This imagery of Yahweh engaged in holy war begins at this point but continues through the early conquest narratives, through prophecy and apocalyptic, into the New Testament. The imagery is encountered in the christological conflict narratives (where demon foes, etc., are encountered), finds a mention in the Pauline Epistles, and is fully developed in the Book of Revelation.

In the second strophe of the poem, the conflict imagery of the first half disappears. Yahweh is now the Divine Shepherd, a graceful and peaceful leadership image of the ancient Near East. The imagery of the passage through the waters is now transferred into a passage through petrified peoples (Philistia, Edom, Moab, Canaan—heralding the exodus route) who stand amazed as the Israelites progress, almost liturgically, into the Promised Land (Lohfink 1969, 79). Of course, all this is the language of theological reflection, since the reality of Israel's entry was a process of forty years of apostasy and struggle. But the emphasis is upon the facility with which God accomplishes his declared purposes. As the Divine Shepherd, Yahweh leads Israel to the Promised Land, presented under the images of sacred mountain and sanctuary (see Ps. 78:54, which refers to the whole of Palestine in this imagery). In the ancient Near East the divine mountain was the focal point of world revelation, and the Promised Land is thus being viewed as the world center from which divine light and truth will emanate.

Another facet of this poem needs consideration at this point. A careful reading of the song betrays obvious contacts with the creation mythologies prevailing during the Mosaic period. There are the pattern of combat in which the sea is involved (albeit as a passive instrument, a fact which serves to underscore the claim made within the poem for Yahweh's incomparability), the victory of the Divine Warrior, the establishment of his sanctuary, and his potential rule over all creation. In Enuma Elish and the Baal epics, the creation accounts of Babylon and Canaan (the creation motifs of the latter are sometimes questioned, but unreasonably so), similar sequences are present (Collins 1977, 99). The redemption of the exodus is poetically being advanced as a new creative act whereby Israel is now brought into being as a political entity. This act of redemption is analyzed as a new creative intrusion, and thus the developing theology of redemption is positively set within the context of the more general purposes for humans and their world as presented in Genesis 1–2.

Covenant and Tabernacle Building (Exod. 15:22–40:38)

Exodus 15:22–19:2 presents the wilderness itinerary and the details of the journey to Sinai. Then 19:3–6 describes Israel's vocation and prefaces verses 8–25, which tell of the preparations for Yahweh's Sinai appearance. Three themes hinted at in verses 3b–4 summarize the progress of the book: (1) redemption from Egypt (punishment visited upon the Egyptians), (2) providential direction on the march ("I bore you on eagles' wings"), and (3) the goal of the journey—worship at Mount Sinai ("I . . . brought you to myself"). Verses 3–4 detail what Yahweh has done for Israel, and verses 5b–6 reply with Israel's vocation. Important is the introductory phrase in verse 5: "if you will obey my voice and keep my covenant." The covenant in mind may be prospective and have Exodus 20 in view. In the Old Testament, however, references to keeping a divine covenant are consistently to a covenant already in existence (Gen. 17:9–10; 1 Kings 11:11; Ps. 78:10; 103:18; 132:12; Ezek. 17:14). It is possible that Exodus 19:5 points back to 6:5 and 3:13–15 and that continuity with the patriarchal covenant is involved here, especially in light of the patriarchal style of address with which Yahweh begins in verse 3. Certainly 19:3–6 forms a unit (note the similar opening and closing phrases at vv. 3b and 6b).

Exodus 19:5–6 then turns to a discussion of Israel's vocation. The key term here is the noun translated "own possession" (or "special possession"), meaning something of special personal worth which is carefully reserved. Most Old Testament uses of the noun are dependent upon Exodus 19:5b–6 (see Deut. 7:6; 14:2; 26:18; Ps. 135:4; Mal. 3:17), but two independent references occur at 1 Chronicles 29:3 and Ecclesiastes 2:8. In the former, David commits not only the resources of the empire, of which he has command by right, to the building of the temple, but also his own personal "treasure." The latter reference concerns what belongs to royalty as personal possessions. In both cases the word refers to a private fortune, as distinguished from the resources of a realm under general control of the monarch. In Exodus 19:5 we should note that this choice of Israel expressed as Yahweh's "own possession" is from among "all peoples." This latter term expresses the family character, and thus the politically undefined nature, of the remaining world. This choice is then justified by the comment "for all the earth is mine." ("For" here probably both summarizes as well as expresses a causal role.) This statement is not an apology for the choice of Israel, but God's reason for the choice, which has the whole world in mind. Israel is separated from all other families to be presented as the ideal political unit. But the aim of her call is that she may be a world influence, a "light for revelation to the Gentiles" (Luke 2:32). There are remarkable overtones of the Abrahamic covenant here in Israel's calling to serve her world by her separateness.

Verse 6 reinforces this calling. Much difficulty has surrounded the phrases "kingdom of priests" and "holy nation." They are best taken as parallels, though there are other possibilities. The word *kingdom* most naturally refers to royal domain. If we take the possessive phrase "of priests" as adjectival, we arrive at the pair "priestly royalty" and "holy nation." These phrases emphasize function rather than institution and signify not Israel's later priesthood, but the typical priestly role in an ancient society. These two parallel phrases elaborate the notion of Israel as God's "own possession." Israel's relationship to the world is likened to that of a priest in an ancient society, who was called to serve the society by differentiating himself from it. Is Israel's priestly role here conceived to be mediatorial? To the degree that Israel is designated to be a servant people in the latter part of the Old Testament, the answer is yes. But Israel's primary role in this connection consisted in attracting the world to her form of government (i.e., the kingdom of God) by her embodied holiness. Of course, the notions of royalty and kingdom in verse 6 point to the ultimate authority of Israel's suzerain, who stands behind Israel's constitution and calls Israel as a political entity into being.

The remainder of Exodus 19 is given over to detailed preparations for the divine appearance, by which the ten "words" (20:1–17) will be introduced. These Ten Commandments together with the social legislation that follows from them are given in chapters 20–23. The text certainly distinguishes the two codes; Exodus 20 is denominated "words" and delivered to all Israel, and chapters 21–23 are styled "ordinances" and derivatively delivered through Moses. The Ten Commandments spell out the boundaries of the relationship established by grace. In keeping with this understanding, we note that the later general word for "law" *(tôrâ)* carries the sense of instruction or guidance. In these terms the Ten Commandments offer a mirror image of how Israel's national life in the land should look, reflecting the relationship of grace. The ten words objectified on Sinai seem merely to have codified the divine will for humankind. Most of their content is contained directly or by implication in the preceding material of Genesis and Exodus. From time to time attempts have been made to identify the form and content of the ten words in ancient Near Eastern parallel codes (or curse materials, state treaties, etc.), but no analogy for such a *collection* can be provided.

In Exodus 24:1–11 the covenant is ratified by a blood rite whose meaning is difficult to assess. The closest parallel to it is the consecration of Aaron in Leviticus 8, where the blood of the ram is sprinkled upon the person of the priest. If we may press such parallels, notes of consecration can be seen in Exodus 24:1–11. In verses 9–11 a covenant meal takes place in which the leaders of Israel and seventy representative elders eat and drink in the presence of the Deity. This is an important incidental piece of information, since it sets the future goal to which the Bible looks in terms of fellowship relationships. This meal on the mountain becomes the focus of later Old Testament projection (cf. Isa. 25:6–8; Rev. 19:7–9).

The exodus age provided Israel with most of its theological language of redemption. Thus, for example, the note of Israel's sonship is present in Exodus 4:22. Important is the introduction of the term *redeem* (6:6; 15:13), a term which becomes prominent theologically in Isaiah 40–55, where the deliverance from exile is described in terms of a second exodus. The term involves the recovery of something that once belonged to an individual or family but became alienated and thus beyond the power of the owner to reclaim. Its use suggests the return of persons or things to their normal position. Thus, as next of kin, God intervenes as Redeemer to secure the return of Israel to her rightful relationship. From Pharaoh he demands his son, who has become enslaved. Under the social regime of the Old Testament, the beneficiary of such an action becomes indebted to the redeemer and is thought to be related to the redeemer in a special way. Israel was thus accustomed to describe herself as bondslaves of Yahweh, as she had once been bondslaves in Egypt. Thus the Old Testament metaphors for worship often tend to be drawn from the sphere of service. By redemption Israel passed into the service of him whose service is perfect freedom. Thus there is an easy transition from the concept of master and servant to king and subject to father and son.

Exodus 25–31 follows upon the covenant ratification but concerns plans to erect the tabernacle and its associated institutions. The blueprint for the tabernacle is offered to Moses on the mountain (25:9), thus establishing its heavenly character. These chapters are not, as commonly supposed, a digression but are really an explanation of the significance of the covenant. Thus they immediately follow its ratification, a step that involves the acceptance of Yahweh's lordship and kingship. Like the later temple, the tabernacle was thought of in Israel as the earthly dwelling or palace of Yahweh (the Hebrew word for "temple" also means "palace"). After the building of the tabernacle, Yahweh is pictured as enthroned in the midst of the tribes, which surround it on four sides.

The detail of Exodus 25–31 concludes with instructions regarding the Sabbath, while chapters 35–40, in which the tabernacle is actually built, commence with similar instructions regarding Sabbath observance. The point is thus made that tabernacle and Sabbath are closely related. The observance of the Sabbath and the building of the tabernacle are simply two sides of the same coin. In this connection we must briefly discuss the idea underlying the Sabbath.

The connection between the Sabbath and creation has been established by Exodus 20:11. The Hebrew root *šabāt* can mean "stop" or "rest," but the underlying note is that which gives completeness, usually by bringing a series to an end (see Gen. 2:1–4), and thus that which provides a culminating point or purpose (Robinson 1980, 38). As an end to the exodus, then, Sabbath concerns suggest building the tabernacle; similar concerns call for building a temple after the conquest of Canaan is complete.

In Exodus 20:11 the notion of the Sabbath has also been brought into theological connection with the important idea of rest. The concept of rest becomes increasingly significant as the biblical goal of redemption is seen as rest in God's presence. The idea underlying the Hebrew concept is that of ease or refreshment, the development of an atmosphere from which tensions of every kind have been removed. Sabbath and rest thus relate to each other as aim and result: *Sabbath* expresses the divine intention for creation (see Gen. 2:1–4a) and thus directs attention to what will be realized in the future, whereas *rest* refers to the nature of the activity once the goal has been realized. The notion of rest from labor referred to in Exodus 23:12 and 34:21 is derived from and related to the pragmatic nature of the then current form of Israelite society. The primary implication of the word, however, is the presence of God in the Promised Land, presented through the concept of tabernacle/temple, which will make the land the Eden, the sanctuary, it was meant to be (see Exod. 15:17). Sabbath and rest coalesce as factors expressing the purpose and result of the exodus.

The actual building of the tabernacle is returned to in Exodus 35–40 and concludes the book. The position and the amount of space devoted to this topic show the author's paramount concern for it. In the tabernacle's erection, we have the response of an Israel that has been invited to redemption. We need to remember that the tabernacle within the camp was a visible reminder of Israel's form of government. As the earthly palace of the heavenly King, the tabernacle pointed to the locus of final political authority in Israel. The worship response for which the tabernacle called was therefore a recognition of divine kingship exercised over Israel and, in this sense, was also a political act. Worship is therefore the protocol by which access to the Divine King may be obtained. The Book of Exodus thus presents Israel as a worshiping community regulated by its Divine King.

The Book of Exodus also addresses, however, the problem of Israel's inadequacy at Sinai and thereafter in the Old Testament in regard to its vocation. This basic unfitness is seen in Exodus 32, in the narrative of the sin of the golden calf, which follows immediately after the tabernacle account of chapters 25–31. This narrative alerts us to the fact that Israel will probably always fail to respond to the ideals set for her in 19:3–6. This probability is confirmed by the actual progress of Israel's history. What will God now do with Israel after chapter 32? It turns out that he is willing to continue with Israel, but only as a result of the extraordinary intercession of Moses reported in chapter 33. Yahweh plans to commence again with Moses alone, as he had done with Abraham (note Moses' appeal to the basic patriarchal promises in 32:13–14). Moses alone will now be the bearer of God's favor (the Hebrew possessive suffix of 33:14, "I will give *you* rest," is singular, thus virtually transferring the promises of 3:13–15 to Moses).

Attention then shifts to the manner in which Yahweh will be present among Israel on the march to Canaan and to the mediatorial role of Moses. Now, for the first time (Exod. 33:7–11), we see mention of the tent of meeting (not to be identified with the tabernacle, which is not yet built), where Moses will meet with Yahweh. In 33:12–17 Moses identifies himself completely with his people. He then pleads that God make a special appearance to him (vv. 18–23), as he had made a special appearance to Israel in chapter 19. The glory for which Moses asks—the hidden nature of the essence of God, which in the Old Testament cannot be revealed—is not shared with him. In verse 19, however, the name "The LORD" (a synonym in that verse for all God's goodness, his covenant faithfulness) is proclaimed to Moses as an expression of the continuity of the promises (McConville 1979, 153–54).

In Exodus 34 the covenant with Israel is renewed but with an important difference. This renewal stems from Yahweh's character alone. "Abounding in steadfast love" (v. 6), Yahweh is willing to go beyond the legal limits of the relationship established and to continue the covenant in spite of the magnitude of Israel's defection. Moses' mediatorial role (referred to in 20:18–20 but not then brought into being) is now dominant. Covenant renewal comes through him, and the words of the covenant are this time delivered to him alone, not to Israel (34:27–28).

Exodus 34:29–35 concludes the covenant cycle of chapters 19–34 and provides a commentary upon what has now become the position of Israel under covenant. Israel, openly addressed in Exodus 20, is now unable to confront Yahweh. The glory which suffuses Moses' face as a result of divine contact and which indicates his unbroken personal relationship with God can no longer be shared with Israel. Moses remains unveiled only in the divine presence or when addressing Israel as mediator. When not delivering the covenant word, he wears the veil, indicating, as Paul explains in 2 Corinthians 3:7–18, the distance between himself and unbelieving, disobedient, and hardened Israel (see especially 2 Cor. 3:14).

Exodus closes with the erection of the tabernacle, which is then filled with the divine presence, Yahweh's glory cloud, which will lead Israel to Canaan (40:34–38). This brings to a conclusion a book whose span has witnessed a great transition in Israel's fortunes wrought by the exodus redemption. From slavery to worship, bondslaves of Yahweh destined for service as the people of God in the Promised Land, which is presented in the Book of Deuteronomy virtually as a reconstituted Eden, Israel has already given sufficient indication within the Book of Exodus of how illusory those goals will become. Yet, given the nature of Israel's God, it will come as no surprise that the ideals of the Sinai covenant will not be jettisoned, but will find new expression in a new covenant. The beneficiaries of that new covenant will recognize that the goal of their redemption is undivided worship in the presence of the God of Israel in the final sanctuary center of the New Jerusalem, which he, as the fulfilment of all things, will bring down as the inauguration of the new creation.

The Book of Exodus exalts the person of Israel's God. It begins with a fresh revelation to Israel in Egypt that Yahweh remains faithful to the patriarchal promises. The call of Moses (chap. 3) is followed by the inevitable clash between the two imperiums, the kingdom of God and the power of darkness expressed in terms of Pharaoh and Egypt, in the plague narratives (chaps. 5–15). The Passover account (chap. 12) is a paradigm of biblical deliverance. The Song of the Sea (15:1–18) sums up the fact of deliverance and its significance as a new creative move from Yahweh and at the same time explores the prospect for Israel's march to the Promised Land in terms of consummate ease. The covenant narratives (chaps. 19–34) confirm the tenor of the Abrahamic covenant and establish a political Israel, bound to Yahweh and to each other by this expression of the divine will. At the same time the covenant narratives indicate the nature of the true Israel, who will be responsive, over against national Israel, whose infidelity to Yahweh from Sinai onward we may expect. Finally, the remaining chapters of Exodus (35–40) remind us that redemption leads inevitably to worship, the pattern for which is given from heaven, and the content of which is basically the acknowledgment of God as King.

3

Leviticus

Two dominant threads run through the fabric of the Book of Leviticus, which begins and ends with Sinai (Lev. 27:34): the goal of holiness for Israel and the need for forgiveness. The ideal of Israel as a holy people is consistently restated as the major theme. However, if the covenant relationship is to be applicable to Israel's national and personal experience, forgiveness, extended through the sacrificial system, is crucial. In the laws concerning sacrifice (chaps. 1–7), the institution of the priesthood (chaps. 8–10), the laws of clean and unclean (chaps. 11–15), the regulations for the Day of Atonement (chap. 16), the so-called holiness code (chaps. 17–26), and the closing chapter concerning dedications (vows and gifts), the concept of holiness is dominant (the word appears 152 times). The notion of holiness is best understood as indicating separateness or consecration. Thus the Book of Leviticus explains what is demanded of Israel as a holy people.

The Sacrificial System (Lev. 1–7)

The divine institution of sacrifice (chaps. 1–7) is clearly given within the framework of the covenant relationships with which the Book of Exodus has left us. The system did not operate as a means whereby God could be approached, but rather as a means whereby covenant relationships could be maintained or repaired. To take the common view of the Old Testament sacrifices as being merely typical or symbolic, but hardly efficacious, is to read into the Old Testament the later conclusions of the Epistle to the Hebrews, drawn in light of the finality of Jesus' sacrifice. Certainly Hebrews dismisses the Old Testament system and reminds us that the blood of bulls and goats could not take away sin (10:4), as it also underscores the fact that the sacrificial system offered no permanent solution for the problem of sin. However, no Old Testament believer would have believed that the system operated merely mechanically. (It is clear from the Prophets and Psalms, though, that a popular attitude to the cult developed which did see the sacrificial system as mechanical.) In the final analysis, it was not the blood of bulls and goats that took away sin, but the fact that the system was the God-appointed means of forgiveness and covenant repair for the period. The clear understanding of Leviticus is that sacrifice did effect atonement (Lev. 4:35), and by it the worshiper was cleansed and purified from sin. What the system did when the worshiper drew near to the sanctuary, killed his own beast, and laid his own hand upon its head, was to underscore the personal recognition that a breach in relationships had occurred. To suggest that the forgiveness offered through the system was only symbolic or typical reduces sacrifice in the Old Testament to a vague and meaningless ritual. This it never was intended to be.

The Book of Leviticus and analogous legislation classify sin under two major headings: unpremeditated (or "unwitting"—Lev. 5:15; Num. 15:29) and premeditated (or "with a high hand"—Lev. 6:1–2; Num. 15:30). Leviticus makes it clear that both of these types could be forgiven (see Lev. 4 for unpremeditated and 6:1–7 for premeditated). However, as in the New Testament, access to the system was denied to the unrepentant. It would seem that unpremeditated sins did not need to be confessed, while confession made it possible for premeditated sins to fall within the system (see Lev. 5:1–6; 16:21; 26:40; Num. 5:6–8) (Milgrom 1975, 195). Forgiveness was ultimately dependent upon divine grace, a fact the Old Testament underscores by reporting occasions when God forgave without the operation of the system (e.g., 2 Sam. 12). Such instances served to remind Israel (as they remind us) that sacrifice was the customary means of approach, but that God's forgiveness was not mechanically distributed in a context in which there was a constant disposition to misunderstand the system.

We are not told in the Old Testament how the system operated, but conclusions may be drawn from the threefold presentation of the order of sacrifice in Leviticus 1–9 (Rainey 1970, 485–98). In 1:1–6:7, the order is burnt, cereal, peace, and then sin and guilt offerings, in what seems a grouping by association. There follows in 6:8–7:38 an order of burnt, cereal, sin, guilt, and then finally peace offerings. The content of this whole passage is described as Torah, or instruction. It seems to be concerned with administrative procedures relating to the manner of offering. But in Leviticus 9 the system is seen in actual operation. This third order of sin, burnt, and peace offerings is affirmed by other sections of the Old Testament where the entire system is presented in actual performance (see also Exod. 29:10–34; Num. 6:14–17; Ezek. 45:13–17; 2 Chron. 29:31–36). The conclusion is that the first priority of the sacrificial system is the need for sin to be forgiven. Personal consecration (burnt offering) follows as a symbol of commitment, and finally the celebration of reconciliation takes place through the peace offerings. While this reasoning may well offer a helpful insight into the overall operation of the sacrificial system, it must be remembered that throughout the Old Testament the respective components of the system (burnt, cereal, sin, peace) are usually presented separately. It is clear that the burnt offering by itself effects atonement (Lev. 1:4; cf. Gen. 8:21), although perhaps in a more general sense than the sin and guilt, or propitiatory, offerings. The burnt offering also witnesses to the worshiper's faith and commitment (cf. Gen. 22 and Exod. 18:11–12). The cereal offering normally accompanied the burnt offerings but could be offered alone. Since the term used to describe the cereal offering is "tribute," it has been suggested that this offering exemplifies the master/servant relationship in which the covenant had placed Israel (Wenham 1979, 69–70).

The peace offering, unlike the burnt offering (which was totally consumed on the altar), was shared between worshipers and priests; only the kidneys and the fat covering the liver were burnt on the altar. Since there is no agreement concerning the meaning of the Hebrew word *šĕlāmîm* (e.g., in Lev. 3:1), the purpose of this offering remains in doubt. The general contextual evidence of the Old Testament suggests that "peace offering" or "fellowship offering" is indeed an appropriate denotation. Neither the peace offering nor the cereal offering by itself is said to effect atonement. Both are dependent upon prior atoning sacrifices.

The propitiatory or purification offerings are dealt with in Leviticus 4:1–6:7. The procedures for these two offerings (purification and reparation) differed sharply from the other three; these differences were observed whether the offerer was a layperson or a priest. The worshiper did not eat this sacrifice; it was given over to the priesthood. Where a priest was involved, after the mandatory portions had been burnt on the altar, the remainder of the carcass was burnt outside the camp. The purpose of these propitiatory offerings was decontamination and cleansing, since sin is an offense against God's holiness. Though the sin offering (purification) and guilt offering (reparation) were related, they involved different rituals and different animals. The guilt offering seems to have expiated trespasses against sacred things or the divine name, with the underlying idea of compensation for losses incurred (Wenham 1979, 111).

Israel's Priesthood (Lev. 8–10)

Following upon the elaboration of the sacrificial system, the consecration of Aaron and the priesthood occurs in chapters 8–10. The consecration narratives tacitly ascribe to Aaron the dignity and authority of a royal figure (Lev. 8). He is for Israel an embodiment of the vocation offered in Exodus 19:3–6. The anointing of Israel's priests and kings indicated their special relationship to Yahweh. The basic function of Israel's priesthood under the leadership of the high priest was to keep Israel holy, to offer decisions as to what was clean and unclean, to keep Israel from everything which could defile, and to make atonement for Israel when defilement had occurred. Aaron's sons were also consecrated to priestly service.

It is often argued that Levitical specialization in the priesthood was a gradual development in the Old Testament. In the pre-Levitical period the priestly role, it is said, was exercised by the head of the house. Certainly this was true of Israel before the exodus, but it may be a misconception to imagine that such a situation continued. In the period up to the later monarchy, sacrifice was offered by individuals (Judg. 6:20–28; 13:15–23; 1 Sam. 6:14–15; 1 Kings 1:9; 18:30–39). But one must differentiate between sacrifice at the central sanctuary and at the local altars. The Levitical priesthood was bound up with the official cult, but there was no interdiction on the practice of local sacrifice, at least in the early period of the monarchy (Haran 1978, 64). As the centrality of Jerusalem became ascendant, this practice may have died out, though the evidence either way is somewhat tenuous.

The role of the priesthood and the progressive degrees of approach to the divine presence which the structure of the tabernacle and its furnishings demanded pointed to the distinction that Israel was to maintain between the sacred and the profane. Probably the distinction between priests and Levites was an original and basic one, bound up with the more general distinctions of access to the sanctuary.

Holiness and Laws of Purity (Lev. 11–15)

Leviticus 11–15 contains laws of purity, distinguishing sharply between what was considered to be clean and what unclean, thus implementing the priestly vocation specified in 10:10. Holiness, we might note, in the first place defines the nature of God as one who is wholly other. The word for holiness is broadly used in Semitic to refer to a quality of the Deity or to divine names, while objects, animals, and persons may be considered to be holy by virtue of their relationship to Yahweh and his service. Of the 842 references to holiness in the Bible, at least 830 refer to Yahweh, his cult, and his people (Houser 1978, 43). In the Book of Leviticus the term is used with reference to God some 14 times, describing his nature, his power, his majesty, and his person. Yahweh as holy is completely separated from human beings, and yet persons and objects may be made holy when dedicated for Yahweh's service by some form of consecration. God as holy is the model for his people and priests, who are also to be holy and who are to evidence a separateness from their world which stamps them as people of God.

Things or persons that are not holy are classed as common or profane. Anything belonging to this sphere is always available for common use, provided it is ceremonially clean, while a holy thing, although always clean, is never available for common use. Any holy thing may be profaned by improper use. God's name, for example, may be profaned by being taken in vain. Profane or common things are further subdivided into clean and unclean. Uncleanness is transmissible, while cleanness is not, and care must be taken by the priests to avoid contact with what is inherently or ritually unclean. No area of life is exempt from the demand to be holy, for Israel is separated as a holy people to Yahweh. Thus the term *holy* is moral as well as ceremonial. In the final analysis, holiness for Israel and her priests involves obedience to the divine commandments.

Recent anthropological studies have suggested that "cleanness" is a broad term encompassing what we would label as normal or acceptable. The distinction between clean and unclean foods seems to have been based upon what was acceptable to the society and what was not. Fish without scales, for example, were viewed as serpentlike and abnormal and therefore unacceptable for eating. Certain bodily discharges that were seen as deviations from the usual are also said to make a person unclean. Some unclean items were unclean only temporarily, for under other circumstances cultic action could be taken to cleanse them. The regulations relating to clean and unclean in chapters 11–15 reinforce the underlying thesis of the Book of Leviticus that holiness, which belongs to God by nature (11:44–45), must be reflected in the life of the elect people.

Day of Atonement (Lev. 16)

The Day of Atonement (chap. 16), perhaps the most significant day in the national calendar, was the day on which the national sins were symbolically atoned for by cleansing the sanctuary. The high priest was specially clad and entered the inner sanctum, or Holy of Holies, for the only time during the year. Dominant in the chapter is the notion of atonement. The meaning of this term, however, is still in dispute. Perhaps in ritual texts such as Leviticus 16 the meaning is "cleansing." Certainly, however, in the more personal sacrificial texts (e.g., 12:7; 14:18; 15:15) a meaning like "ransom" seems more appropriate. The notions of both ransom and cleansing are required to account for the New Testament understanding of the death of Christ. In any case, the Day of Atonement legislation, with its elaborate procedures for the cleansing of the tabernacle, complements and concludes the extended section on clean and unclean (chaps. 11–15).

Holiness Code (Lev. 17–26)

The holiness code of chapters 17–26 emphasizes the more positive aspect of biblical holiness. It is not merely withdrawal from what is tainted, but it is the exhibition of the wholeness and completeness which characterizes God himself and which must therefore be the property of his people (see, e.g., 19:2; 20:7, 26; 21:6–7). Thus laws calling for separation (chaps. 17–18) are complemented by material dealing with moral (and ceremonial) requirements (chaps. 19–20). The remaining chapters of this section consist of laws for the priesthood (chaps. 21–22) and for the cultic observances that are more generally required of the people (chaps. 23–25). The section concludes in chapter 26 with an exhortation to holiness and a list of accompanying blessings and curses.

Chapter 27 discusses vows and dedicatory gifts and closes the book. Perhaps it may be seen as the proper human response to chapter 26, the divine announcement bearing upon Israel's future (Wenham 1979, 336). In any case, its concern is with what is to be dedicated and thus belongs to God—the subject matter of the whole book.

The Book of Leviticus demands that the people of God reflect his character both in their cultic worship as well as in personal deportment. God as holy (11:44–45) serves as the model for his people, since the very purpose of their redemption is that they might reflect his nature. Particular attention is paid in this book to the priesthood and the cult: to the priesthood, since by their separation they emphasize the role of the nation as a whole, and to the cult, since Israel's worship must reflect the authority base to which it is subject.

But Leviticus is a book operating within a context of grace. God has redeemed Israel, separated the people from their world (18:24), and given them laws by which they are to live (v. 5) and by which the land to which he is bringing them is to be protected (chap. 26). In the final sense Leviticus is a political document describing Israel as a theocracy, an entity ruled by God. God is to be obeyed because of his holiness, demonstrated in the saving history of Israel; underlying the demands for ritual and personal purity in Leviticus is the theology of redemption (11:45; 22:32–33; 25:38, 55; 26:13, 45). He is thus to be served exclusively and completely. The book is thus concerned not with antiquarian or peripheral issues, but with the very practical issue of how life within the covenant is to be maintained. Obedience within this framework is the final requirement. As Israel and the Israelite reflected the law that was the product of their covenant connection, they were impelled by the divine injunction, "You shall therefore keep my statutes and my ordinances, by doing which a man shall live; I am the LORD" (18:5).

4

Numbers

The Book of Numbers opens with Israel still at Sinai, one month after the erection of the tabernacle and thirteen months after the completion of the exodus. The book ends with Israel in the plains of Moab some forty years later, poised to enter the Promised Land after repeated national failures. It is thus the narrative of a spiritual pilgrimage. Israel's continuance as a people with the possibility of inheriting the promise of the land is entirely due to the superintendence of her affairs by God, who never ceases to strive with her infidelity during this desert experience. The wanderings through the wilderness (the Hebrew title of the book means simply "In the Wilderness") are calculated to teach Israel the essence of obedience. These lessons are designed to place before Israel once again the ideal to which she should politically and personally correspond.

In the wanderings of this period the national characteristics that we have already seen displayed in the failure at Sinai (Exod. 32) are clearly in evidence again. The Book of Numbers thus carries with it the message of further national failure, a failure which typifies the manner in which

Israel will live out her national history in the Promised Land. This wilderness period was a time of testing and sifting for Israel, providing occasion after occasion on which Israel could rise to a position of national trust in God, which would have brought blessing. But the unhappy message of the book is that a period of great national failure occurred at a time when significant formative influences should have been at work. From this period the nation never in fact recovered, and the remainder of the Old Testament presents the history of an Israel provided with countless unrealized opportunities to become what they were meant to be—a separated people of God. Thus, when Ezekiel reviews the history of Israel and speaks to a nation now in exile (Ezek. 20), he passes over the period of the monarchy without reference, confining his attention to decisions taken by Israel during the wilderness period that were responsible for her present exilic distress. At the same time, however, Ezekiel, like the other prophets of the Old Testament, sees the wilderness period as the time when the ideal governmental structures for Israel were established. When he turns to the future constitution of Israel (Ezek. 40–48), he takes his model for the community of the end time from the wilderness period and its institutions.

The theme of the people of God on the march to the Promised Land connects Numbers to the Book of Hebrews in the New Testament. Unlike Hebrews, however, the Book of Numbers deals with Israel's rejection of rather than commitment to an ideal whereby the Promised Land would be secured. We cannot come to the end of the Book of Numbers without feeling that the future for national Israel now stands very much in the balance. In this sense Numbers is a very human book, not only serving to indicate the opportunities which were wasted by Israel in a most spiritually favored situation, but also demonstrating the manner in which rebellion progressively hardened the national heart. Numbers has the following divisions:

> **1:1–10:10** Israel at Sinai: Legislation for the ideal Israel
> **10:11–22:1** Rebellion in the wilderness
> **22:2–36:13** In the plains of Moab
> **22:2–24:25** Balaam
> **25–36**   Preparations for the entry into Canaan

The Ideal Israel (Num. 1:1–10:10)

The first six chapters introduce us to the ideal for Israel in this period. The census of Numbers 1 tells us that the multitudinous descendants of Jacob have now become a great people. Though primarily concerned to display fitness for battle (1:2–3, 20, etc.), the census also serves to indicate how each Israelite clan contributes to the wider whole and to stress the family links, and thus the total unity prevailing, among the tribes. The tribes are arranged in battle order around the tabernacle (chap. 2), the symbol of Israel's leadership by God and his kingship. This is an interesting concept, to which Ezekiel returns in his reapportionment of the Promised Land in Ezekiel 48. With such a concept we have begun this book on a high note of national discipline. Israel is equipped for conquest, with the symbols of her charter and authority in the midst of her camp. In a sense the message of the book is met here, for it is by discipline, self-control, and divine national regulation that the Promised Land will be attained. Moreover, the presence of Yahweh in the midst of the camp is the sole guarantee of victory (cf. 14:44). This presence of Yahweh as King is symbolized by the dark heavy cloud which covers the tabernacle.

This cloud, also known as the glory cloud, precedes Israel on her march, not only providing her with direction during the journey, but also regulating its stages (see 9:15–23; 12:5–10). The glory cloud is thus God's manifested presence, serving both to save and to judge Israel during this wilderness period. After the census of the Levites is taken (chaps. 3–4) and a poll tax provided for, chapters 5–6 concern the question of ridding the camp of contamination. Chapters 1–6 are brought to a somewhat logical conclusion with the Nazirite vow, which represents an ideal act of dedication. The Aaronic blessing follows, in which God's intention for Israel is again repeated. Numbers 7–9 details events such as tribal offerings for the tabernacle, the dedication of the Levites, and the institution of the second Passover, all of which happened within the period covered by chapters 1–6. The manner in which the glory cloud guided is described (9:15–23), and further instruction to coordinate movement is given (10:1–10).

Through the Wilderness (Num. 10:11–22:1)

The second major division is concerned with the theme of God's guidance through the wilderness. God leads his people like a shepherd (Num. 27:17), and they set off in battle order, led by Judah, with the cloud preceding (10:11–28). As proof that they are the people of God, God feeds them in the wilderness with manna and quails and provides them with water from the rock (11:7, 31–32; 20:11). Chapters 11–21 exhibit Israel under testing from hunger (chap. 11), leadership struggles (chaps. 12, 16–17), and fear of adversaries, as a result of which they are unwilling to enter the adjacent Promised Land (chaps. 13–14). These trials were designed to fit them for entry into the land, which is presented in Eden-like terms (13:23–27). While Israel will eventually arrive at

Jericho, temporarily purified and thus invincible (26:63–65), Numbers 10:11–22:1 is designed to show us the disastrous results of Israel's contact with the profane in the wilderness and her incessant murmurings in spite of the continued divine providence and presence (Exod. 15:22–16:36).

Virtually none of the Israelites of the exodus period, not even Moses himself, survive the time of testing in the wilderness. Of the adult males, Caleb and Joshua, who returned with a favorable report from the Promised Land (Num. 14:6), are the exceptions. Still, Moses is presented in this book as the supreme commander in almost royal terms. He makes the final decisions, regulates the cult, and above all is the true prophet and intercessor for the community (11:24–25; 12:6–8). But even he exceeds his authority and strikes the rock rather than merely addressing a word to it in Yahweh's name (20:10–13). Wilderness trials of this character reduce Israel from a largely disciplined congregation at the commencement of the book to an unruly mob of petulant, fearful people who eventually try the patience of their leader beyond its limits. These chapters deal with a time of transition. The exodus generation does not survive the wilderness because, when they arrived at Kadesh-barnea (13:26), a highly suitable point of entry from the south into the Promised Land, they refused to heed Caleb and Joshua's promising report. This, moreover, took place within two years of the exodus!

Numbers thus relates the account of two generations: one that perishes in the wilderness through unbelief, and one that is placed in the plains of Moab with the striking advantage of having seen firsthand the disastrous results of disobedience. They repeat, however, the curious and continual paradox of the Old Testament. Once they enter the land, Israel shows the same tendencies and behavior patterns as the first generation, putting the whole nation proleptically into another wilderness situation, which finally led to the later exile.

After Aaron's authority has been vindicated against the priestly revolts in Numbers 16–17, further instruction aimed at cultic regulation is given (chaps. 18–19), which again emphasizes the national need for purity and separation: God's purposes for Israel have not lapsed, rebellion notwithstanding. Numbers 20:1–22:1 takes us from Kadesh to the plains of Moab.

A turning point comes with the victory of Israel over the Canaanites at Hormah (21:3). A previous defeat at Hormah (14:45), after an abortive attempt by the old generation to enter the land, had signaled their role from that time on as aimless pilgrims. Yet there is no indication that this new generation will fare better than their fathers. Murmuring resurfaces immediately after the victory at Hormah (21:4–9), and the judgment must be assuaged by the brazen serpent. Chapters 21–26 then deal with the fortunes of the new generation after this heartening victory in the south and the subsequent defeat of Sihon the Ammonite and Og of Bashan.

In the Plains of Moab (Num. 22:2–36:13)

While Israel encamps on the plains of Moab, spiritual opposition in the form of Balaam the Mesopotamian seer is held in check by God (chaps. 22–24). Balaam must bless, though called by Balak of Moab to curse. The tenor of this blessing is that the Abrahamic promises will shortly be realized: a multitudinous people in the Promised Land, living in peace. Characteristically, this further documentation of the divine intention for Israel is followed by the act of dire apostasy at Baal-peor (25:1–15), provoked by contact with the Midianites. In the manner of Exodus 32, this outbreak is dealt with by faithful priests. A new census called for in Numbers 26 indicates that the forty years of wandering are over, and a new beginning is heralded. Many parallels can be drawn between the people of the census of Numbers 26, which begins a new phase for Israel, and the congregation of the earlier census. In addition to the fact that in each case the census list makes a fresh start for Israel, it is to be noted that (1) a legal discourse involving women is present in Numbers 5 and 27, and laws regarding vows appear in Numbers 6 and 30; (2) the celebration of the Passover in Numbers 9 finds a parallel in regulations for that feast in 28:16–25; (3) the Midianites who impel Israel to apostasy in chapter 25 are punished by Israel in chapter 31; (4) Israel's wilderness journey in the first half of the book is recapitulated in chapter 33; (5) the list of twelve spies in Numbers 13, one from each tribe, is matched by a list of tribal leaders in Numbers 34 who will be engaged in land allotment; (6) Numbers 15 gives laws relating to sacrificial offerings, as Numbers 28–29 does concerning regulation of feast days; and (7) a provision for the Levites at Numbers 18:21–32 is matched by the provision of Levitical cities in Numbers 35 (Olson 1985, 87–88).

Since the occupancy of the land is in view, chapters 27–30 concern laws relating to its possession and retention (repetition of the sacrificial code in brief, in chaps. 28–29, particularly in regard to public sacrifices) and material relating to inheritance (27:1–11) and to succession in Israel's leadership (vv. 12–23). Numbers 31–32 paves the way for the entry by recounting the defeat of the Midianite confederation and the settlement of the Transjordanian tribes (Reuben, Gad, and part of Manasseh). A presentation of the wilderness itinerary, including achievements and obstacles overcome, follows (chap. 33). Finally, chapters 34–36, in view of the impending entry, are given over to particular instructions about the land (descriptions of borders, provision for cities of refuge, etc.).

These years in the wilderness established the character of later Israel. Testing produced occasional faithfulness, but mainly it led to repeated displays of apostasy. This massive army of Israel, with which the book began, moved irresolutely from place to place, organized for battle, meeting no enemy except the righteous God. The people continually offended him and consequently were brought into judgment for their rebellion. When they did engage in rare skirmishes in the wilderness, it was the power of God, not their prowess, that provided the victory. Despite the faithlessness of Israel, Numbers reports Yahweh as holding true to his promise. Thus, though one Israel dies out in the wilderness, it is replaced by another of comparable size (Num. 26). Aaron is replaced by his son Eleazar (20:28), as Moses is by Joshua (27:12–23).

The Book of Numbers is in essence two-sided. The somber side is the side of judgment. After the wonderful experience of exodus and Sinai, it is a tragic record of so many lost opportunities. Positively, however, the Book of Numbers is concerned, as Leviticus is, to establish the very sharp contrast for Israel between the sacred and the profane. The message of the book very clearly is that if Israel wishes to enjoy the blessings of the Land of Promise, they must follow God's unfailing guidance and keep themselves unspotted from the world.

5

Deuteronomy

Structure of Deuteronomy

The Book of Deuteronomy records addresses of Moses to Israel in the plains of Moab and about to enter the Promised Land. Three farewell speeches of Moses are recorded, each of the latter two building upon the previous speech. The first, after the introduction to the book, commences at 1:6 and consists of a survey of Yahweh's activity on Israel's behalf during her wanderings extending from Horeb to the Jordan (1:6–3:29). It concludes with an exhortatory section in which Moses appeals for Israel's obedience (4:1–40). There follows a brief appendix (vv. 41–43) which refers to the establishment of the cities of refuge. The second address commences with a brief introduction in 4:44–49 and continues as the heart of the book until the end of chapter 28. The third address, Deuteronomy 29–30, is an appeal to accept the implications of the Sinai covenant that have been expanded upon in the previous addresses. The options of "life" in the covenant or "death" (i.e., exclusion from the Promised Land) are placed before Israel (30:15–20). Chapters 31–34 are additional material which primarily seeks to provide for a successor to Moses and to sum up his achievements.

With good reason scholars in recent years have seen very definite parallels between the structure of the Book of Deuteronomy and the form of the ancient Near Eastern state treaty, an instrument by which diplomatic relationships between powers were regulated. Such treaties are best known from Hittite archives (ca. 1400–1200 B.C.) and in their ideal but extrapolated form consist of (1) preamble, (2) historical prolog, (3) stipulations, (4) covenant sanctions, (5) ratification, and (6) blessings and curses. Requirements for periodic readings could be included. While this form does not match exactly the material of Deuteronomy, the fit is close enough to suggest that comparison is justified. Such modifications as exist would have been undertaken by the author to provide for the necessary theological adjustments. The most serious difference is that Deuteronomy has to do with covenant renewal, and not with initiation. Since most of the theological emphases of Deuteronomy are spread throughout the exhortatory sections of the book, our discussion must be thematic rather than sequential.

Themes of Deuteronomy

Land

The most compelling feature of the book is the persistent theme of Israel's occupying the land and the theological significance of the land in Israel's experience. This theme is well caught in Deuteronomy 26, a chapter which reflects the attitude of the grateful pilgrim who comes before Yahweh at the central sanctuary on the occasion of the Feast of First Fruits (Pentecost). Returning thanks for the gift of the land, the worshiper confessionally affirms that the land has come to Israel as a result of the fidelity of Yahweh to the patriarchal promises (v. 3). The non-Palestinian origin of Israel's fathers is recognized, as are the Egyptian sojourn and the significance of the exodus.

The matter of the land must be taken further here because of the emphasis placed upon it in Deuteronomy and its paramount importance for Israel's political history. The Book of Deuteronomy is almost entirely given over to the prospect of entry into Canaan and how Israel must deport itself nationally once it is there. This emphasis upon the land complements the emphasis of the Book of Exodus—the redemptive process, that is, the rescue of the people of God, and the definition of their status and function. While Exodus deals with the matter of Israel's redemption, Deuteronomy at its very commencement delimits the boundaries of Israel's Land of Promise (Deut. 1:7–8, where the boundaries detailed by

Moses are substantially those of Gen. 15:18–21). Deuteronomy 1:10–11 continues the Abrahamic note with reference to the multitudinous character of Israel, leaving us in no doubt as to what the theological bent of this last book of the Pentateuch will be.

Returning to chapter 26, we find that heavy stress is laid upon the land as a gift, yet at the same time, through the language of inheritance (v. 1), assertions are made that Israel has legal and binding rights to it. The paradox of the gift is therefore presented to us: before Israel may inherit it (26:1), Yahweh must dispossess the present occupants. It is, on the one hand, God's bounty to Israel, hers by right. On the other hand, she must take it by conquest (Miller 1969, 455). The notion of a deity's owning national territory was generally accepted in the ancient Near East (von Waldow 1974, 494–95). For Israel it was a potentially dangerous notion, since she was entering territory whose owner from another point of view was Baal, the god of fertility, storms, and war. The capriciousness which characterized the blessings of the fertility deities in the ancient world is rejected in Deuteronomy 27–28 in favor of a system of blessing and curses which followed respectively from covenant response or rejection. In the Old Testament it was always easy to transfer religious conceptions and to mix faiths; thus the Book of Deuteronomy constantly warns against the acceptance of Canaanite practices. The book makes it clear that Yahweh's ownership of Palestine arises from his sovereignty over all things, from his lordship of creation (Deut. 32:8–9, LXX). Canaan was thus Israel's inheritance, given to her by Yahweh, who owned all lands (Josh. 23:4). The key term used in the book to describe the character of the inheritance, "heritage," has the firm meaning of landed property which has been apportioned to an individual from a larger whole (von Waldow 1974, 494). Thus Yahweh's lordship of the land was acknowledged. Since the land was Yahweh's, it could not be sold, and thus the rights of particular Israelite subgroupings were preserved by complicated rules of land tenure, namely, the laws of the Sabbath and Jubilee years. To some extent these laws may always have been idealistic (they are detailed in Lev. 25, but seem never to have been implemented), but they did preserve an understanding of Israel's right relationship to the land.

Holy War

Since the land, though a gift, had to be taken, the Book of Deuteronomy develops the important theology of holy (i.e., of Yahweh) war to give expression to this truth. We recall that Israel had recanted her unbelief and tried abortively to enter the land from the south (Num. 14:40–45; Deut. 1:41–45). Thus Deuteronomy commences with the awareness that the land can be Israel's only if Yahweh gives it to her. He will add the land, and he alone will be responsible for the remarkable series of victories that will put it in her possession. Thus a theology of conquest arises, stemming, to be sure, from Israel's past history, but more so from the nature of Israel's Deity. In this way the tensions between the land as a gift and as an object to be conquered and possessed are resolved. The Book of Deuteronomy thus assumes a particularly martial character, and references to the manner of conquest are scattered throughout the book (see, e.g., 6:19; 7:1–11; 9:1–3; 11:23–25; 12:29–31; chap. 20). Opposition to the entry can be expected. Israel must be disciplined to enter and to occupy the land, but in the final analysis Yahweh will give it to them.

Promised Land as Sanctuary

The view of Canaan as God's Promised Land, in which Israel is to live as an ideal political unit in service to Yahweh, is developed further by a depiction of the land in Eden-like terms as a highly desirable and fruitful place (Deut. 8:7–9; 11:10–12) and thus as a sanctuary. We have been prepared for this by Exodus 15:17, where the land is described as God's holy mountain and sanctuary. Deuteronomy richly develops this thought. The land is presented as a good land, "flowing with milk and honey," whose hills are copper (Deut. 6:3; 8:7–9, etc.). In such a land, fulness of life and prosperity will be enjoyed. Israel will be blessed above all peoples (7:14), and all sickness will be removed as well as every threat to Israel's security (v. 15). God's particular care will always be on the land, and it will be the object of his special attention (11:11–12).

Parallels may be drawn between Adam in Eden and Israel in Canaan. Like Adam (Gen. 2:8), Israel was formed outside of the land. Placed in the land by God, she was given a code which was to regulate life there. In the land she was promised particular access to the divine presence, but the threat existed that if the regulations were not kept, she would be expelled from the land. Even before the entry, what had become a reality for Adam (expulsion from the land) became a threat for Israel (Deut. 28:63–68; see Lohfink 1969, 162).

In these circumstances, as we might expect, the boundaries of the Promised Land are always carefully defined. This demarcation is always in terms of possessions west of Jordan. Such weight is placed upon the crossing of the Jordan that the verb "to cross" can be used to express the actual conquest of the land (Deut. 6:1). It is always made clear that the possession of the land is in fulfilment of promises given to the fathers. Not only are the boundaries of the land Abrahamic, but the manner of taking possession of it recalls the injunction to Abraham. Israel is told that every place upon which the sole of her foot will tread shall be hers (Deut. 11:24). We are not far here from the legal terminology of Genesis 13:17, where, given the land in prospect, Abram is invited to walk the length and breadth of it.

Since the land is viewed as a sanctuary, it is appropriate that a central shrine should have been marked out at that point where the twelve tribes in regular festival pilgrimages were to recognize the nature of Yahweh's rule. It is often suggested that this law of the sole altar in chapter 12 indicates that Deuteronomy was the book discovered in Josiah's time (2 Kings 22:10–20). But it is clear that the material of Deuteronomy basically reflects an earlier period and that the law of the one sanctuary is a fundamental provision of the book. Perhaps the formula "the place which the LORD your God shall choose" (Deut. 12:5) establishes the principle of the sole altar but leaves open the particular site, for the time being, though in any case the emphasis is upon Yahweh's choice (McConville 1984, 31–32) and not upon the place. It is noteworthy, in connection with the sanctuary, that the key chapter of Deuteronomy 12 opens (vv. 1–4) and closes (vv. 29–31) with a polemic directed against Canaanite gods.

Rest

Bound up with the land is the important question of "rest." The ceremony of Deuteronomy 26, which is the worshipers' response to the gift of the land, follows the detail of 25:17–19, which declares that, when enemies round about have been dealt with, then "rest" in the land will follow. The gifts of 26:1–2 are the grateful response to that fact. This concept of rest finds frequent expression (3:20; 12:9; 25:19) and is bound up with the notion of a pleasant life in the land (15:4; 23:20; 28:8; 30:16), free from all the threats of enemies. Israel is to enjoy without threat the blessings of creation in her Eden-like situation. Like Adam in the garden, Israel is meant to enjoy the blessings of creation and to worship before God in a situation of ever-increasing awareness of the significance of the divine presence. Deuteronomy is insistent that only a correct view of Yahweh and a proper response to his gift can secure this rest. We are therefore not surprised to find that the important chapter 12, which deals with the centralization of the sanctuary, treats rest and sanctuary as interdependent notions (vv. 10–11). When Yahweh has given Israel "rest," then he "will make his name dwell" at the central sanctuary.

Important also is the association of rest with the concept of the Sabbath in 5:12–15. There the fourth commandment is linked directly to redemption, unlike its counterpart in Exodus 20:11, where Sabbath and creation are joined. Such different representations are really complementary, however, for redemption from Egypt ushered in a new-creation atmosphere, returning Israel to an Eden-like environment. Such a rest was thus seen as the result of the entry into the land. Unfortunately, as we know from the Old Testament, this rest was never fully realized. Even the New Testament believer sees this rest, the ultimate in salvation blessing, as a prospect (Heb. 4:6–11).

Law and Love

After Deuteronomy 26:12–15 has dealt with the giving of tithes to the underprivileged, the topic changes to the law and thus to Israel's response to the covenant by which the land would be retained (vv. 16–19). The matter of Torah, or law, is one which the Book of Deuteronomy ranges widely over, applying its tenor both to the individual (which explains the frequent use of the second-person singular) and to the nation. Important for our understanding of the major role which law plays in Deuteronomy is the explanation given in 6:20–25. When a son asks his father about the meaning of the law, the answer is to be given that the law is a witness to something which stands behind it and accounts for it—the great redemption from Egypt. The law is to be understood in the light of the context of grace in which it was given (Exod. 20:1–2). Law expounds the nature of the relationship brought into being by redemption. Without a prior redemption there would have been no basis for the operation of law (Toombs 1965, 400). Though law later degenerates into a narrow legalism as it becomes increasingly externalized in pious circles, the true nature of Torah was never lost. This explains the very easy accommodation in the New Testament of law and gospel.

Complementing law in Deuteronomy is the command to love God, which in turn is set against the background of God's love and choice of Israel. The totality of the law is thus comprehended in one demand (Deut. 6:4–5). Love, however, is more than mere affection or devotion. Love always appears in association with some activity: walking in his ways (10:12), keeping his commandments (5:10), obeying his voice (13:4). Love thus demands that the person engage in practices that demonstrate covenant fidelity. Love, though never a slavish obedience to rules but rather a growing understanding of and a commitment to the divine will, involves a demonstration of what God requires, or law. We need to understand the context in which love and the demands that flow from it are set within the Book of Deuteronomy. Israel is constantly reminded of her previous servitude in Egypt. Redemption has now made her a bondslave to Yahweh. The nature of this respectful obedience is also stressed by use of the father-son terminology (8:5; 14:1). Deuteronomy also gives attention to the concept of fear as a further response to Yahweh. Fear and love are sometimes set side by side and seem thus to be used interchangeably (10:12–22).

Fear, however, finds its roots in the Sinai experience of Israel, where divine holiness was disclosed. It is thus the element of dread and respectful awe that the Sinai experience evoked (5:29; 6:2). Fear demands a proper attitude before Yahweh, specifically, love, and its outworking in practical action (Kooy 1975, 106–16). The generation of the exodus is to fear God by keeping his commandments (6:24–25). Love is thus a calculated course of action which in turn may lead to a national (or individual) character. Love depends upon instruction to make the path of duty plain (6:4–9; 11:18–21; 31:12). Loving God means the keeping of his commandments—not, however, out of a bald sense of duty, but in grateful national response to the redemption provided. In terms similar to Paul's, love is the practical response of obedience from which a heightened faith emerges (cf. Rom. 1:5). Deuteronomy seeks not a joyless service but a set of responses which stem from deep conviction lodged in the national and personal heart. Deuteronomy never fails to draw attention to the interiority of the covenant (6:5; 10:12; 26:16; 30:14). Thus not coerced obedience but trustful behavior stemming from a changed heart is what the book seeks. The requirement of obedience is the note on which the summarizing chapter 26 ends. The aim of the Mosaic declaration is to bring into being and maintain Israel as a holy people (v. 19).

In the plains of Moab the vocation of Israel is again set before her. The implications of the choices that this vocation implies appear in chapters 27–28. The differing ways of life which will result from obedience to or rejection of the divine will, and the blessings or curses which will flow from the acceptance or rejection of the covenant, are laid out. Finally, Moses closes with a call for Israel to choose fulness of life in the land, which would be the realization of the Abrahamic relationship (30:15–20).

Deuteronomic Humanitarianism

In essence, Deuteronomy is never interested merely in providing civil or social legislation by which the community may be regulated. That is why the exposition of the social codes differs from Exodus 21–23, even though the detail is similar or even identical. There is a pronounced humanitarian bent in Deuteronomy (cf. Deut. 15:12–18 with Exod. 21:2–11; see also Deut. 22:13–19; 25:13–16, etc.). From beginning to end, we are confronted with a preached ethic; Torah is expounded and explained in pronouncedly sermonic and exhortatory terms. Laws providing for civil regulation, settlement of civil suits, or property matters, which are dominant in Exodus 21–23, barely rate a mention (Weinfeld 1972, 282–97). The author centers his attention on human welfare, underscoring the laws that relate to human life and personal happiness. Deuteronomy is concerned to emphasize Israel's relationship to Yahweh and therefore that of Israelite to Israelite. In keeping with this focus, the major statement concerning Yahweh—"The LORD our God is one LORD"

(6:4)—is not a statement regarding God's essential nature, his ontological indivisibility; rather, it concerns the exclusive demand that Israel's life and worship be directed to him.

If Israel's heart is fixed on Yahweh, if he is worshiped as he should be, and if the covenant is thereby kept, then the blessing of life in the good land that Yahweh has chosen will result. Israel is to learn from the past and actualize the Sinai covenant in her national experience. Will Israel do so? Deuteronomy essentially raises this question as Israel stands in the plains of Moab. Will she in fact choose life or death? Subsequent history will indicate the series of disastrous choices to which Israel committed herself.

An Overview of the Pentateuch

The Book of Deuteronomy draws together the promise theology which was presented to Israel in the successive Abrahamic and Sinaitic covenants. In this sense it serves a summarizing function, binding together people and land as a unit, seeing the future of Israel as bound up with the land. If we begin our assessment of the history of Israel from Genesis 12 onward, Deuteronomy provides a nexus of promise and potential fulfilment.

Patriarchal Genesis deals with the formation of the twelve tribes. Exodus sees the provision of land through redemption as facilitating Israel's vocation to be a witnessing people of God, exhibiting an ideal political structure. Leviticus provides legislation whereby the tensions between actual human experience and covenant expectations could be met. Its major purpose, however, is to underscore the nature of Israel as a holy people. Numbers records Israel's trek from Sinai to the plains of Moab, while Deuteronomy calls upon Israel to reflect upon her past history of salvation and to recognize that her future depends upon actualization of the Sinai covenant.

Only the barest hints, it would seem, of contact with Genesis 1–11 appear in the rest of the Pentateuch. A doctrine of creation does, however, underlie Israel's concept of redemption. That is presented in Exodus 15, not only by the basic structure of that poem, which reveals contact with the common creation accounts of the day, but by the purpose of the exodus itself, which would place Israel in a new sanctuary situation, a land (Yahweh's mountain) which would be the point of revelatory contact for the world at large. This latter intention recalls strikingly the more general mandate given to humankind in Eden at the beginning. The link between Sabbath and creation provided by Exodus 20:11 reminds us also of the forward-looking nature of Israel's covenant theology. In these senses the positive notes of Genesis 1–2 are carried forward. At the same time the frustration of Genesis 3–11 is already evident in Israel's history from her national formation at Sinai onward. A widening gap develops between the ideal postulated for Israel and the reality which her history begins to exhibit. Exodus 19–34 clearly indicates that not all Israel are in fact the true Israel.

The dichotomy between the correspondences to Genesis 1–2 and those to the cold realities of Genesis 3–11 is very apparent in the Book of Numbers and in the blessing-and-curse structure of both Leviticus and Deuteronomy, particularly in the series of choices which Deuteronomy places before Israel. We see reflected in the Pentateuch's history of Israel both the possibilities provided for in Genesis 1–2 and the disappointments encountered in Genesis 3–11. In this sense the remainder of the Pentateuch offers a comment on Genesis 1–11. By the time that the covenantal theology of Israel is fully developed in the Book of Deuteronomy, a program to which the rest of the Old Testament remains committed, the national failure of Israel has been anticipated. The Pentateuch makes it clear, however, that this failure in no way vitiates the eschatology already developed in these books. A people of God will be constructed and will enjoy the ideal of rest in a Promised Land. God will be her God and will indwell her forever!

It should be clear to the reader that with the Pentateuch the theological framework of the Old Testament and indeed the Bible has been erected. It is the task of the historical books, to which we now turn our attention, to trace the progress of national Israel further, building upon the structures provided by the first five books of the Bible and elaborating them in a way completely consistent with the Pentateuchal ideals.

Part 2

The Books of the Prophets: The Former Prophets

6

Joshua

The intent of the Book of Joshua to fulfil the program of the Book of Deuteronomy is very clear. The book commences with preparations for immediate entry into the Promised Land and concludes with the covenant renewed by the twelve tribes, among whom the land has been divided. The contents of the book may be summarized as follows:

1:1–5:12	Preparations for the invasion of Canaan
5:13–12:24	Three-pronged invasion of Canaan
13–19	Distribution of land among the tribes
20–21	Cities of refuge and Levitical cities
22	Integration of the Transjordanian tribes
23	Joshua's closing address
24	Covenant assembly at Shechem

The book thus deals with the acquisition and maintenance of the land. It has a close theological relationship with the Book of Deuteronomy (Wenham 1971, 148). Deuteronomy's sermonic exhortations to Israel and blueprint for the occupancy of the land are translated into the practical obedience which the Book of Joshua displays. However, the emphasis within the Book of Joshua lies upon Yahweh—his fidelity to the covenant promises and his willingness to put them into practical effect. Joshua is an optimistic book: with the burials of Joshua and Eleazar, it closes on a note of an era successfully ended, as it opened with the ushering in of the new era in which Mosaic exhortation was to give way to implementation. In leading the conquest Joshua is portrayed throughout as Moses' successor and his virtual extension. Indeed, the close relationship between Deuteronomy and Joshua calls to mind that between Luke and Acts.

Conquest (Josh. 1–12)

Joshua 1 sets the tone for the book. The key address of verses 1–9 emphasizes Yahweh's role in the conquest: in verses 2–6 especially, he is the giver of the land and thus the faithful fulfiller of the patriarchal promises. It is clear that Israel will receive the land because Yahweh will take it (v. 5). The undertones of the holy-war theology of Joshua are thus emerging, as is Israel's obligation to be a covenant people (vv. 7–9). Joshua has only to adhere to the relationship through trustful obedience to Torah precepts. The summary first chapter ends on this note. Additionally, the Deuteronomic promise of "rest" in the land (v. 13), though incidentally introduced in this chapter, sets before us again the goal of the conquest.

The prospects held out in Joshua 1 are transferred into initial achievement by the end of Joshua 11. The theological summary of 11:23 reports that the conquest of which Yahweh is the architect has been completed in response to the promises given to Moses. The division of the land to all Israel is anticipated, and with it will come fulfilment of the promise of rest. Chapters 2–5 deal with the mission of the spies, the crossing of the Jordan, presented in liturgical terms as a divine progress (see chap. 3), and the reconstitution of the New Israel of this second generation at Gilgal (chaps. 4–5). Note that there has been no emphasis upon circumcision as an all-Israelite rite since Genesis 17, a fact which adds to the new-era note in the narrative. The Gilgal Passover formally brings the wilderness wanderings to a conclusion (Josh. 5:10–12). Yahweh now comes as Divine Warrior to this newly constituted people (note "I have *now* come" in v. 14). The conquest is now to begin for a purified Israel.

The ease of the conquest of Jericho serves as a paradigm for the manner in which Yahweh will dispossess Canaan and make it sacred space. Jericho (chap. 6) is dedicated to Yahweh by an elaborate act of worship before the blowing of the trumpets which announce his presence and, after the last circumambulation of the city, signify its capture. Israel embarks upon a holy war and not a war of conquest from which material benefits may be derived. This distinction is emphasized by detailing the requirements of the ban, whereby the spoils of conquest are to be dedicated to Yahweh. The story of Achan and Ai (Josh. 7) serves as a quick reminder of what Israel will do if left to herself. Achan's breach of the ban brings disaster upon all Israel. Ai is then given to a chastened people by Yahweh, after which a rededication ceremony is held, again reminding Israel of the centrality of Torah for success (8:30–35).

The type of unthinking political compromise in which Israel later indulged is prefigured by the ill-advised compact with the Gibeonites in Joshua 9. The south and its city-states are then miraculously delivered to Israel by Yahweh, with the ban, this time, completely observed (chap. 10). The conquest of the north is recorded in chapter 11, and chapter 12 provides a list of defeated kings.

Division of the Land (Josh. 13–21)

Chapters 13–21 detail the division of the land. This phase likewise proceeds under divine direction (in chaps. 13–14 note the use of the lot and the express dependence upon divine initiative). The provision for Levitical cities at the end of the distribution again focuses our attention upon the centrality of Torah teaching and its cruciality for Israel's tenure in the land. The unity of all Israel is the aim, despite the division which the Jordan has imposed (see chap. 22, where the ill-advised attempt by the Transjordanian tribes to build an altar on the west bank is noted).

Covenant Renewal (Josh. 23–24)

In his closing address Joshua reviews the divine achievement and gives timely warnings to Israel. Rest, in the sense of general occupation of the Promised Land, has now been achieved. Although "very much land" (13:1) remains to be possessed, at least in broad terms Israel has been established in the land and is now instructed how to keep it. This charge involves adherence to the Mosaic law and the sole worship of Yahweh (23:6–8), the recognition of the land as Yahweh's gift (vv. 9–11), the maintenance of the special character of Israel by avoiding intermarriage with other nations (vv. 12–13), and above all, complete fidelity to the demands of the covenant (vv. 15–16). The book closes with covenant renewal and national rededication at Shechem (24:1–28); there is also indication that with the deaths of Joshua and Eleazar, the leaders of the wilderness period, Israel now faces another period of transition (vv. 29–33).

Joshua ends with the proclamation of Yahweh's rule over Israel. The book has focused upon his fidelity to patriarchal promises. Politically the stage has now been set for Israel to fulfil her Abrahamic mandate. Little has been seen of Israel's response, for it has been a book about the divine acts of Yahweh. The Book of Judges, by contrast, transfers the focus from Yahweh to Israel, and the results are disastrous.

7

Judges

The Book of Judges is the account of the results of Israel's failure to complete the mandate for conquest issued in Deuteronomy and Joshua. Judges 1 surveys the later geographical placement of the tribes (from Judah to Dan, south to north) and points to the pattern of irresolution, absorption of foreign elements, and gradual tribal disintegration which foreshadows the remainder of the book. However, there is a movement at the close of the book (chaps. 19–21) toward recovery of the unity which characterized the earlier conquest period. We may outline the Book of Judges as follows:

1:1–3:6	Introduction to the period of the judges
3:7–16:31	The exploits of the heroic figures
17–21	Two appendixes about life during the period
17–18	The migration of the tribe of Dan
19–21	The guilt and punishment of the tribe of Benjamin

In the main body of the book (3:7–16:31), Israel lurches from crisis to crisis because of the apostasy produced inevitably by failure to separate

69

herself from the inhabitants of the land. The angelic messenger of 2:1–5 simply reinforces the message previously delivered through Joshua: covenant infidelity will inevitably bring judgment, for which the tribes must now prepare themselves. The superficiality of Israel's response to inspired leadership is pointed out in 2:6–10. The Israelite nation throughout the Old Testament period would always be prompted to obedience by divinely given leadership, and its spiritual health at any period would largely depend upon the vigor of the leadership exercised. Reformation under such leadership would be effected, but the basic national attitude of a halfhearted response to the great saving events of the past would continue. This tendency inevitably made the reform movements short-lived.

The Book of Judges provides clear illustrations and foreshadowings of the deficiencies in spiritual attitude which would plague Israel throughout Old Testament times. The sorry history of this period is summarized in 2:11–23: (1) Israel identifies herself with Canaanite society, indulging in apostasy; (2) as punishment, she suffers an attack upon the land by one foreign invader after another; (3) Yahweh exhibits his graciousness and his fidelity to the covenant by raising up inspired leadership, or judges, by whom Israel is delivered; and (4) after the death of the judge, there is the inevitable spiritual lapse, with the resultant repetition of the cycle. This is the basic pattern of Judges 1–16. Next, chapters 17–18 deal with the migration of the tribe of Dan from south to far north and the tribal corruption of the period. As we have noted, a certain unity surfaces again as the tribes join in holy war against the offending tribe of Benjamin (chaps. 19–20). The Book of Judges concludes with the twelve tribes united, Benjamin reintegrated, and the cult located at a central shrine. This shrine is Shiloh (chap. 21), which will be rejected in the early chapters of Samuel. Since the dubious character of the shrine seems underscored by the tribal activities conducted there in Judges 21, the note on which the Book of Judges concludes does not inspire the reader with any degree of confidence in the future of Israel or in her capacity to overcome difficulties.

Israel's Judges (Judg. 3–16)

The core of the book (chaps. 3–16) contains the exploits of the great heroic figures of the time, who are raised up by Yahweh to "save" Israel and who "judge" Israel thereafter, for the remainder of their lifetime. The verb *judge* generally bears a wider meaning in the Book of Judges than the narrower judicial sense that it comes to have later in the Old Testament, namely, the forensic sense with which we most naturally associate it. The word earlier carried the meanings of "administer," "govern," and "rule." Thus the individual heroes of the period (of whom the noun *judge* is rarely used) are major authority figures and must be seen as governing representatively over Israel on behalf of Yahweh, who is the true Judge (11:27). Such a conclusion is supported by the fact that the Spirit of Yahweh rushes upon so many of the heroic figures (3:10; 6:34; 11:29; 14:6). I have argued in more detail elsewhere the case associating the Spirit with divine rule (Dumbrell 1974, 1–10). Divine kingship seems to have been exercised in this surrogate manner by the heroic figures during the period of the judges.

In keeping with this emphasis upon divine rule is the background of the judges themselves. Rarely do they stem from influential families. Gideon was the youngest in his somewhat obscure family, and his clan the smallest in his tribe. Deborah was a woman and thus one to whom leadership would not have been normally entrusted. Jephthah was of very dubious descent and a bandit by profession. Only in the case of Ehud (3:15) is something resembling a genealogy presented. Again, none of these heroic figures seems to have been associated with any significant power base such as Gilgal, Shechem, Bethel, or Shiloh. Not many mighty, not many noble were called (Malamat 1976, 161–63)!

Indeed, Israel during this period was judged by a number of men about whom no heroic narratives have been written. It is customary to point to two lists of what are called minor judges (10:1–5; 12:8–15), whose limited personal details are presented in a stereotyped fashion. It is unwise, however, to conclude that these men are lesser figures or that they exercised a different function during the period. Generally speaking, the same terminology is used of them as is used of the so-called major judges. In 10:1–2, for example, Tola "arose to deliver Israel" and "judged Israel." Probably a principle of selectivity has operated in the presentation of the materials of this epoch, as seems clear from the fact that we encounter twelve judges in the book. Commencing with Othniel (chap. 3) and concluding with Samson (chaps. 14–16), the order of judges is geographic by tribe of origin, ranging from Judah in the deep south in the initial incident to Dan in the far north (the final position of this tribe after migration). No tribe contributed more than one major judge, and in each case the foreign aggressor is different.

Israel in the Judges Period

It is also customarily suggested that the Book of Judges exhibits merely local incidents involving isolated tribes of Israel. This idea is usually accompanied by the further assumption that the religious and political unity of the twelve tribes was either a fiction of the Old Testament period or was only in the process of formation during the era of the judges. However, no book in the Old Testament uses the term "Israel" or the phrase "all Israel" more frequently. From beginning to end of the book, we are concerned with what will happen representatively to "all Israel." Since each local event in a small territory like Palestine inevitably influences the whole, each event assumes in the mind of the writer an "all-Israelite" dimension.

Furthermore, the incidents themselves are rarely portrayed as affecting only one tribe. Othniel (3:7–11), for whom details are sketchy, serves as a model for all later figures. We deduce that Othniel himself is a Judahite, but the foreign threat is directed against all Israel, in divine response to apostasy throughout Israel. (The aggressor Cushan-rishathaim has proved difficult to locate geographically, though some have suggested that a general Mesopotamian incursion underlies this narrative.) Ehud of Benjamin rallies all Israel (3:27); Deborah (chap. 5) unites the tribes of the center and the north; Gideon (chaps. 6–8) is associated not only with Manasseh, his tribe, but with Asher, Naphtali, and Zebulun (all in the far north, while the Midianite offensive against which they are gathered seems to have swept also through the south [see 6:4]), and later seeks help from Ephraim (7:24). There appears to have been a central assembly by all Israel at Mizpah (10:17) to consider the Ammonite threat, at which Jephthah is appointed judge. Judah as well as Dan (then in the far south) is affected by the Philistine invasion, for which Samson is raised up. Thus the authority of the judge always transcends both his or her tribe and locality. In any case, as noted, local incidents in such a small area would have quickly assumed a national significance. The case for a confederacy of twelve tribes, united in entry into and exit from Egypt, recipients of the Sinai covenant, and together involved in conquest, not only is made by the detail of the early historical books, including Judges, but is moreover required to account for the Israel which we see united in a request for kingship in Samuel's period.

The Purpose of Judges

We may take it, then, that the Book of Judges is vitally concerned with the preservation of Israel's unity. Something more detailed, however, must now be said about the specific purpose of the Book of Judges and its contribution to the progressively developing theology of the Old Testament canon.

The book's final verse—"In those days there was no king in Israel; every man did what was right in his own eyes" (21:25)—appears at first sight to affirm that the unity of Israel, so much an issue for the writer, can be preserved only by the type of political movement now to be undertaken, that is, from a tribal society to an urbanized society under dynastic kingship. The difficulty about such a view of 21:25 is that kingship as an office is so roundly condemned within the book itself. Gideon, the great hero of Israel, pointedly refuses kingship, dynastic kingship in particular (8:23). In doing so, he draws attention to the reality of Yahweh's kingship, which must always be recognized by Israel and from which the earthly office that Israel wished to bestow on him would presumably detract. Kingship is ridiculed in the fable of Jotham (9:7–15) as that at which only charlatans and adventurers aim. The only "king" in the Book of Judges is Abimelech, the half-Canaanite son of Gideon, who brutally seizes power after the death of his father and exercises an abortive reign in Shechem. That reign, in fact, is the very antithesis of judgeship. What is emphasized about Abimelech (family background, establishment of institutional government, mercenary backing, and power base) receives no mention at all in the cases of the other heroic figures who are the successes of the book.

Perhaps the concluding comment of Judges 21:25 is to be taken in another way. The Book of Judges is inextricably bound up with the view of history propounded by the Former Prophets (Joshua through 2 Kings). These books include a cycle of narratives which appears to have stemmed from prophetic sources and to be very critical of the kingship exercised within Israel (and later Judah) up to the exile, even though the prophetic movement endorsed the theological aims of the Davidic covenant. Thus it is likely that the general antimonarchical stance of the Former Prophets is reflected in Judges, since the Former Prophets' view of Israel and its infidelity is clearly evident also. What the comment of Judges 21:25 may be reflecting upon is the remarkable persistence of Israel, notwithstanding her sustained apostasy during the period and her continued attempts to undo herself. It is remarkable that, after such a chaotic period when the people did what was right in their own eyes and when social abuses were so glaring as virtually to need no extended comment, Yahweh was still not prepared to give up on Israel. There still remained a future for this historical people of God, in spite of Israel herself. But just as during the preceding period, it would be Yahweh—and he alone—who would account for the continuance of Israel. He himself would be the architect of his people's lives, his promises would control Israel's future, and his rule alone could provide for its continuance.

The Book of Judges emphasizes, by its episodic parade of leadership raised up spontaneously by Yahweh to meet the crises of the time, the character of Israel as a theocracy. Everything in these bizarre accounts serves to commend God's direct leadership of his people in this period as the sole guarantee that Israel will have a future. The real Judge behind the scenes is Yahweh (11:27). It always has been and always will be the kingship of God which sustains the nation. The sad truth is that because of Israel's neglect of Yahweh's rule, prompted largely by the inopportune and inadvisable behavior of her kings, Yahweh will finally give up on Israel and give her over to exile. But at the time the Book of Judges concludes, Israel still has a future. Of course, the closing verse of the book foreshadows human kingship. It is another matter, however, whether it commends it. It merely sees Israel as standing before a new phase in its political future. For the character of that future we now turn to the Books of Samuel.

8

Samuel

The Books of Samuel provide a natural continuation for the Book of Judges. We begin the two books with action located at the corrupt shrine of Shiloh, staffed by a degenerate priesthood. The quiet piety of Hannah (1 Sam. 1) provides a fitting contrast to the censured conduct of Eli and his two sons, Phinehas and Hophni. We conclude 2 Samuel with David's purchase of the temple site from Araunah the Jebusite (2 Sam. 24) and are thus on the threshold of the movement of the shrine permanently to Jerusalem. The total vision which these two books provide seems to be that of a movement of the shrine from Shiloh to Jerusalem, a movement which in itself provides for the reversal of the situation in regard to formal worship which we see prevailing in 1 Samuel 1–3. Since worship, as we have already noted, is the official response in the cult to Yahweh's kingship, such a movement from Shiloh to Jerusalem really involves a progressive renewal, the development of a proper attitude to divine authority. The Books of Samuel thus operate as a theological endorsement of the kingship of Yahweh, rejected so frequently by Israel during the period of the judges. In the course of these books, the

offices of Israelite prophecy and kingship also emerge, making it plain
that the function of these two offices is to contribute to a correct understanding of Yahweh's relationship to Israel. The plan of the Books of
Samuel is as follows:

1 Sam.	1–3	The early history of Samuel, Israel's last judge
	4:1–7:2	The capture of the ark
	7:3–17	Samuel as judge of Israel
	8–12	Competing ideologies of kingship
	13–15	The abortive kingship of Saul
1 Sam. 16–		
2 Sam. 5		David's rise to power
2 Sam.	6–7	The Davidic covenant
	8	The Davidic conquests
	9–20	The reign of King David
	21–24	The appendixes
	21:1–14	Gibeon and the guilt of Saul
	21:15–22	Heroic tales of the Philistine wars
	22	David's psalm of thanksgiving
	23:1–7	David's testimony
	23:8–39	Military lists of the kingdom
	24	The divine provision of the temple site

Samuel's Roles (1 Sam. 1–3)

In chapters 1–3 of 1 Samuel the later ministry of Samuel as prophet,
priest (a term which is never specifically applied to Samuel), and judge of
Israel is anticipated. As priest, Samuel is apprenticed to Eli at Shiloh,
while as the replacement for Eli, he is Israel's judge (see 4:18). As the last
of the judges (note Samuel's role in chap. 7), he ushers in the period of the
monarchy and draws the era of the judges to a close. But it is upon the
note of prophecy that the first three chapters, which introduce Samuel,
end. This note is in itself clear evidence of a reversal of a situation in
which there has been "no frequent vision" (3:1). Since these first three
chapters move from despair to hope—a movement reflected by the parallels constructed between the barrenness of Hannah in chapter 1 and the
opening of the prophetic word through Samuel (Janzen 1983, 91), we conclude that this reversal is effected by the word of Yahweh in prophetic
pronouncement. It is noteworthy that the Song of Hannah focuses on the
theme of reversal (2:1–10). In this way the details of the song provide a
theological introduction to the two books of Samuel, just as the poetry
at the end of 2 Samuel (22:1–23:7) sums up the contribution of the
books. Since the books have much to do with the establishment of messianic kingship as representative of divine rule, it is appropriate that
1 Samuel 2:1–10 should end on that note. (This theme is not unexpected,

in view of Deut. 17:14–20; consider also the promise given to the barren Sarah [Gen. 17:16] in a situation somewhat analogous to that of Hannah.]

The Ark of the Covenant (1 Sam. 4–6)

Chapters 4–6, from which Samuel is absent, consider the fortunes of the ark, and thus another facet of divine leadership. It is clear that the successive defeats of Israel by the Philistines have been brought about by the hand of Yahweh, which was experienced formerly in the exodus and is now turned against Israel (see 1 Sam. 4:3, 8; 5:4, 6, 11). Yahweh's intervention results in the prophesied death of Eli and his house (2:34) and the "exile" of the ark. Yahweh thus virtually withdraws himself from the Promised Land, in what the writer interprets as a reverse exodus. Yahweh has gone into exile, leaving Israel in the Promised Land! Again we are left wondering whether there will now be a future for the people of God (A. F. Campbell 1975, 83).

Our doubts are temporarily removed by the return of the ark at the conclusion of 1 Samuel 6. But the penalty inflicted upon the inhabitants of Beth-shemesh who gaze into the ark indicates that there is the element of mystery about Yahweh which will always rebuke Israelite presumption or attempts at manipulation (vv. 19–20). The ark then remains at Kiriath-jearim for the next twenty years, on what was at that time the virtual border of Israelite-occupied territory within Canaan. It resides within the household of Abinadab, who ominously is the father of the ill-fated Uzzah of 2 Samuel 6:3. Its return under David (2 Sam. 6) will inaugurate a new theological era, just as the voluntary exile of Yahweh concludes the period of the judges.

Kingship (1 Sam. 7–12)

Chapters 7–12 now introduce the Israelite monarchy. In 7:6 we see Samuel operating as the last judge of Israel, the architect of victory who saves Israel from external aggression and then protects her internally by wise administration (vv. 14–15). In view of these details, the particular request for a king in chapter 8 is baffling, although kingship is expected and has been sanctioned. Paradoxically, however, Samuel's family has gone the way of the house of Eli (8:1–3). The request for a king is put by the elders of Israel in terms which provoke the tensions of the next few chapters. "Appoint for us a king to govern [Heb. 'judge'] us like all the nations," they say (v. 5, repeated in vv. 19–20). The fact that this request echoes the anticipation of Deuteronomy 17:14 does not lessen the difficulties which the request provokes.

The request is granted by Yahweh (1 Sam. 8:22), but there is an inherent incompatibility in it which the events and dialogs of the next few chapters are given to resolving. The basic difficulty is the nature of the kingship which the elders have in view. Kingship like that of the other nations would be dynastic, bureaucratic, tightly regulated, and thus quite antithetical to the concept of judgeship with which the request was linked (cf. v. 5). Dynastic kingship would eliminate from Israel the spontaneity and direction by Yahweh which judgeship had provided, thus cutting the cord of Yahweh's spiritual guidance of Israel by providing for an ordered succession. Moreover, the demand to be "like the other nations" carries with it a virtual unilateral withdrawal from the Sinai covenant. As noted, the phrase is used in Deuteronomy 17:14, but even there only Israel's demand is presented, a demand which is then responded to correctively by Moses (vv. 14–20).

The Sinai covenant (Exod. 19:3–6) had foreshadowed a separated Israel who would witness to her world by her distinctiveness. Clearly the demand for kingship must be adjusted to become compatible with covenant. We shall see that this adjustment is achieved by the time we reach 1 Samuel 12. The matter is resolved in two ways within these chapters, after Samuel has first outlined the implications of Israel's request (chap. 8). In the first place, the office of prophet as an ongoing institution is brought into being in chapter 9. The call of Samuel to exercise this function (v. 9 seems to refer to the change in status and designation of Samuel from that point onward) is a direct rejoinder to the request for kingship and thus seems designed to ward off any threat to Israel's covenant base which kingship may present. Samuel's prophetic role in relation to the emerging kingship of Saul is clearly designed to provide a system of checks and balances whereby kingship, with all its dangers of independent action, would not put the covenant at risk. The struggle of prophecy and kingship, of spiritual goals versus political aims, characterizes the subsequent history of Israel until the exile of north (722 B.C.) and south (587/586 B.C.).

The second movement in 1 Samuel 9–12 comes by the gradual integration of kingship itself as a covenant office. This movement happens in two ways. First, there is the development of a theology of kingship which separates it from the surrounding models that had so heavily influenced the elders of Israel. Here the sequences in both the choices of Saul and David need to be noted carefully (Knierim 1968, 30–32). Since what happens in their cases is not repeated elsewhere in the Old Testament, an ideal framework of kingship is being erected by their calls. Saul is first divinely selected (9:16), is brought to the prophet by whom he will be anointed (10:1), and then is endowed for his office with the Spirit (vv. 6–13). Finally, Saul is publicly attested by his victory over the Ammonites (chap. 11). Similarly, David is selected (16:1), is anointed by Samuel in the midst of his brothers (v. 13), and receives the Spirit for rule (v. 13). The Spirit then leaves Saul (v. 14), indicating the transfer of authority and thereby making it clear that the gift of the Spirit is bound up with the office of leadership in Israel. Finally, like Saul, David is attested before all Israel (chap. 17).

It is to be noted that in both cases the anointing constructs a relationship between the king and Yahweh, not between the king and people (Mettinger 1976, 191), whereby the Israelite king is then called Yahweh's messiah. While the term *messiah* means merely "anointed," in the Old Testament the word becomes specialized to refer to Davidic kingship in Israel, and thus it forms a set of expectations that finally leads to Jesus of Nazareth, King of Israel (John 1:49). Performed by Yahweh's representative, anointing here seems to be the confirmation of election (cf. Exod. 29:6–7; Lev. 8:9–12, for somewhat similar analogies). Though anointing is occasionally referred to until the exile (especially, as noted in Malamat 1968, 140, where succession is contested; see 2 Kings 23:30) and thus seems to have been practiced, no northern king after Saul is ever called messiah as indicative of the precise relationship set up. Establishing the close personal relationship that it does, anointing may have involved a contractual obligation. It seems, in any case, to have provided authorization to act. Thereafter the king is Yahweh's representative, his messiah. (David's continued use of "messiah" in referring to Saul [1 Sam. 24:6, etc.] indicates that only Yahweh could abrogate the relationship, just as he had begun it.)

With the erection of the office of kingship, then, an undergirding theology of ideal kingship has been supplied. We come to expect office and theology to develop together as Old Testament institutions are formed (cf. the priesthood). The office of messiah is thus not one which grows out of disappointment with the empirical monarchy, a psychological improbability in any case, but is one which arises with the advent of kingship itself. It is noteworthy that the four elements (choice, anointing, gift of the Spirit, and mighty acts) are not again seen associated with kingship beyond Saul and David until we arrive at the ideal kingship demonstrated in the ministry of Jesus of Nazareth (Knierim 1968, 43–44).

The second way in which emerging kingship is integrated into the covenant is seen in the narrative structure of 1 Samuel 11–12. After Saul's victory over the Ammonites, Israel assembles at Gilgal (11:14–15) to "renew the kingdom" ("kingship," NIV). Saul's kingship is not being referred to, since it has so far not suffered a threat and the verb *renew* elsewhere in this specific usage means to repair something already in a state of deterioration (cf. Isa. 61:4; 2 Chron. 15:8; 24:4, 12; Ps. 51:12;

104:30; Job 10:17; Lam. 5:21). The context suggests that it is in fact Yahweh's endangered kingship over Israel which stands in need of renewal. Since this assembly is called together at Gilgal, the first point of entry into Canaan and the place where the "New Israel" was then convened (Josh. 5:2–9), the appropriateness of the site for the occasion is obvious. Saul is indeed made king in this context (11:15), but only after Yahweh's kingship over Israel has been renewed in verse 14 (Vannoy 1978, 81).

First Samuel 12 seems also to occur at Gilgal (no change in site is indicated) and focuses on renewal of the covenant. Samuel gives an account of his own ministry but then puts Israel on trial, pointing to the breach of covenant which their choice of a king has constituted. Far from being his farewell speech, chapter 12 outlines Samuel's continued role as Israel's intercessor (vv. 23–25) and thus as the ultimate guide of the new order. With 1 Samuel 12 kingship of a modified character has been engrafted into the Sinai arrangement. It is clear from chapters 13–15, however, that the experiment with Saul has proved a failure. While the breach with Samuel appears to be minor, Saul defies the order to wait until Samuel comes to Mizpah. In chapter 14 Saul is cultically overcircumspect, thereby alienating mobilized Israel in the matter of his food taboo and the proposed death of Jonathan. In chapter 15, the issue over the destruction of the Amalekites brings Saul and Samuel into sharp conflict, with Saul initiating a clear breach of the holy-war code in the matter of objects and persons spared. The issue, however, that clearly divides the two personalities is that of relative authority. Kingship must submit to prophecy; the contemplated office of kingship requires divine guidance for success. We understand, therefore, the necessity of a further theological movement of the type embodied in 2 Samuel 7.

David's Rise to Power and the Davidic Covenant (1 Sam. 16–2 Sam. 7)

David's rise to power (1 Sam. 16–2 Sam. 5) may be quickly passed over. These chapters deal with the patient manner in which David waits for power and the gradual dissolution of Saul as a personality till his death in 1 Samuel 31. They also lay the groundwork for the essential network of personal relationships which David exploits when once he comes to power. These chapters are also concerned to distance David from any hint of complicity in the fall of the house of Saul and the passage of Saul's kingdom to David (McCarter 1980, 499).

After the capture of Jerusalem in 2 Samuel 5, most of Palestine falls into David's hands. This expansion of territory follows the anointing of David by Israel to be their unifying king (v. 3). The Philistines, Canaanites, and others are incorporated into his growing empire. Fortified by this success, David attempts in chapter 6 to bring the ark back from its exile in Kiriath-jearim and thus to centralize all of Israel's sacral traditions in his new capital. He draws rebuke, however, for this move is blatantly political. Later, escorted by the necessary Levites, the ark returns to the center of Israel's religious life—but only with Yahweh's sanction. This return spells the rejection of the house of Saul, a step made clear at the close of chapter 6 by the dismissal of Michal, the daughter of Saul.

Chapters 6 and 7 are fundamental. The former deals with provision for divine rule from Jerusalem by the return of the ark, while the latter deals with the provision of an enduring dynasty for David. Thus we have divine kingship in view under the guise of concern for the proper lodging of the ark in an establishment of its own (a temple which will betoken Yahweh's kingship). We also have as an issue the Davidic dynasty and thus royal stewardship which serves the temple. This pattern, basically of temple in 2 Samuel 6 (and thus divine kingship) and dynastic kingship in chapter 7, conforms to the ancient Near Eastern order, whereby provision of a residence for the deity must precede provision for the city-state ruler, who is a servant of the deity concerned.

David is first refused permission to build the temple, with the reasons advanced in 2 Samuel 7:5–7. The refusal is not absolute, however, and thus not a prophetic victory over the more centralizing priestly forces, for Solomon is later to receive permission to build (v. 13). This chapter really concerns the basic role of David as the giver of the political rest that stems from the conquest completed (Carlson 1964, 119). As the chapter progresses, it is clear that the rest from enemies "round about" of which verse 1 speaks is inconclusive, since the real blessings to flow from complete occupancy of the Promised Land have not yet been produced. Under David and the conquests that lead to empire (chaps. 8–10), control over Palestine is finally realized politically. Thus the conquest begun by Joshua but left incomplete by the judges (7:11) is ended. Verses 8–9a review David's career to that point in time, leaving us in no doubt of the exalted station to which he has been elevated (note the language of vv. 5–7; David as Yahweh's "servant" is Israel's shepherd).

In 2 Samuel 7:9b–11 the prospects of David are then considered. Yahweh will (1) make "a great name" for David (v. 9b, clearly reminiscent of Gen. 12:2 and the Abrahamic promises), (2) appoint a "place" for Israel ("place" is the distinct term in Deuteronomy for the Promised Land, particularly as outlined in promise to Abraham; cf. Deut. 11:24 with Gen. 15:18), and (3) give David rest from all his enemies round about (v. 11) (Carlson 1964, 116–17). In short, David's greatness must be established, Israel's living space determined, and the conquest completed before Yahweh will undertake to erect his sanctuary. But Yahweh himself will build it, since he will provide the circumstances on which construction will depend: the riches of empire previously conquered by David and the accession of Solomon the builder. The refusal of verse 5 thus defers temple building until Yahweh has acted further. It also operates as a mild rebuke, for this temple is not a static dwelling which Yahweh will inhabit (note "dwell" in v. 5). Yahweh will not be confined in houses built with hands, for the very heaven of heavens cannot contain him (1 Kings 8:27). Nor can a person build such a house; note Yahweh's question in 2 Samuel 7:5: "Would *you* build *me* a house?"

The eternal character of Davidic kingship is established in absolute terms (2 Sam. 7:13b). Thus the necessary steps beyond the interim kingship of Saul's have now been taken. The remainder of 2 Samuel, which is largely given over to more somber presentations of David, who is involved in court intrigue, family difficulties, and so forth, reminds us that such a promise of continuity establishes the office and not David the man and his physical line. The Old Testament thus oscillates between describing the Davidic covenant as eternal (the word *covenant* is not mentioned in 2 Sam. 7, but is found in 2 Sam. 23:5; Ps. 89:33–37) and describing it as conditional (1 Kings 2:4; 8:25; 9:4–5; Ps. 89:29–32; 132:12). Such an oscillation is designed to draw a distinction between, on the one hand, the promises and blessings to David which would not fail and, on the other, the punishment and fate of specific individuals within the line of promise. In physical terms the line of David foundered in 587/586 B.C. with the fall of Jerusalem, but in spiritual terms a promise such as 2 Samuel 7:13 directs us to look for ultimate fulfilment to the Christology of the New Testament.

The tenor of David's prayer in 2 Samuel 7:18–29 indicates the degree to which he has understood the nature of the divine commitment made in the first half of the chapter. Particularly puzzling, however, is David's summation of what has preceded: "this is the law for man" (v. 19, RSV margin). In view of the extrabiblical parallels for this phrase, it is best taken as "this [i.e., the detail of the first half of the chapter] is the manner in which human destiny is to unfold" (Kaiser 1974, 314). The thrust of the Abrahamic promises operative through Israel has now been revealed as henceforth bound up with Davidic kingship.

Empire and Division (2 Sam. 8–20)

In 2 Samuel 8–10 the Davidic empire is extended. David is thus presented as the architect of conquest. Being preoccupied, he could not be the temple builder (1 Kings 5:3; cf. 1 Chron. 22:8; 28:3). Solomon, as the man of rest (1 Kings 5:4), will be the temple builder. His prosperity is an index of the conquest sanctified and the Abrahamic promises fulfilled, at least in Israel's political history (note the Abrahamic tenor of 1 Kings 4:20 and 5:4, where the Solomonic era is seen as the great age of fulfilment). Yet the fact that the ideal borders of the Promised Land were never secured by David (Tyre and Sidon were never included in the Davidic empire) might suggest to us that the scheme of 2 Samuel 7, according to which temple building is to follow conquest, is an idealization which was never translated into biblical reality.

Indeed, we recognize that 2 Samuel 11–20 is given over to the depiction of David's fall from grace and his essential human weakness. Discord is sown among members of David's family and between north and south by David's actions. The thrust of these chapters is to deflate the character of David, just as the force of 1 Samuel 16–2 Samuel 5 was to idealize it. The final chapters of 2 Samuel indicate that the Davidic promises would not be fulfilled by sound political management, but only by the intervention of Yahweh through the history of salvation. Second Samuel 9–20 and 1 Kings 1–2 have commonly been termed the succession narrative and have been viewed as dealing with the problems of dynasty. But this is to overlook the fact that it is David who is at the center of 2 Samuel 9–20 and that the Books of Samuel are more concerned with temple and divine kingship than they are with David's own reign.

The Temple Site (2 Sam. 24)

The final four chapters of 2 Samuel are carefully structured. They begin and conclude with narratives which emphasize the fragility of the Israelite monarchy (Saul's in 21:1–14, David's in chap. 24). Chapters 21:15–22 and 23:8–39, heroic narratives related to the Philistine wars and military lists, bracket a central poetical section (22:1–23:7) offering a theological summary of the two books. Chapter 22 follows David's rise to power and implicitly offers reasons for it, while 23:1–7 presents the Israelite king as the ideal Israelite, ruling by the fear of God and thus bringing blessings and life. Chapter 24, David's ill-advised census of Israel, followed by the purchase of the temple site, concludes the books. The mention of Uriah the Hittite at the close of chapter 23 prepares us for the outburst of divine anger which the matter of the census provokes against David for his having been seduced by political realities to number an Israel which cannot be numbered (perhaps he had a standing army and taxation in view). David, Israel's shepherd, is then smitten through his flock. As shepherd he must make a sevenfold restitution (cf. 24:15 with 18:3; see Carlson 1964, 204). The temple site is chosen and purchased by Yahweh's direction. The books close by underscoring the sovereignty of Yahweh in the conduct of Israel's affairs and in the unfolding of her history.

In summary, 1 and 2 Samuel concern Yahweh's sovereign conduct of Israel's affairs and inform us of how difficult and indeed impossible it proved to be for Israel to recognize it. The movement between the two books has been from sovereignty ignored (1 Sam. 1–3) to sovereignty expressed (2 Sam. 24), from an indifferent response to divine kingship (1 Sam. 1–3) to the required response to divine kingship (2 Sam. 24). They place before Israel the prospect of a future as the people of God. It will be the function of the Books of Kings to comment upon how the opportunities afforded to Israel were transferred into historical reality.

9

Kings

The Books of Kings chronicle the growth and development of the Davidic empire to economic greatness and political influence. Solomon's reign (1 Kings 1–11) witnesses the transition to dynastic kingship, accompanied by all the difficulties foreshadowed by Samuel. Within the two books, the building of the temple (1 Kings 6–8) provides a sound theological basis for the continuance of Davidic monarchy, just as the political factors which develop during Solomon's reign threaten to undo such continuity. This fact presages, for all the magnificent conceptions of empire with which we commence Kings, the demise of empire which we meet in 2 Kings 25. The Books of Kings unfold as follows:

1 Kings	1–11	The reign of Solomon
	12–13	The division of the kingdom
	14–16	The history of Israel and Judah to the advent of Elijah
1 Kings 17– 2 Kings 1		The exploits of Elijah the prophet
2 Kings	2–8	Elisha
	9–17	From Jehu of Israel to the fall of Samaria
	18–25	The last kings of Judah

The Reign of Solomon (1 Kings 1–11)

The march to dynastic state involves for Solomon a break with the older tribal structure of Israel (1 Kings 4); he divides the realm into economic districts, significantly excluding Judah from the burden of making contributions. After the difficult matters of succession have been dealt with (chaps. 1–2), the dream of Solomon at Gibeon (3:3–9) provides legitimacy for his reign. Its content anticipates the writer's presentation of Solomon's reign: justice and administration (3:4–4:19); building operations which bring honor to Solomon (4:20–9:23); and Solomon's wealth and international reputation (9:26–10:29; see Porten 1967, 125–26). The sins and punishment of Solomon conclude the account (chap. 11).

The reign of Solomon is treated, as we have indicated, as the great age of the fulfilment of promises. So the Abrahamic promise that Israel would become a great nation, too numerous to be counted, is pondered in 1 Kings 3:8; 4:20. That Israel would occupy Canaan and achieve rest from her enemies is alluded to in 5:4–5. That the son of David would build the temple is fulfilled in chapters 6–8 in an operation which lasts twenty years. When the ark is deposited in the temple sanctuary, the exodus cloud fills the temple and thus brings the period of the exodus to a formal close, with all political goals having been achieved. The Sinai and Davidic covenants are now formally linked together.

But Solomon's tenure is also an age of thoroughgoing theological defection. A royal nobility develops during this period, laying to rest the older tribal democracy. A vast array of foreign alliances is erected. These fly in the face of the older holy-war theology, which demanded faith in Yahweh's person for Israel's protection and not in foreign policy. North is eventually sundered from south by the ill-advised concentration upon the south and the location of resources there. This latter policy is dictated by the political realities of the time when, halfway through the reign of Solomon, the twenty-second (Libyan) dynasty comes to power in Egypt, destroying the entente between Israel and Egypt. As a result, the north is virtually abandoned, and valuable trade routes are surrendered to the emerging Aramean states. Solomon's policy of forced labor (5:13; cf. 9:20–21) strikes at older concepts of egalitarianism. Extravagant building projects and the taxation measures associated with them as well as the sale of Israelite territory (9:10–14) alienate the north (Halpern 1974, 522).

But the splendor of Solomon's reign—his patronage of the arts (1 Kings 4:29–34) and the wealth that poured into his coffers as a result of his long-time control of the trading routes and his mercantile alliance with Hiram of Tyre (5:1–12)—also had a positive effect. The visit of the queen of Sheba (chap. 10) not only reflected the international reaction to

Solomon's kingdom (ruling, as he did, over Israel's ideal borders from the Euphrates to Egypt [1 Kings 4:21]), but it seems to have provided the paradigm from which the later prophetic vision of the eschatological pilgrimage of the nations to Jerusalem was drawn. In coming to Solomon and acknowledging the source of his wealth, influence, and wisdom (10:9), the Sabean queen, the ruler of probably the largest trading empire of its day, brought her world with her (10:24). Her visit and her acclamation of Israel's God were a confirmation of the promises to Abraham (Gen. 12:3) and provided inspiration for the later prophetic vision that saw Gentile kingdoms coming into Jerusalem to receive wisdom and Torah from Yahweh's shrine.

A Divided Israel (1 Kings 12–13)

This idealized picture of the kingdom (with which the Books of Chronicles conclude the Solomonic account) is shattered by the sober presentation of Solomon's apostasy. His downfall is evidenced particularly in the matter of foreign alliances, with which foreign marriages would inevitably have been connected (1 Kings 11). The kingdom, rife with potential divisions, is torn from him by the prophetic movement based in Shiloh (vv. 26–40). After Solomon's death, only two tribes remain in the south—Judah and Benjamin. The division occurs in chapter 12, where Jeroboam, the one-time forced-labor supervisor in the north, capitalizes upon the ineptness of Solomon's son Rehoboam and leads the northern ten tribes into secession as the kingdom of Israel. Jeroboam moves beyond his prophetic mandate in setting up two alternate shrines to Jerusalem, Dan in the far north and Bethel in the extreme south of the new kingdom of Israel. The religious moves of Jeroboam in chapter 12 seem to have been an artful gesture to draw support from the older sacral traditions familiar to the average Israelite and traceable to the exodus and conquest period. However, the prophetic editor is not impressed with this attempt to return to a pre-Jerusalem tradition of multiple sanctuaries and sees Jeroboam's move as tantamount to a repetition of Exodus 32 (cf. 1 Kings 12:28 and Exod. 32:4). This rejection of Jerusalem by the north comes as the great apostasy of the period and keeps south and north apart thereafter.

The prophetic rebuke and dismissal come for Jeroboam in 1 Kings 13. The house of David and Jerusalem are reaffirmed in verses 1–10; then the theme of obedience to the voice of true prophecy is highlighted (vv. 11–34). It is clear that Josiah is to be the second David, the restorer of the kingdom and the reviver of the fortunes of empire, bringing north and south together again, as his ancestor had done (13:2).

The prophetic movement continues to be active in the affairs of the apostate north. Successive northern dynasties are brought down by the prophetic word—Baasha's is replaced by Omri's dynasty (Omri, Ahab, Ahaziah, and Jehoram; see 1 Kings 16:1, 7), which in turn is ended in about 842 by Elijah's word pronounced through Elisha (19:16; 2 Kings 9:1–2). Jehu's dynasty of four (Jehu, Jehoahaz, Joash, and Jeroboam II) is also brought to an end by prophetic assault (cf. Amos 7:9), while the fall of the north is announced by Hosea and Amos.

Elijah and the House of Omri
(1 Kings 16–2 Kings 1)

Omri, a significant early king of Israel, founded a dynasty of four. He bought the hill of Samaria as a site for his capital (1 Kings 16:24). The fact that it was purchased has led to the supposition that it was not at that time Israelite territory. There are some parallels to the action of David in choosing Jerusalem as a neutral and central site for his kingdom. Barely six verses are devoted by the biblical writer to Omri, though a century later in Assyrian records the kingdom of Israel was still called by his name. We must not regard this lack of detail regarding Omri, however, as indicating a lack of interest in history on the part of the writer. The Books of Kings are prophetic works, a theological interpretation which displays a sense of what was ultimately important for the history of the people of God. Omri's foreign policy called for the restoration of good relationships with Judah, close ties with the Phoenicians, and a strong hand against the east and north. Omri consolidated his position with a marriage pact uniting Jezebel, the daughter of the king of Tyre, with his son Ahab; a further alliance between Israel and Judah involved the marriage of Ahab's sister (or daughter) to Jehoram (2 Kings 8:26), son of Jehoshaphat, king of Judah. Moab was defeated. The times seem to have been a period of great economic prosperity and expansion for both north and south (1 Kings 22:44–50), but with an inevitable religious decline, especially in the north (arrested, to some extent, in the south by the reforming Jehoshaphat).

During the reigns of Omri and Ahab, great surrenders were made to foreign religious influences, particularly to the worship of Baal of Tyre. Ahab built a temple for Baal in Samaria as part of a chain of concessions made to Canaanite interests (1 Kings 16:32). Such compromises provoked a religious crisis in Israel. In chapter 17, in response to the growing syncretism, Elijah appears suddenly on the scene from the Transjordan region. The gauntlet is thrown down by Elijah, and the issue of Yahweh or Baal (a choice which may well have puzzled the average Israelite, who seems to have identified Yahweh with Baal) is settled on Mount Carmel (chap. 18). The call by Elijah for undivided allegiance to Yahweh is virtually a recall to the Sinai relationship (note the tenor of 18:21) and thus to covenant renewal for the north. Elijah's challenge is met by silence on the part of the spectators, and then Yahweh himself asserts his sole sovereignty, as he had done on Sinai, by fire in a spectacular theophany (v. 38). Like Moses at Sinai, Elijah then turns the sword on the apostates (v. 40), having previously made clear by his selection of twelve stones to repair an older altar the indivisibility of the people of God (vv. 30–32).

The national question having been settled, 1 Kings 19 directs us to the inner life of Elijah himself. His life now sought by Jezebel, he turns back for strength to the source of Israel's original experience, to Sinai itself. Sustained by an angelic presence, he finally reaches what seems to have been the scene of the original theophany to Moses, at an analogous phase in that great man's ministry (note *"the* cave" in 1 Kings 19:9 [Heb.]; cf. Exod. 33:22). We note the obvious Mosaic posture into which Elijah is cast throughout the whole of the narratives.

The new theophany that Elijah receives assumes a different form. It entails a divine question as to the reason for Elijah's journey to Sinai and Elijah's response that he is the sole believer amongst an otherwise apostate Israel (1 Kings 19:10). Repetition of the question and answer indicates that what Elijah has heard as a result of the theophany is unsatisfactory and puzzling to him. Accompanying (but not constituting) the theophany are the traditional elements of earthquake, wind, and fire, in which expectedly there is no direct divine manifestation. Heralded by the clamant elements, the divine appearance comes as expected after them as what the Hebrew text designates "the voice of drawn-out silence" (v. 12). We should not interpret this incident, as some have supposed, as the replacement of strident Baalism with the still small voice of prophecy, since the effect of the theophany is unperceived by Elijah and the prophetic voice is neither still nor small. Nor does it signal the end of the dramatic in Israel's experience of Yahweh, since the theophanic tradition continues throughout the Old Testament. However we may interpret this passage, the eerie phenomena draw Elijah out of the cave to be questioned a second time as to the reason for his return (v. 13).

We may draw two conclusions here. First, since nothing concrete comes from the encounter related in 1 Kings 19:11–13, we may assume that Yahweh has nothing further to add to what was delivered upon Sinai in Exodus 19–34. Second, by implication, Elijah would have been better employed by being about the kingdom business elsewhere (1 Kings 19:15–16)! In any case, he does not carry the spiritual burden alone. The notion of a godly remnant, a unit within the nation, is now brought into prominence for the first time in the Old Testament. There are seven thousand who have not bowed the knee to Baal (v. 18)!

With this incident the place of the Israelite prophet as an international figure begins to emerge. Elijah is commissioned to anoint Hazael king of Syria and Jehu king of Israel. Elijah is also to anoint his successor (the only attested case of prophetic anointing in the Old Testament); clearly the purpose is to present Elisha as an extension of Elijah, authorized by him for office. The remainder of the narratives in 1 Kings largely concern the conduct of Israel and Judah in concert in the Aramean wars. We note, though, Elijah's firm adherence to Pentateuchal law in the matter of the sale of Naboth's vineyard (1 Kings 21).

Elisha and the Fall of the North (2 Kings 2–17)

Virtually the first third of 2 Kings represents an extended description of the ministry of Elisha. By the extensive space devoted to both figures, the editor shows the significance of the prophetic ministries of Elijah and Elisha. The centrality in these two books accorded to the work of prophecy during the monarchical period emphasizes the key role of prophecy.

The activity of prophecy in the monarchical period is underscored by reports in the early chapters of 2 Kings of "the sons of the prophets" (2:3, 5, 15, etc.)—a term used in the Old Testament to denote prophetic activity in different periods without any necessary relationship between the groups being referred to. The long arm of Elijah reaches to the revolt initiated by Elisha, in which the usurper Jehu brings down the house of Omri and the last vestiges of Baalism in the north (chaps. 9–10). The history of the northern kingdom of Israel is brought to its end with the fall of Samaria (722 B.C.). A prophetic commentary upon the reason—failure to heed the prophetic word—is attached (chap. 17).

Josiah and the Fall of Jerusalem (2 Kings 22–25)

Our attention switches to the south. With the reforming reign of Hezekiah, its reversal under his son Manasseh, and then the advent of Josiah (2 Kings 22–23), the hopes projected by the prophetic movement in 1 Kings 13 are fulfilled. A comparison with the account of Josiah's reforms in 2 Chronicles 34 indicates that the report of the reforms has been condensed in 2 Kings to throw major emphasis upon the finding of the book of the law in 621 B.C. (Josiah's eighteenth year). Second Kings 23:4–20 seems to condense the three-stage reform movement of Chronicles (with only v. 4 necessarily referring to Josiah's eighteenth year). Thus the major part of the reforms (which involved the extirpation of Canaanite, not Assyrian, practices) were conducted before the book of the law on which they seem to depend was actually found (cf. 2 Chron. 34:1–13 with v. 14).

In view of the tenor of 2 Kings 22–23, where phrases reminiscent of Deuteronomy occur ("walk after the LORD"; "keep his commandments and his testimonies and his statutes"; "with all his heart and all his soul"; "words of this covenant" [23:3]), the identification of the book of the law with the Book of Deuteronomy seems very plausible—the more so as the book of the law contains a clear threat of judgment upon national evils (22:13) and an emphasis upon covenant (23:2). However, it is difficult to explain the finding of Deuteronomy in 621 B.C. Both Josiah's reforms (which, as I have pointed out, mainly preceded this finding) and those of Hezekiah (reported in 2 Chronicles and substantially identical with Josiah's) show familiarity with the demands of a book such as Deuteronomy. The nineteenth-century theories that the finding was a pious fiction to give ancient authority to Deuteronomy, which allegedly was composed at this time, are not only intrinsically improbable (in view of the undoubted antiquity of the contents of Deuteronomy) but are at variance with the detail of Chronicles and Kings previously referred to. What was found in the temple at this time was perhaps a document on the duties of the king, prepared for the royal court and incorporating the obligations and covenant responsibilities of the Jerusalem kings. The nature of any conclusions in this area, however, must remain tentative.

For his piety Josiah went down to his grave with his kingdom intact (the apparent meaning of "in peace" in 2 Kings 22:20). But the accumulated sins of the southern kingdom, particularly the apostasy of Manasseh, required the end of the Jewish state. It is later clear from the Book of Jeremiah that the Josianic reforms, like the preceding reforms of Hezekiah, were only superficial, leaving the deep-rooted problem of Israelite apostasy untouched (Jer. 44:7–10, etc.). Even Josiah's more thorough reforms (the high places were defiled to prevent their subsequent use, etc.) did not last, though the focus of both reforming kings was the temple, the symbol of divine authority. It is thus a somewhat fitting commentary upon the failure of the monarchical period that the Books of Kings end with the temple in ruins and thus divine authority withdrawn from the Promised Land.

The Purpose of Kings

The Books of Kings deal with the issue of the decline and fall of the Davidic empire and the reasons for it. The whole history of this period is cast into the familiar pattern of rebellion and punishment, totally unrelieved except by the personalities of the reforming southern kings—Josiah, Hezekiah, and, to a much lesser degree, Asa, Jehoshaphat, and Joash. For the writer, the north was doomed by its religious secession from Jerusalem. Israel is thus shown to have chosen, in the Promised Land, the path of death she had been advised to shun in Deuteronomy 30. On the other hand, Yahweh perseveres with the south with King Josiah as the new David. But here the accumulation of sins, particularly from the age of Manasseh (2 Kings 21), is too much even for a reformer like Josiah, and thus the end comes in 587/586 B.C. for Jerusalem. It is clear, as we have already noted, that these books interpret history theologically, from a prophetic perspective, a fact confirmed by the many appeals to fulfilment of prophecies, previously uttered, which the Books of Kings make throughout.

While the issue dealt with in Kings is clear, there has been a division of opinion as to whether the books offer any message of hope for the future to the exiles. Has the history of Israel come to an end with the exile, now that all the externals (temple, cult, priesthood, kingship, even land) have gone? Some have seen in the message of Jehoiachin's elevation from prison in Babylon a note of hope being offered to Israel as the period closes (2 Kings 25:27–30). But Jehoiachin, the Davidic king in exile, is now dead. He indeed was released, but the portrayal of the Davidic monarch, eating defiled food puppetlike at a pagan king's table, contrasts markedly with that of the faithful Jew, Daniel, whose conduct of no compromise in Daniel 1 indicates a faith which would survive the exile. We are thus left with the distinct impression that once again a question mark has been raised over the future of Israel. The monarchical period began with the recognition of the need for a more ordered institutional life under Yahweh's leadership (Judg. 21:25). The period witnessed the growth of Israel's institutional life but also the progressive denial of the authority of Yahweh by gross acts of apostasy. Two questions therefore emerge as a result of the events of 587/586 B.C. and the destruction of Jerusalem, which the Books of Kings report as they close. Would Israel ever learn that God-given institutions must be protected from corruption? And more important, would Yahweh be prepared to begin again? Perhaps those who see in the release of Jehoiachin a slim note of hope have a point here. Perhaps this indirect reference to the promises given to the Davidic line (2 Sam. 7) is just a glimmer that in the midst of despair and uncertainty, Yahweh would still remain faithful to his promises. How this faithfulness would express itself and be worked out in terms of a possible revival of the Israelite state, the prophecies relating to the exilic period make clear.

We have now completed our survey of the Former Prophets. We began with very high hopes being expressed in the Book of Joshua for Israel in the land. This optimistic note was deflated, however, by the Book of

Judges. Yet the fidelity of Yahweh to his patriarchal promises finally saw the full establishment of the Israelite state under Solomon and the building of the temple, which crowned the conquest. The period as a whole, however, continued the attitudes of unfaithfulness and apostasy, seen in national Israel since its Sinai foundation. The collapse of the Israelite state saw the failure of a national experiment. This failure seemed to make it clear that neither a national state nor a system of institutionalized religious practices would henceforth be the carrier of the promises to Abraham. With the fall of the Israelite state, the dawn of the New Testament age had virtually begun. For after the exile, though many attempts to revive the past would be made, it would eventually become clear that the visible carrier of the promises would not finally be physical Israel as such, but a community of faith. In retrospect this had always been so. The exile would serve to underline this biblical truth.

Part **3**

The Books of the Prophets:
The Latter Prophets

10

Isaiah

Prophecy in General

In the sense of possession by a power beyond oneself, prophecy is an old phenomenon in the ancient Near East. Revelation by dream and by trance is commonly reported from extrabiblical sources. In the twentieth century, ecstasy has been viewed by many as the hallmark of Israelite prophecy. Here much depends upon the matter of definition. If by "ecstasy" we mean the manner of the divine-human communication, then this is a factor which the Old Testament generally plays down. If we mean by it the suppression of personality during the conveyance of the message, then ecstasy is not present in the Old Testament. More recently, however, the definition of "ecstasy" has been widened to include controlled trancelike states; this sense would have to be admitted as a prophetic manifestation. But the personality of the prophet is never obliterated in Old Testament prophecy, and in this sense ecstasy does not occur. Again it is clear that the phenomenon of prophecy was not confined to a particular class, for men of very differing backgrounds appear to have received calls. Moreover, the manner of the call was never standardized. The call itself provided authorization, and for this reason Old Testament prophets were not anointed. Much consideration has been given to the relationship of prophecy to Israel's cultic responses. While this issue probably cannot be resolved, prophecy of every kind betrays more than a passing interest in what went on at the official sanctuaries.

But sociological and phenomenological questions of this character ought not to cloud our eyes to the fact that Old Testament prophecy as instituted was a continuant of the Mosaic office and therefore covenant-centered (Deut. 18:15–22). Like Moses, the prophets offered what was given on Sinai and reapplied it to current social, religious, and economic questions. They were therefore not innovators. They dealt with a faith once delivered which needed to be possessed by the communities of their day, for whom they brought constant new application of old truths. Since the Israelite prophet was primarily a covenant mediator, his appearance and intervention meant that covenant breach in some shape had occurred. Thus the prophetic ministry was most normally associated, up to the exile at least, with impending judgment. But their message was actually a saving message. For unless the sin of Israel was so deeply ingrained that it could not be eradicated, the threat of judgment was an implicit invitation to repentance.

Israel's prophets spoke with the authority of the sender. For warrant for their message they appealed to participation in the deliberations of the heavenly council (see Isa. 6; Jer. 23:18), where the message had been heard and whence commissioning proceeded. As opposed to the more formally appointed kingship, Israelite prophecy was a Spirit-filled office which continued the charismatic type of ministry of the judges period. We now turn to consider the implications and effects of the prophetic message to Israel. Here we shall move away from chronological order, taking the major prophets first and then considering briefly the message of the remaining twelve so-called minor prophets.

Literary and Theological Unity of Isaiah

The question of the literary and theological unity of the Book of Isaiah has consumed the interest of nineteenth- and twentieth-century researchers. Since the epoch-making commentary of Bernhard Duhm (1892), the division of the book into three segments (chaps. 1–39, 40–55, 56–66), each with its own historical or thematic interest, has been widely accepted in biblical scholarship. The problem with such an approach is that it fails to explain the fact that the Book of Isaiah was received into the canon as a unity. This fact suggests that the sixty-six chapters manifest a literary cohesiveness which may be related to a major purpose the book is seeking to convey. To postulate a school of disciples (cf. Isa. 8:16) as responsible for the whole book, continuing the tradition begun by an Isaiah of Jerusalem, is an interesting hypothesis but one that only "explains" one unknown by another.

Recent discussion has tended to look more for inner theological connections which bind the book together. Factors such as divine kingship, the notion of holiness, the Davidic and Zionistic emphasis of much of the book (Davidic only in chaps. 1–39, however), as well as the very high ethical tone of the whole, have been cited as general tendencies giving a common theological direction. At the same time B. S. Childs (1979, 325–34) has suggested that Isaiah 40–55 functions as prophetic interpretation and elaboration of the traditions of chapters 1–39. Childs and others have seen Isaiah 56–66 as elaborating and applying the message of chapters 40–55.

Approaches of this character (particularly attempts to interrelate the materials of the book by viewing chaps. 1–39 as initial prophecy upon which the successive sections build) have been helpful, but are not sufficiently precise. If the book is read as a unit, one overmastering theme may be seen to effectively unite the whole: Yahweh's interest in and devotion to the city of Jerusalem. Of course, other subthemes abound in a book of this length and character, and they have rightly been identified (holiness, divine kingship, etc.). But when we are considering the major contribution to the canon which the book makes, the interest in the fate of the historical Jerusalem and the future hopes bound up with the notion of Jerusalem are central. This concern provides for the theological cohesion of Isaiah and gives it its unitary stamp.

The thesis of Jerusalem as the integrating factor in the book finds support not only from the initial emphasis placed upon Jerusalem in Isaiah 1 and then again in conclusion in chapter 66, but also in the internal structuring of the various subsections of the book (chaps. 1–12, 13–23, 24–27, 28–33, 34–35, 36–39, 40–55, and 56–66). In each subsection, the interest in Jerusalem is dominant and threads often somewhat disparate topics together.

Isaiah 1 presents us with the picture of a decadent Jerusalem whose sacrifices can no longer be accepted and whose prayers must be turned aside. This chapter functions as an introduction not only to chapters 1–12, but to the whole book. Appropriately, therefore, the prophecy concludes (66:20–24) with the emergence of a New Jerusalem as God's holy mountain to which the world will go up in a pilgrimage of worship. From the final chapters it becomes clear that the notion of the New Jerusalem is intimately linked with the prophecy of a new creation (65:17–18).

This New Jerusalem in fact functions as a symbol of the new age and is presented in the conclusion as an obvious offset to the city with which the book begins.

We should note that the emphasis on Jerusalem is not found merely at the beginning and the end of the book. The first half of Isaiah ends in chapter 39 with a threat of exile pronounced upon King Hezekiah and his city, Jerusalem. The second half of the book begins with an announcement of a prospective return from exile (40:1). Immediately the prophet translates the "comfort" to be extended to "my people" into a tender speaking to Jerusalem (v. 2). Indeed the entire focus of the introduction to this section of the book (vv. 1–11) is upon Jerusalem (cf. the correlation between vv. 1–2 and 9–11). Once the general tenor of the return has been discussed in chapters 40–48, Jerusalem/Zion becomes the point of direct focus in 49–55. The Zion theme also begins and ends the final section (chaps. 56–66).

The purpose of the Book of Isaiah is to account for the difference between the initial and final portraits of Jerusalem (cf. chap. 1 with 65–66). Bearing in mind the broad movement of the entire prophecy, we now turn to the individual sections of the book and to the series of interconnections which serve to keep the Jerusalem theme before us. We may outline the Book of Isaiah as follows:

1–12 The call of Isaiah and the commencement of his ministry in Jerusalem (ca. 740–732 B.C.)
13–23 Oracles against the foreign nations
24–27 The emergence of the city of God: The apocalypse of Isaiah
28–33 Judah and Jerusalem in Hezekiah's time (ca. 715–687 B.C.)
34–35 The ransom of the redeemed
36–39 The siege of Jerusalem in 701 B.C.
40–55 The work of the Servant
  40:1–11   Prolog
  40:12–48:22 The second exodus
  49–55   The restoration of Jerusalem
56–66 The earthly and the New Jerusalem

Promise and Threat (Isa. 1–12)

The content of Isaiah 1–12 alternates between the motifs of promise and threat (Ackroyd 1978, 16–48), effectively introducing the outline of chapters 1–39 as mainly threat and 40–66 as predominantly promise. Thus Isaiah 1 is plainly threat against Jerusalem, while 2:1–4 outlines the prophetic hope for Zion (a prophetic notion obviously developed prior to Isaiah's time). This hope is greatly expanded by chapters 60–62. Isaiah 2:5–22 is a threat directed against a Jerusalem society given over to pride and idolatry. The threat continues in chapter 3, which deals with the Jerusalem leadership and the social upheavals occasioned by the reversal of roles in society. This alternation of motifs continues with the promise of a return of the remnant to Zion in chapter 4 and the lament over the impending rejection of Judah and Jerusalem in 5:1–7. A series of seven woes against prevailing social conditions appears in 5:8–10:4, interrupted by 6:1–9:7. The remainder of chapter 10 is interwoven with oracles concerning divine punishment to be visited upon Judah and Jerusalem and then upon arrogant Assyria. A complementary message of hope, pointing to an ideal community established under messianic leadership, is presented in 11:1–9, followed by a picture of the new age initiated by a new exodus (vv. 10–16). A salvation hymn (chap. 12) completes this first section and concludes on the note of praise to be uttered by the inhabitants of Zion in whose midst Yahweh will dwell.

Isaiah 1 is undoubtedly the key to the book. It is a thoroughgoing indictment of the failure of Israel to be the people of God and a rejection of Jerusalem, the political and cultic center. Verses 2–3 discuss the covenant breach; verses 4–9, Israel's refusal to be God's people; verses 10–20, the problem of the perverted cult. Verses 21–23 resume the indictment of verses 2–3, verses 24–26 then deal with the threat of punishment, and verses 27–31 issue a verdict which reveals for the first time in the Old Testament an emergence of two groups within the nation—the wicked who will be punished and the righteous remnant who will be redeemed.

What accounts for the savage nature of this divine assault upon Jerusalem in Isaiah 1? Here it may be helpful to turn to 6:1–9:7, an apparently intrusive element into the structure of threat and promise which prevails in Isaiah 1–12. Chapter 6 contains the call of the prophet and directs our attention toward his vocation and the difficulties which he will have to confront. It is significant that Isaiah's call is narrated in connection with chapters 7–9, which deal with the fate of the house of David. Given the pattern of threat and promise which we have found in the surrounding chapters, we expect it also in 6:1–9:7. Chapters 6–8 deal with judgment directed against the Davidic house in Jerusalem and the resulting desolation which is to come upon the city. Isaiah 9:1–7 returns us to an idealized picture of Davidic leadership to be brought about by divine intervention at a later period.

Isaiah 6 begins with an account of the prophet's call in the year of Uzziah's death. Uzziah's long reign of fifty-two years had marked for the south a return to Davidic and Solomonic greatness. However, in the year of the death of this king, Isaiah is encouraged by his vision of the Lord (v. 1), *the* King (v. 5), to put politics into their proper perspective. He thereby comes to realize that Judah's security and continuance depend on Yahweh's guidance within history, not on the deft political kingship or the foreign alliances which have served to hold the southern kingdom together. The scene which Isaiah beholds seems to be the heavenly council in session, Yahweh surrounded by his royal court. The question under discussion, as the later context indicates, is the coming judgment upon Jerusalem (vv. 8–10). Isaiah sees Yahweh sitting ominously upon his throne, a normal judgment posture (cf. the judgment vision of Micaiah in 1 Kings 22:19).

Important for the understanding of what is being conveyed to Isaiah are the actions of the seraphim, who are offering a doxology in response to the heavenly judgment (Isa. 6:3). In the light of what they do in heaven, Isaiah realizes that he is a man of unclean lips and dwells in the midst of a people of unclean lips (v. 5). This is not merely the language of prophetic diffidence, since verse 5 presupposes that what characterizes Isaiah also characterizes Judah. This language points to the proper response from pure lips to Yahweh's kingship, namely, the seraphim's worship, which acknowledges his sovereignty. At once Isaiah realizes that his own and Judah's failure to reflect Yahweh's kingship at the center of Israel's covenant life, the cult, accounts for the tremendous decline from prosperity to desolation which this chapter projects. We see clearly the reasons underlying the sweeping condemnation of worship and sanctuary in 1:10–20.

The eschatology of the Book of Isaiah aims at reversing the situation described in chapter 1. That is perhaps the reason for what seems a new introduction in 2:1; certainly it is the reason for the presentation of the prospect for Jerusalem which we find in 2:2–4. I have argued elsewhere (1977, 39–41) that the Zion imagery in Isaiah 2:2–4 received its impetus from the choice of Jerusalem in 2 Samuel 6. The particular form which the hope concerning Jerusalem developed was influenced by the contours of the Solomonic empire, particularly as acknowledged by the visit of the queen of Sheba (1 Kings 10) as representative of her world. Her "hard questions" (v. 1) were responded to by Solomon's wisdom. This incident anticipates the picture developed in Isaiah 2:2–4, where the chosen city Jerusalem becomes the redemptive center of the world and a towering mountain, the place of divine revelation. Nations that had previously assailed Jerusalem will come in pilgrimage for the divine will. The nations will come to Yahweh as Judge (i.e., world King) for law. Since "law" is paralleled by the general expression "word of the LORD" (v. 3), we are not dealing with a prescriptive code but with divine instruction understood in the broadest terms, divine regulation of the affairs of the world in the new age. This passage affirms international submission to divine kingship. Nothing concerning the Davidic traditions is stated here or in the extensive expansion which this passage undergoes in chapters 60–62. This eschatology of 2:2–4 becomes basic in chapters 40–66. But throughout chapters 1–12 (indeed, chaps. 1–39), the vulnerability of Jerusalem is made plain (1:21; 10:24–32; cf. 18:7; 24:10; 29:1–8; 32:13–14), while at the same time it is emphasized that the Zion ideal would survive (7:1–9; 10:24–34; cf. 14:28–32; 17:12–14; 29:1–8; 30:27–33; chap. 31).

We have noted, within the pattern of oscillation between threat and promise directed at Judah and Jerusalem in Isaiah 1–12, the intrusion of 6:1–9:7, in which the same pattern of threat and promise emerges. While these chapters deal mainly with the rejection of Davidic kingship and the eventual substitution of ideal kingship, the notion of a remnant—a community within a community—receives prominent attention. Within chapters 7–9 the house of David (currently represented by Ahaz) is rejected, while the future is tied to the motif of a faithful remnant who will emerge from the coming disaster. It is probable that the name of the prophet's son Shearjashub ("a remnant shall return" [7:3]) foreshadows the community who will turn in repentance and faith to Yahweh. This faith community provides the positive side of the double-edged sign of Immanuel ("God with us"—in judgment or salvation!) which is to confront the world (7:14; 8:8). If the latter half of 7:15 may be translated as a purpose clause ("in order that he may know how to refuse the evil and choose the good"), as Joseph Jensen (1979, 228) argues, and not as a temporal clause, then the announced birth of a child to a young woman could involve a reversal of Israel's fortunes in the far distant future (i.e., far beyond the immediate Assyrian crisis) and be a promise which concerns the house of David (cf. 7:13) more than it does Ahaz, the current ruler. Certainly the highly developed pictures of a God-given ruler in 9:1–7 (and 11:1–10) cannot have reference to contemporary leadership. Appropriately, the hymn of chapter 12 ends the first section of the book by noting that prophetic expectation calls for the presence of the Holy One of Israel in the midst of Zion and her inhabitants.

Oracles Against Foreign Nations (Isa. 13–23)

Chapters 13–23 are prophecies against foreign nations. The origin of this genre of prophecy is difficult to establish. There is much to be said for the view that the judgment oracles against foreign nations are offshoots of the Zion traditions. We should consider, however, the manner in which such oracles are employed. The link that joins chapters 13–23 together is their concern with nations which have encountered or will encounter Assyrian rule or threats and will take part in useless coalitions against Assyria (Erlandsson 1970, 102). Thus there seems to be implied condemnation in these chapters for (1) Judean attempts to establish diplomatic contacts with Babylon (chaps. 13–14); (2) Philistia (14:29–32—here the alliance policy is rejected out of hand, since Yahweh has founded Zion and he will protect it); (3) Ethiopia (18:1–5—here it is noted that Yahweh himself will intervene before the final harvest, that is, before complete destruction by Assyria; perhaps vv. 6–7 refer to the subsequent fate of the Assyrians and their submission to Yahweh in Zion); and (4) Egypt, whose undependability is stressed in chapter 19. Chapters 15–16 are directed against Moab and may refer to the abortive stand by that state against Tiglath-pileser III in 734 B.C. The oracles suggest that Moab would pay the price for its failure to recognize the fulfillment of Yahweh's historical purposes through the Assyrian menace. The threat against Damascus (17:1–11) seems to fall into the same category and time. Isaiah 21:1–10 links the names of Elam, Media, and Babylon together and could thus point to a time of around 700 B.C., when the fortunes of those three nations converged and they were dealt with by Assyria, which appears to be the devastator of verse 2. The message of verses 1–10 is clear: no nation is to repose its hope in the doomed Babylon. Verses 11–17 appear to be related to Assyrian campaigns of the period against the Arab peoples. Isaiah 22 refers to political measures taken when Jerusalem was threatened during the reign of Hezekiah. Jerusalem society is attacked for its reliance upon physical defenses and not upon Yahweh in its time of need. Finally, Tyre and Sidon, which were involved in the western coalition against Assyria (ca. 734 B.C.) and had strong commercial links with Judah, are the subjects of chapter 23.

The recurring theme of Isaiah 13–23 is that faith in Yahweh's purposes and not foreign policies will protect Jerusalem. Yahweh will crush Assyria, and he alone is the guarantor of Zion's security (14:27–32). Perhaps 17:12–14 refers to an attack upon Zion, with the attackers being described in the typical chaos imagery of "many waters." This attack is thwarted by Yahweh at the last moment. Chapters 13–23 thus carry forward the dominant Jerusalem theme struck in chapters 1–12.

The City of God (Isa. 24–27)

Chapters 24–27 do not interrupt the course of the prophecy but are tied to the rest of the book by a heavy Zionistic emphasis, although it remains difficult to identify precisely the two cities involved. They may be Babylon and Zion, or, perhaps more likely, the wicked city of these chapters may be Jerusalem (see 24:10; 25:2) in contrast to the Zion in which God will reign (24:23). The appearance of Yahweh with his elders in this last reference may be reminiscent of Exodus 24. Yahweh as a replacement for the sun and the moon (Isa. 24:23) heralds the introduction of the new age at the end of a chapter given over largely to a cosmic catastrophe engulfing the city (perhaps Jerusalem, as is suggested by the language of vv. 5, 13).

In these chapters sifting judgment has been pronounced upon the earth, with the focus on one particular city (Isa. 24:1–13, 17–23). The righteous who wait for this judgment lift up their voices in an interlude of praise (vv. 14–16). Yahweh's victory (vv. 21–23) leads to a song of praise in 25:1–5, followed by a feast upon the (world) mountain (vv. 6–8), with an appropriate response by the faithful. The reference to Moab in these final verses is difficult but may depict the victory in terms of a new entry into the Promised Land (Millar 1976, 18). Zion offers a song of trustful confidence (26:1–6), while verses 7–19 broadly deal with the life of the final age which Yahweh has brought about. Yahweh's control over death (v. 19) is now revealed. The oscillation of motifs continues with a short lament (vv. 20–21) and the assurance that Yahweh will slay the dragon, thus removing any threats to the new age (27:1). Isaiah 27:2–6 reverses the Song of the Vineyard (5:1–7). In 27:7–11 we return to the theme of punishment to come upon Jerusalem, while verses 12–13 close the chapter with a picture of an eschatological return to the Promised Land by Israel's scattered people, all coming to worship on God's holy hill of Zion. Thus, while the obscurity of these chapters is tantalizing, their Jerusalem emphasis is undeniable.

The Certainty of Divine Defense (Isa. 28–33)

In the absence of specific detail chapters 28–33 are difficult to date precisely. This difficulty is reflected in the very different positions taken by the commentators concerning them. There is nothing in this section to disprove the position that it deals in the main with Assyrian activity directed against Judah and Jerusalem in the later period of the reign of Hezekiah (715–687 B.C.). The reference in 28:1–4 to Samaria ("Ephraim") and thus to the northern kingdom, however, presupposes a time prior to the fall of that city in 722 B.C. Editorially the chapters are unified by the introductory formula "woe to . . ." (28:1; 29:1, 15; 30:1; 31:1; 33:1). The details of these chapters confirm their Zion bent and call upon that city and her people to rely upon her cornerstone, the temple in Jerusalem. The themes of the importance of avoiding foreign alliances and the certainty of Yahweh's defense of Jerusalem are characteristic of these chapters.

In chapter 28 verses 1–4 offer judgment upon Samaria; verses 5–6, salvation for the remnant in Israel; verses 7–13, condemnation of Judean indulgence; and verses 14–22, a rejection of Jerusalem leadership, which trusted in political agreements. The cornerstone on which faith ought to have relied is Zion herself (v. 16). The community of faith is thus called to take their stand upon God's purposes bound up with Jerusalem while Yahweh conducts his strange work of sifting and punishing. Verses 23–29 offer to the faithful an assurance of God's perfect timing in the unfolding of events.

In the Ariel paragraph, 29:1–8, Yahweh first occasions the siege of Jerusalem and then relieves it. Verses 9–12 trace the spiritual lethargy of the people of Jerusalem, a lethargy resulting from a basic religious insecurity (vv. 13–14) which must draw punishment. Verses 15–24 threaten the perverse but promise salvation to the meek. A golden age will then result. Isaiah 30:1–5 condemns trust in Egypt. Verses 6–7 seem to belong to the same period and strike the same note, but the details are in doubt. Perhaps ambassadors are en route to Egypt (v. 6), but Egypt's help will be worthless (v. 7). Verses 8–18, after calling on the prophet to summarize his message of salvation, detail the consequences of rejecting it. For the community of salvation, however, who dwell in Jerusalem (vv. 19–26), blessings await in the form of the defeat of the oppressor and the full transformation of the cosmic order. The consequences for the oppressors of history, with Assyria particularly in view, are then graphically outlined (vv. 27–33).

The contrast between the search for support (from Egypt) and the true source of Zion's protection continues in chapter 31. The hymn of chapter 32 appears to draw out the consequences of the new era of deliverance which is granted to Zion. Just government will prevail (vv. 1–2), sensitivity and understanding will be the property of all in the new age (vv. 3–5), and a contrast between the former and the latter leadership is provided (vv. 6–8). The reference to the siege of Jerusalem by Sennacherib in 701 B.C. seems continued in the bitter attack on the women of Jerusalem (vv. 9–14), whose reversal of social roles has been characteristic of the conduct which has brought Jerusalem down (cf. 3:16–26). There follows in 32:15–20 a section which ushers in the ensuing age of salvation, when all life will be regulated by the divine Spirit that is poured out.

The Zion emphasis seems clear in the closing hymn (chap. 33), whose theme is the defeat of a powerful enemy of Jerusalem and the ultimate glorification of Zion. Chapter 33 is heavily Zion-oriented and, though difficult to date, might also be ascribed to the period of Yahweh's deliverance of Jerusalem in 701 B.C. The argument in these chapters is at times difficult to unravel, but they make it clear that Yahweh is the ultimate defender of Jerusalem, though that city must first pass through the fires of judgment.

Destruction and Deliverance (Isa. 34–35)

In the next section, a clear contrast between chapters 34 and 35 is provided by the Zion motif. Aggression in the shape of the old enemy, Edom, is ranged against Zion (Isa. 34; cf. Ezek. 35). But Edom will be destroyed, allowing the redeemed of the Lord to return through a transformed wilderness to Zion (Isa. 35). These two eschatological chapters are often linked by commentators with the material of chapters 40–55. The very general character of their projections, however, makes their presence in the first half of the prophecy perfectly natural. Conveying a comprehensive sense of the future of the people of God, Zion functions as the world center.

The Siege of Jerusalem (Isa. 36–39)

The last four chapters of the first half of the prophecy (chaps. 36–39) deal with the historical situation immediately preceding the siege of Jerusalem in 701 B.C. Isaiah 39 closes with a prophecy of exile, but refers primarily to the deportation of the Jerusalem leadership (vv. 5–8). Thus the first half of the book has ended with a prophecy of virtual destruction and the cessation of the Davidic house (vv. 6–7). The unremitting prophecies directed against Jerusalem in Isaiah 1 are still in view, though at the same time throughout chapters 1–39 there has been an emphasis maintained upon the role appointed for the eschatological Zion of 2:2–4.

The Ministry of the Servant (Isa. 40–55)

We are now in a position to discuss the material of Isaiah 40–66, having noted the consistent threat in chapters 1–39 of the impending destruction of Jerusalem and the equally consistent eschatological note of God's protective role to be exercised on behalf of Zion and the remnant who will populate it. We now turn to note how these twin themes are worked out in chapters 40–66. Chapters 40–55 represent almost pure eschatology, while chapters 56–66 offer a blend of history and eschatology. In terms of the overall structure we thus have the following arrangement:

1–12 History and eschatology
13–23 History
24–27 Eschatology
28–33 History
34–35 Eschatology
36–39 History
40–55 Eschatology
56–66 History and eschatology

In Isaiah 40–66 the theology of a renewed city of God is taken up in earnest. Following hard upon the promise of exile and the threat to Jerusalem with which chapters 1–39 have concluded, 40:1–11 begins with an emphatic word of comfort extended to Jerusalem. The structure of 40:1–11, which introduces chapters 40–55, must be carefully noted. Material related to Jerusalem is found in 40:1–2 and 9–11, with both sets of verses bound internally by thematic considerations. Thus verse 2 contains the causal clauses which provide the ground for the statement of verse 1. There are two commands in verse 1 and two more in verse 2, which seem to unite the two verses; in fact, whenever a double command occurs in chapters 40–55 (as it does in 40:1), it is followed by further commands (see 51:9, 17; 57:14; 62:10). Not only is Isaiah 40:9–11 linked by the Jerusalem theme to verses 1–2, but we also note that three "behold" clauses in verses 9–10 balance the three causal clauses of verse 2. Like verses 1–2, verses 9–11 begin with a command and continue with a double command ("lift up"). In turn the two passages encase material relating to a new exodus. Verses 3–5 refer to the preparation of a divine way through the wilderness, and verses 6–8 make it clear that this will happen as a result of the proclamation of the divine Word. Note that the three themes of verses 1–11 (consolation for Jerusalem, the new exodus from Babylon, and the power of the divine Word, which accounts for all transformations) also relate to the content of 40:12–55:13. The message of 40:1–2, 9–11, is developed by 49:1–52:12; next, 40:3–5, which concerns the return to Jerusalem considered as a new exodus, is taken further in 40:12–48:22; finally, 40:6–8, dealing with the power of the divine Word to effect final change, finds emphasis in the material of 52:13–55:13 (Kiesow 1979, 165).

Sorrow has been removed from Jerusalem, her period of suffering is over, and the covenant language of 40:1 ("my people" and "your God") foreshadows the reinauguration of the Sinai covenant, which the second-exodus language of the prophecy supports. Comfort for "my people" (v. 1) will issue in the restoration of Jerusalem's people and place (v. 2); in other words, the Abrahamic promises have been united in the major symbol of restored Jerusalem. The message of comfort is basically a simple one, which the shepherd language used of Yahweh in verses 9–11 elucidates. God is coming as King and will dwell in Zion (cf. 52:7)! By a new exodus engineered by Israel's God, the covenant will be reestablished for the people of God who are to be gathered to the divine center, Jerusalem.

Isaiah 40:12–42:4 forms a continuous argument. The crucial figure of the Servant is presented in 42:1–4 in both royal and prophetic terms. The fact that so many theories have been constructed about the person of the Servant (from individual figures such as Jeremiah the prophet or King

Jehoiachin to corporate, faithful Israel) means that the identity of the Servant is not so important. Rather, it is his function which is to be emphasized. He is doubtless an idealized figure, perhaps the believing community within Israel, whose ministry will control Israel's future and that of the world. Though ostensibly unimpressive, his ministry of suffering will result in the pilgrimage of the Gentile world to the divine center, Zion, and thus in the fulfilment of the eschatology of 2:2–4. The term that threads the argument of 40:12–42:4 together is mišpāṭ, "justice," which in the total context seems to mean Yahweh's control of the present course of history, which Israel regards as misdirected (Beuken 1972, 1–30). Israel's complaints implied in 40:12–31 and her present plight in the grip of foreign powers (chap. 41) will be redressed by the ministry of the Servant!

The remainder of the material through Isaiah 48 cannot be dealt with in detail here, but the emphasis in these chapters is upon the impending return, the overthrow of idolatrous Babylon, and the role of Cyrus. Chapters 49–55 discuss the question of Zion's future. This new phase of the prophecy begins with reference to the ministry of the Servant (Isa. 49:1–6), as a result of which kings stand up to watch the return of Israel in processional exodus to the Promised Land (vv. 7–13; cf. Exod. 15:12–18). Yahweh has not forgotten Jerusalem (Isa. 49:14–26), for the relationship engraved on his palms is clearly unbreakable (v. 16). The nations that have oppressed Israel will return her.

The exile is for discipline, not divorce (50:1–3). Verses 4–11 offer a message to the Servant to persevere and call on the exiles to respond to his voice. Isaiah 51:1–8 addresses a faithful Israel who will inherit the promises, while verses 9–11 spell out the return to Jerusalem in terms of a new creation. Verses 12–16 offer consolation to Jerusalem, for Yahweh stands behind her and the covenant is thus to be restored. Jerusalem is then called upon to rouse herself (vv. 17–20), since her cup of wrath will be passed on to Babylon (vv. 21–23). She is to put on garments appropriate to the new age (i.e., queenly robes—52:1–6). Then 52:7–10 provides a climax to the expectation of 40:1–2, 9–11, and the return to Jerusalem viewed prophetically as completed is seen to parallel the exodus from Egypt (52:11–12).

What follows is a commentary explaining how this return has been achieved, namely, through the ministry of the Servant, who has suffered so extremely (52:13–53:12). The disfigured Servant, whose ministry was nonetheless so effective, is presented in 52:13–15. Then in 53:1–9 we seem to be confronted by the confession of the Gentile kings of 52:15, who stand astonished at the new exodus and restoration. Next comes a prophetic (vv. 10–11) and a divine (v. 12) assessment of the Servant's ministry. It is clear that the Servant's ministry has made possible this great change involving the return of God's people to his city. The confession of the kings thus bears eloquent testimony to the eschatology of 2:2–4.

A bewildering array of covenant language in Isaiah 54 draws out the consequences which this ministry of what seems paradoxically "servant Israel" has had for Israel and her world. Israel's total covenant expectations have been realized through the ministry of this Servant. Abrahamic (vv. 1–3), Sinaitic (vv. 4–8), and Noachian (vv. 9–10) language is employed before the extravagant imagery depicting Zion's rebuilding and repopulation occurs in verses 11–17. From the restored Jerusalem, in a manner reminiscent of the description in Ezekiel 47:1–12, waters of life flow (Isa. 55:1–2), while all the people of Jerusalem are now sharers in the promises of the Davidic covenant and are thus, like David, kings and priests (vv. 3–5).

The Inheritance of the Remnant (Isa. 56–66)

Isaiah 56–66 expands the material of chapters 40–55, with more reference to the divisions within the community: salvation is confined to the faithful (the position also in chaps. 40–55) and is not given to the nation as a whole. The covenantal, new-creational emphasis of chapters 40–55 is carried forward here, again with special emphasis being accorded to Zion. An international pilgrimage to a sacred mountain, presumably Jerusalem (56:1–8), begins the sequence of these chapters, just as the note of a similar pilgrimage ends it (66:18–24). While the detail of these chapters cannot be treated here, mention must be made of the manner in which the promises of 2:2–4 are expanded in chapters 60–62.

Isaiah 60:1–9 resumes the themes of chapters 49–55, but with the expectation of the return to Zion as imminent. Verses 10–22 describe the manner of the return. The wealth of nations and peoples led by their rulers will stream into the renewed Jerusalem; this will be in fulfilment of the Abrahamic promises (vv. 21–22). In 61:1–3 a servant personage announces the victory. Verses 4–11 are concerned with the physical reconstruction of Zion, which is to be populated by priest-kings (v. 6), with world homage being offered to the bride Zion (v. 10), and with an attendant transformation of physical nature.

The particular election of Zion to privilege is the subject of Isaiah 62. She is vindicated and restored (vv. 1–2a), a new name is given to her (vv. 2b–4a), and her future is referred to in the covenant imagery of marriage (vv. 4b–5). Zion's security is the tenor of verses 6–9, while the call to the people of God to enter Jerusalem as a sanctified people and to occupy that holy space completes the chapter (vv. 10–12).

Two communities are in view in chapters 56–66. Only a small group will experience the promised return. In 65:19, for example, we are dealing with the concept of "my people" as opposed to those who "forget my holy mountain" (v. 11). In verses 17–25 the elect people of God (the remnant of chaps. 1–39) enjoy the blessings of the new age resulting from divine intervention. Yahweh revives the theme of the New Jerusalem as he "roars" from his heavenly temple (66:5–6). Judgment upon his enemies follows. The metaphor of Zion's miraculous delivery of many children (vv. 7–9) points not only to fulfilment of the Abrahamic covenant, but to the suddenness of the transition to the new age (Hanson 1975, 183). Again, such a consolation is available only for those who "rejoice with Jerusalem" (v. 10). Traditional imagery returns in the description of the new age (vv. 12–14) and Yahweh's coming in judgment as the Divine Warrior (vv. 15–16). Beyond this judgment the end is heralded by the return of the chosen to Zion (vv. 18–24). The book concludes with a picture of uninterrupted temple worship by all, which is the consummation of history.

The Book of Isaiah moves from the perverse worship offered by physical Jerusalem under judgment, arising from the neglect of Yahweh's kingship, to the worship of Yahweh in the New Jerusalem. Gradually, in the course of this great book, Jerusalem becomes a major biblical symbol uniting city and saved community, combining sacred space and sanctified people. Isaiah makes it clear that there can be no thought of a restored Israel without a prior restoration of Zion. For it is Yahweh's presence alone which makes Israel the people of God. Davidic king and temple have little space devoted to them in the latter half of the book, for there Isaiah talks about the ultimate end. His Zion is an ideal—the perfected community, the righteous people of God.

As a political concept, however, Isaiah's notion of Jerusalem reminds us that God's saving activity occurs within history. Out of the Babylons of this world, God will save his people. He will found for them a city, a unified political community, of which he is the Maker and the Builder. The Babel concept of Genesis 11 will thus be reversed. Isaiah's conception of the New Jerusalem is the replacement for the ill-conceived humanistic dream of the tower builders of Babel. All the world is now related to the divine center, Jerusalem.

The function of the Book of Isaiah is to put this theology of the center before us. But the historical setting of this symbolism alerts us to the fact that eschatology builds upon prior history and projects a historical fulfilment. The Book of Isaiah takes the salvation history bound up with the original choice of Jerusalem and turns it into a magnificent concept of a populated city of God.

11

Jeremiah

The Book of Jeremiah is the most political of all the Old Testament prophecies. It covers the period from 627 B.C. (which was either the year of his birth or of the beginning of his ministry—it all depends on the interpretation given to Jer. 1:1–2) to 582, a few years beyond the fall of the Judean state. In a broad sense the book reviews the period of Judah's history which included the reforms of Josiah (639–609 B.C.) and the reigns of three of his sons, Jehoahaz (609 B.C.), Jehoiakim (609–598 B.C.), and Zedekiah (597–587/586 B.C.), and one grandson, Jehoiachin (598–597 B.C., when he was exiled to Babylon). It thus covers the period of hope engendered by the reforms of Josiah to the fall of Jerusalem, which revealed their superficiality. During the period of Jeremiah, Assyria fell to Babylon (virtually, with the fall of Nineveh in 612 B.C.; actually, with the second battle of Carchemish in 605 B.C.). The Book of Jeremiah defies precise dissection, since it seems to have been organized topically rather than chronologically, but the outline below represents a general consensus. (It needs to be noted that in the Septuagint the oracles against foreign nations [chaps. 46–51] follow 25:13.)

The Purpose of Jeremiah's Call

Every exposition of the Book of Jeremiah must take into account the peculiar nature of Jeremiah's call. Jeremiah is appointed as a prophet to the nations, or Gentiles (cf. the manner in which Paul, relating his conversion in Gal. 1:15, obviously refers to Jeremiah's call). The call narrative of Jeremiah is enclosed by his commission (Jer. 1:5, 10); its nature, peculiar to Jeremiah among Old Testament prophets, determines the character of his message. We must give due consideration also to the fact that oracles against the foreign nations (arranged in a broad geographical order: Egypt, Philistia, Moab, Ammon, Edom, Damascus, Kedar, Elam, and then finally and emphatically, Babylon) virtually conclude the book, since 51:64 forms an inclusion with 1:1. The underlying motif of these oracles is the failure of the nations merely to be the rod of Yahweh's anger. The historical reality of the advent of Babylon is underscored by the formal conclusion to the Book of Jeremiah, chapter 52, which is a historical appendix referring to the fall of Jerusalem.

Jeremiah thus comes before us as the prophet who ushers in the "times of the Gentiles." His ministry formally brings the history of the divided kingdom to a close and describes events leading to the fateful and historically decisive fall of Jerusalem and the reasons for it. Jeremiah is thus the first genuine internationalist of the Old Testament period.

The decisive emphasis of the Book of Jeremiah is his summons to the world to face the new reality which has come into being, to recognize that God has given world leadership to the state of Babylon and to his servant Nebuchadrezzar (25:9). Placing the oracles against the foreign nations at the end of the book (chaps. 46–51) emphasizes this, as does the conclusion of the book by its narration of the fall of Jerusalem (chap. 52). The function of the Book of Jeremiah may therefore be to introduce us to a new state of Israelite salvation history and the end of an era. The Josianic reforms had revived dreams of Davidic grandeur. But the years of Jeremiah's ministry saw an increasing declension from the Josianic ideals, a nation given over to apostasy and idolatry and thus deserving of the most severe covenant curse which Deuteronomy 28 pronounced—the loss of the Promised Land itself. With the fall of Jerusalem, all the externals of the faith had gone: temple, Davidic kingship, ark, sacrifice, priesthood, and then the land itself. The Book of Jeremiah raises the obvious question, How intrinsic were all of these externals to the true nature of Israel? How would Israel be identified in the absence of the precise geographical and religious markers by which she had become known?

Where is the true Israel? is thus the major question which the Book of Jeremiah raises. This concern is voiced at a time when the advent of the age of the Gentiles would bring to an end the Israelite state and submerge the people of God in the midst of a sea of peoples. Would there be a future for Israel, and what would be this future? Would it be to build up what had been demolished? Would a new individualism replace the rejected nationalism? What would the impending exile, which Jeremiah describes at length, mean for the ongoing history of Israel?

With the dissolution of nationalism in Jeremiah's times, the way is now open for the emergence of the heavily individualistic apocalyptic movement, appropriately in exile (e.g., Daniel). Of course, like his fellow preexilic prophets, Jeremiah looks beyond the disaster to the reconstitution of the people of God. His expectation is cast into the familiar terms of a new exodus, the return to the land, and a new covenant. Jeremiah 31:35–40 hints that a new covenant would necessarily operate within the contours of a new creation, as Isaiah and Ezekiel both additionally make clear. Accordingly, Jeremiah looks for an idealized return to the land. That an actual return from exile, as was hoped for by the exilic prophets, did not materialize did not mean that expectations for such a return were abandoned. They were simply postponed, for we cannot speak of a failure of prophecy merely on account of its nonfulfilment in a particular historical era of expectation.

The Compilation of the Book of Jeremiah

A brief analysis of the literary complexity of Jeremiah must be offered, since the book is a diffuse collection of oracles, not necessarily arranged chronologically, and often following no discernible order. Difficulties of this character led earlier commentators to divide the book into three groupings of material: poetry, first-person prose, and third-person prose. It was suggested that the poetic sections of the book were the oldest, offering insights into the career of Jeremiah and his preaching ministry. These parts were then complemented by a first-person prose account written by Baruch, Jeremiah's secretary. He was responsible for the reading of Jeremiah's scroll before King Jehoiakim (Jer. 36) in 605 B.C. Though analogous to Shaphan's reading of the law before Josiah (2 Kings 22), Baruch's reading had startlingly different results.

It has been suggested that this material was then supplemented by prose accounts in the third person (e.g., 3:6–13; 7:1–8:3; 11:1–14; 18:1–12; 21:1–10; 22:1–5; 25:1–11; 29:1–23; 32:1–2, 6–16, 24–44; and portions of chaps. 34–45). It is said that these sections echo the prose style of the so-called Deuteronomistic history (Joshua–2 Kings, to which the Book of Deuteronomy is alleged to be the introduction). This view, however, says little more than that the prose accounts of the Book of Jeremiah reflect the qualities of the normal prose accounts of the Old Testament. I do not propose to discuss recent refinements of the literary analysis of the Book of Jeremiah. They have tended to take two directions, namely, to label the Baruch materials as a Deuteronomic editorial device, thus reducing three components to two, or to suppose that the third-person prose accounts are homiletical expansions from the hands of those responsible for the other stylized biographical accounts. Questions of this character (and the solutions offered) are notoriously subjective and often deflect us from the major task before us, namely, that of making sense of the book as it presently stands arranged, with all its diversity of content. Although we may differ widely on particular details, we cannot miss the major emphasis of the book: with the fall of Jerusalem, about which the rulers of Jeremiah's time were earnestly warned by the prophet, a new age in Israel's relationship with Yahweh has arrived.

Jeremiah's Earliest Oracles (Jer. 1:5–20:18)

Chapters 1–20, which have been identified as a major section of the book, are framed by references to Jeremiah's birth (Lundbom 1975, 28). They end on a note of somber gloom driving us back to 1:5. We are then left with the success of Jeremiah's message of terrible judgment but also with the tensions that it has provoked within his character. A break certainly comes after chapter 20, for Jeremiah 21 begins the first datable biographical prose in the book. It has been proposed that chapters 1–20 constitute the scroll read by Baruch before Jehoiakim (chap. 36). However that may be, most scholars do believe that these chapters represent the earliest material of Jeremiah's ministry. It is possible that chapters 2–6 are to be related to Josiah's time and thus give evidence of the inconsistency of the Josianic reforms, while chapters 7–20 may relate to the reign of Jehoiakim. It must be said, however, that if Jeremiah 1:2 refers to the date of the prophet's birth, no material in Jeremiah can with certainty be dated to the period of Josiah.

Generally speaking, chapters 2–3 contain poems lamenting the covenant disloyalty of Judah. Making wide appeal to the exodus traditions (2:1–3), they evoke the older covenant language and motifs of Israel as bride. The poems include instances of historical lapses into idolatry (vv. 4–13), now prevalent within Judah, and apostasy (presented as harlotry in the manner of Hosea, with whose language and imagery there is a remarkable affinity in the early chapters). By entering into political alliances (vv. 14–19) and religious affiliations, Judah has plainly broken the Sinai covenant and has rejected its call for exclusive worship. Baal worship has multiplied in profligate abandon (vv. 20–28). Israel has in fact broken the marriage relationship (3:1–5), a breach to which Jeremiah again refers when the issue of the new covenant is raised (31:31–34). Judah has done likewise (3:6–11). Yet, brighter days could come for both north and south. They would be days in which the older reliance upon externals (temple, land, cult, etc.) would be abandoned—even the ark of the covenant (3:16) replaced as a symbol—days in which Jerusalem would once again be Yahweh's throne, and the world would gather in prophetic pilgrimage to Zion, to Jerusalem, and the divisions between north and south would be obliterated (vv. 12–18).

The prophecy then continues by asserting the truth that the necessary response is the repentance of north and south (3:19–4:4). But in 4:5–31 a dreadful prospect is placed before the nation. The as yet unnamed terrible foe from the north (later to be identified with Babylon) will execute a bitter retribution, the scope of which requires the image of a graphic reversal of creation to depict the horror of what will break loose (vv. 23–28). The theme of Israel's idolatry and complacency being judged by means of an incursion from the numinous "north" is taken further in Jeremiah 5. The attack is in fact mounted in 6:1–8. Jeremiah's inability to command a hearing with Yahweh's Word will inevitably mean destruction for Judah by the very same Word (vv. 9–15). Demands for obedience and not sacrifice (vv. 16–21) are counterposed by the reported advance of the dreaded foe (vv. 22–26). The prophet endeavors vainly in the face of the approaching foe to sift Judah for what may be saved (vv. 27–30).

Chapters 7–10 are integrated by the major theme of institutional religion which has become apostate and the punishment which necessarily follows (Thompson 1980, 271–339). Jeremiah's renowned temple sermon is delivered in chapter 7 and is appropriately assigned to the first year of Jehoiakim (i.e., 609 B.C.; cf. Jer. 26:1). Jeremiah now becomes more overtly political. Current prophecy which seeks to promote misconstrued Zion ideals, and which sees the temple as a talisman guaranteeing, by its mere presence, the existence of Jerusalem and its future, is condemned in Jeremiah 7 and throughout chapters 26–29. Clearly the people have failed to recognize the temple as the locus of Yahweh's kingdom rule, the final point of authority. Reliance upon the externals of worship, which, when properly exercised, should be the response to Yahweh's kingship, leads Judah to ruin. The outstanding feature of this sermon is the play upon the word *place* in the twin sense of temple (7:3) and Promised Land (v. 7), the latter a customary use of the word in Deuteronomy. The message is very clear—a right attitude to the temple would have secured the Promised Land. The official cult is roundly attacked by Jeremiah in this chapter (vv. 21–26), who apparently rejects not sacrifice itself, but only the misplaced emphasis which has been put upon the system. Thus temple, sacrifices, priesthood, and land are all condemned by Jeremiah in this attack, and their end is foreshadowed. There is also the indication within the chapter that the Josianic reforms, which were to guarantee the survival of the state, have now been jettisoned. For example, idolatrous practices flourish again in the valley of Topheth (7:29–8:3), practices which Josiah had purged (2 Kings 23:10).

The theme of "the foe from the north" is taken further in the section from 8:4 to 10:25, which continues to deal with the inevitable judgment of Judah for her corruption and impenitence (8:4–13). This theme of impending attack (8:14–17; 9:17–22; 10:17–25) is interspersed with laments from Jeremiah over the prospect (8:18–9:1; 9:2–9; 9:10–16) and with a wisdom piece reflecting on the true grounds for confidence (vv. 23–26). An attack upon idolatry (10:1–16) stresses the incomparability, power, and kingship of Yahweh over all nations (note the remarkable title "King of the nations" in v. 7, a title which underscores the thematic interest of Jeremiah). Yahweh will bring judgment upon Judah by the foe (vv. 17–25).

Jeremiah 11:1–20:18 intensifies the emphasis of the earlier chapters. The divisions and subdivisions to be made within this section are by no means clear. Jeremiah 11:1–17 deals with problems stemming from the broken covenant, namely, the loss of the land that the covenant had given. Threats are uttered against Jeremiah, the covenant messenger (11:18–12:6). Jeremiah 12:7–17 applies the extreme covenant curse, the loss of the land for covenant breach, against Judah. Prophetic strictures directed against Judah's pride take the form of a symbolic action involving a linen girdle (13:1–11), a further parable (vv. 12–14), urgings to repent (vv. 15–17), and a lament over the royal house (vv. 18–19) and over Jerusalem (vv. 20–27). Further material bearing upon the crimes of Judah, which are to be punished by drought and banishment into exile, follows in 14:1–15:9. The prophecy then assumes a particularly personal note until 20:18; most of the introspective reflections by Jeremiah on his lot and ministry, the so-called confessions, are found here (15:10–21; 17:14–18; 18:19–23; 20:7–13, 14–18; cf. also 11:18–20; 12:1–6). These confessions are cast into the familiar language of Psalms and cult, but it would be wrong to eliminate the personal element from them. The point of these confessions seems to be, however, that Jeremiah is in fact speaking for the people in their corporate agony. Yet his solitariness, misery, and incalculable personal pain at the treatment he has received from his fellow citizens and Yahweh cannot be reduced in these poems merely to the language of a national confessor.

Jeremiah's inner conflict and Yahweh's response to it are portrayed in 15:10–21. His loneliness in ministry (16:1–9) necessarily separates him from an idolatrous nation (vv. 10–13) that must be exiled. The possibility of a new exodus, however, is immediately raised (vv. 14–15), only to be balanced in the oscillation that the book constantly exhibits by a threat of impending judgment from which none will escape (vv. 16–18). Yet the future of Israel remains implicitly secure for Jeremiah, since this somber chapter concludes on a passage reflecting the eschatology of a Gentile pilgrimage and the conversion of the nations (vv. 19–21).

Judah's deeply ingrained corruption (17:1–4) is then reflected upon as stemming from trust having been placed in human beings and not Yahweh (vv. 5–8). The human heart is naturally corrupt (vv. 9–11), and Yahweh is Israel's only hope (vv. 12–13). After a personal lament again expressing Jeremiah's reluctance for ministry (vv. 14–18), a charge to keep the Sabbath and thereby to protect Davidic kingship, Jerusalem, and temple, completes the chapter (vv. 19–27). The parable of the potter, in which possibilities for Israel are raised (18:1–12) and its implications for Israel discussed (vv. 13–17), is followed in chapter 18 by the seeming rejection of hope for Israel, since threats against Jeremiah's life (vv. 18–23) complete the chapter. A symbolic presentation of judgment against Judah by the public breaking of the potter's vessel and Jeremiah's arrest (19:1–20:6) are followed by introspective reflections upon his call (20:7–13). This first major section of the prophecy is completed by Jeremiah's lamenting his birth (vv. 14–18), returning us thus to 1:5 and at the same time underscoring the reality of the judgment which, at the beginning of the prophecy, Jeremiah was commissioned to pronounce.

Oracles Against the House of David and Foreign Nations (Jer. 21–25)

These chapters assume a more public and detached tone. A review of Judean kingship is first conducted, with the conclusion that Davidic kingship as exercised must lead the nation into exile (Jer. 21:1–10 is di-

rected against Zedekiah, vv. 11–14 against Davidic kingship generally).
A model for kingship (clearly drawn from Josiah) is offered in 22:1–9, followed by a series of judgments leveled at Josiah's successors: Jehoahaz
(vv. 10–12), Jehoiakim (vv. 13–19), and Jehoiachin (vv. 20–30), Zedekiah
having been dealt with in chapter 21. The end of human kingship is announced, since Jehoiachin, the last surviving king of Judah, is to be written down as childless in the genealogies (22:30), even though in exile he
was the father of at least five children. Yet Jeremiah does not repudiate
the Davidic covenant, for God himself will establish shepherds in the
future for Judah (23:1–4). The righteous Branch who will be raised up for
David in the uncertain future bears the name "Yahweh is our righteousness" (v. 6), a direct reversal of Zedekiah's ("my righteousness is Yahweh"). This is a clear denunciation by Jeremiah of Judah's present
ruling house.

The denunciation of leadership now moves into the area from which
leadership ought to have been displayed. The prophetic movement is
arraigned in 23:9–40. We remind ourselves here that prophecy was in-
augurated in the Book of 1 Samuel concurrently with kingship. The implications of that correlation were clear. Prophecy was to carry the final
political voice in Israel and was, by its superintendence of political institutions, to keep Israel firmly within an orbit of divine government. Although, as we observed, the prophetic movement was active in the north
until the exile, the authority of the southern court seems to have made it
difficult for a strong prophetic voice to emerge in the south. Attention is
drawn to this weakness by Jeremiah's strictures. Of course, the great
classical prophets of the south (e.g., Isaiah and Jeremiah) are exceptions.
In general, however, the prophetic movement in the south seems to have
capitulated to what may, as a result of the Davidic covenant (2 Sam. 7),
have been regarded as the prerogatives of kingship in Jerusalem.

The future of the people of God is seen as lying with the community
to be exiled (Jer. 24). In prophetic symbolism, which was used for the purpose of more graphic presentation, Jeremiah contrasted the "good figs,"
who went into captivity, to the "bad figs," who remained behind after the
exile of Jehoiachin and most of the officialdom in 597 B.C. Undoubtedly
Jeremiah is supporting a popular conviction, arising after this removal of
Jehoiachin, that the exiled community provides the grounds for hope.
But he has already rejected the popular confidence reposed in Jehoiachin
(22:20–30), and he qualifies the popular expectation by insisting that the
exile will prove to be a beneficial factor in Judah's history only because
God would produce "good figs" among the exiles by giving them a heart
to know him (24:7). This message anticipates something of what will be
said in the new-covenant passage (31:31–34).

In Jeremiah 25 Judah is placed among the nations of the world, all of whom must submit to Babylon. This matter is taken further in chapters 46–52 and forms the closing insistence of the book. Thus by the end of chapter 25, nation, land, priesthood, cult, kingship, and even the ark have been disowned. The institutional fabric of Israel has been rejected, and world leadership has been transferred to Yahweh's strange servant, Nebuchadrezzar (25:9). Jeremiah has thus prepared Judah for the grim reality of the coming days when Israel will cease to exist as a geographical entity, never in fact to be restored to its preexilic dimensions. His message has been very clear: exile will mean a new beginning, the calling of a new people.

Israel Under the Word (Jer. 26–36)

Jeremiah 26–36 is a collection of oracles and sayings presented for the most part within a narrative framework. The unit begins with the repetition of the temple sermon, which in itself marks out a new phase of the prophecy. It ends with Baruch's reading of the scroll before Jehoiakim, who is presented as a counter-Josiah who destroys "the book of the law" rather than heeding it. The introductory chapter (26) again provides the ground of hope for Judah, namely, submission to Yahweh's authority, which the temple symbolizes. The concluding chapter (36) notes the rejection of the Word by the Davidic king. Immediately after the temple sermon, Jeremiah, by his symbolic action of assuming a yoke of bondage (27:1–11), throws down the gauntlet to the Jerusalem prophets. This passage reports the attempted formation of a western coalition against Babylon, encouraged by prophetic elements in Judah which Jeremiah labels false (vv. 12–22). This stance provokes his celebrated clash with Hananiah, spokesman for the prophetic group, and ends in Hananiah's death (chap. 28). Jeremiah sends a letter to those who were deported in 597 B.C., urging them to accept the conditions of exile and to come to terms with the prospect of a long period of absence (chap. 29). The seventy years specified (v. 10) may be a round number alluding to the period of Sabbath rest which the land now deserves (cf. Lev. 26:34).

The problem that faces the audience of Jeremiah at this point is the evaluation of the respective prophetic criteria. Basic tests of true prophecy were proposed in Deuteronomy, namely, consistency (13:1–5), subordination to the Mosaic pattern (18:15), and fulfilment (v. 22). Hananiah comes before the people as an advocate of the Zion traditions and the inviolability of Jerusalem and its temple. Jeremiah has rejected these traditions, however, because of their lack of correspondence to the historical reality of his day; they actually amount to his personal definition of falsity. His position is made all the clearer by prefacing the temple sermon to the issue of what constitutes true prophecy. It is clear for Jeremiah that the popular appeal to inviolability has been in the interests of the status quo, which Yahweh has now rejected. We see this clearly in retrospect. Of course, Jeremiah's audience had no such advantage. An additional problem they faced was the absence of other than subjective criteria by which true and false prophecy, in their own contexts, could have been distinguished.

The book of consolation (Jer. 30–33), so styled because of its hopeful content, deals with the restoration of Israel's fortunes, her land, and her institutions. Central to this section is the prophecy of the new covenant (31:31–34). This prophecy posits a new exodus as a prerequisite to establishment of the new covenant and a new entry into the Promised Land as the issue of it. Because of the impending change in Israel's political situation, a review of the Sinai covenant, which had brought the political constitution of Israel into being, is undertaken. Though there is no mention of the new covenant's exercising influence beyond Israel nor of a world pilgrimage of the nations, so characteristic of the prophetic eschatology, the emphases of 31:35–40 combine to affirm an international context. These verses refer to the certainty of God's new-covenant purposes as grounded within the order of creation itself (vv. 35–37), and to the (muted) note of the New Jerusalem (vv. 38–40), which will function as the world center. Jeremiah 30–31 is almost exclusively given over to the return of the exiled and divided nation and its reestablishment as one people. By his new-covenant doctrine of one Israel, Jeremiah is building a bridge between Israel's past and her future hope. Note especially the structure of 31:31–34, where future hope is juxtaposed with the negative past.

The announcement of Jeremiah 31:31, "Behold, the days are coming," points to an age in transition. To judge from its use elsewhere in the Old Testament, this phrase refers to the uncertain future, whether near or remote. The emphasis upon the divine initiative makes it clear that the covenant will be divinely imposed, not negotiated. This accords with the manner in which all divine covenants in the Old Testament were delivered. Yahweh will "cut" (i.e., initiate), a word that always refers to the beginning of a covenantal arrangement, though the subject of the formula may not always be the initiator of the arrangement. Since the Sinai covenant is clearly the model which Jeremiah has chosen for his meditation, some specific redemptive intervention in the manner of the exodus seems to be contemplated to bring this new arrangement into being.

Jeremiah's contemplated covenant is described as "new." There is possible ambiguity here, for the Hebrew word can refer to temporal (Exod. 1:8; Deut. 32:17; 1 Sam. 6:7; Eccles. 1:10) or qualitative (Lam. 3:22–23) newness. Perhaps we are to balance both nuances of the word here and suggest a new dimension of faith to be imported into Israel as a result of the exile, yet not so radical a dimension that it constitutes a complete break with the past.

That the new covenant will be continuous with the old and will deal with present historical difficulties is signified by the fact that it will be made with the traditional geographical entities, north and south, referred to in Jeremiah 31:31 as "the house of Israel" and "the house of Judah." Like the notion advanced in Ezekiel 37:15–28, the recall from exile will involve a divine grafting which makes the two warring brothers one. It is sometimes argued that "the house of Judah" in Jeremiah 31:31 is a scribal addition, since only "the house of Israel" occurs in verse 33. But the thought is rather that the imposition of the new covenant will mean the healing of the long-standing breaches between the two kingdoms. It will give expression to the prophetic conviction that there can be, and has ever been, only one unified people of God.

Yet in indicating that the new covenant will not be like the Sinai covenant in its tenor or type, Jeremiah 31:32 moves us into a new phase. We can hardly expect that the new covenant will display a greater expression of grace than the great redemptive act of the exodus. It would also be a mistake to see the new covenant as grace and the old as "demand." Rather, 31:32 stresses the fallibility of the Sinai covenant. That covenant was able to be breached by Israel and was continually breached ("my covenant which they broke"). The pathetic national response to the reforms of Josiah was living proof of this fact. But Yahweh had maintained his commitment to Sinai despite the continuing provocations of Israel. The divine fidelity to the Sinai arrangement is referred to in 31:32 under the familiar prophetic symbolism of marriage. No divorce was possible under the old arrangement, and though Israel had been an unfaithful wife, the bond still held. By contrast it will not be possible to breach the new covenant—and herein certainly lies an element of newness! Both parties will keep the new arrangement!

The matter of newness seems to be fully displayed in Jeremiah 31:33, where the note of the law in the heart is taken up. The problems under the old covenant had arisen on the human level. Would not therefore a radical inward change both personally and nationally be necessary to create the response to Yahweh for which the new covenant would call? Obviously it would, but it would be wrong to suggest that the Sinai covenant, which is clearly in view, had not entailed some degree of inward change.

True, the demand for inward change under the Sinai covenant had not resulted in a national transformation. Nevertheless, the Sinai covenant was an idealization which had aimed at such a transformation. The reference to law in Jeremiah 31:33 causes us to reflect further upon the relationship of covenant and law in the Old Testament. These terms are interdependent, with "covenant" implying a response and "law," as response, indicating a prior relationship. It would be a mistake, however, to think of covenant law as a theology of demand, since law pointed to the contours within which the relationship operated. Law was guidance for living, not an outward arbitrary demand. No demand could be expected where grace had not first operated. Thus there could be no separation of Torah from the whole covenant framework.

Later in Israel's history, and contrary to Yahweh's original intention, a tendency to separate law and promise surfaced. Obedience to the law, however, was incumbent upon all those within the framework of grace (see Deut. 6:20–25). Moreover, in Deuteronomy it was always presumed that the place of the law was in the national (and personal) heart (6:4–6; 11:18). Perhaps the oscillation between the second-person plural and second-person singular in the exhortations of Deuteronomy was a device consciously employed to address national Israel through Israelites. The notion of the law in the heart is usually advanced by command in Deuteronomy (e.g., 6:4–5), but such references point to the ideal state desired and presumably envisaged as possible. The demand for "circumcision of the heart" is similarly made (e.g., 10:16) and seems a requirement to which Israel must rise. But in Moses' moving final address, Israel is addressed as in exile (chap. 30). The recall of the nation is anticipated, but only after Yahweh, as he must do if the law is to be obeyed, has circumcised the heart (v. 6).

Salvation of the individual in the Old Testament presupposes the "law in the heart." Thus the demand for the purification of the heart, the creation of a clean heart in personal renewal, is frequent in the Old Testament. Contrition always stems from the heart (Ps. 51:10, 17; 73:1; Prov. 22:11; Isa. 57:15). Jeremiah makes it clear that a national change of heart would mean a return to Yahweh and uses the language of circumcision in this connection (Jer. 4:4; cf. 9:25–26). Indeed, the law in the heart is always required for the possibility of spiritual experience in the Old Testament (Ps. 37:31; 40:8). In Isaiah 51:7, which addresses the exiles, the prospect of a return to Jerusalem and a new covenant is advanced to "you who know righteousness, the people in whose heart is my law."

Of course there are tensions between the placement of the law in the heart by God and the obedience which stems from it, but such tensions are not confined to the Old Testament. They are also inherent in the struggles between flesh and spirit in the New Testament. It would thus go beyond the evidence to suggest that the newness of the new covenant consists solely in the emphasis upon the inwardness of the law. When the Old Testament insists that the law in the heart is essential for spiritual experience, it does not suppose that the individual has put it there. Thus to suggest that Jeremiah is breaking new ground in 31:33 may be to go too far. Moreover, this verse closes with the traditional covenant formula, derivable from Sinai, "I will be their God, and they shall be my people." Jeremiah 31:33 may be plausibly viewed as saying no more than that Yahweh is returning to the idealism of the Sinai period in this new-covenant relationship. Granted that the law in the heart is a factor common to both the Sinai and new covenants, the problem that remains is how the perfect expression of this new relationship, implicitly demanded by verse 32, will be manifested in the new age. As the major statement emphasizing the radical discontinuity of the new covenant, verse 34 takes us further.

With Jeremiah 31:34 we do seem to have reached the climax of the presentation and to have entered a new phase of human experience. The divine initiative of verse 33 is now seen to issue into something more than was possible through Sinai. The wording "no longer" of verse 34 moves us to the radical character of the change which is contemplated. Because the old system was mediated, it required constant institutional support. No such support will be needed in the new situation. No more exhortation will be required to produce constancy in the relationship! All will be deeply and consciously involved in the new expression of the covenant in the coming days (note the use of "know," a verb often employed in the Old Testament to convey deep intimacy). A new set of circumstances is envisaged which takes us beyond the framework of human limitation within which spiritual experience has had to operate in Jeremiah's day and ours.

What makes the new covenant truly new becomes evident at the end of Jeremiah 31:34. In the new age, says Yahweh, "I will forgive their iniquity, and I will remember their sin no more." Forgiveness in the Old Testament was normally extended through the sacrificial system, which was efficacious for sins confessed. But in the new age, sin will be more than forgiven—it will be "not remembered"! This is a remarkable statement, and its tenor must be appreciated. There is a technical use of vocabulary here, for "remembering" in the Old Testament is not limited to the power of psychological recall. Particularly when describing Yahweh, "remembering" implies the reactivating of an issue, the taking of action to effect a new condition whose rationale stems from some past event. God thus "remembered" Noah and caused the waters to abate (Gen. 8:1). He also "remembered" Hannah (1 Sam. 1:19), and the promise of a son became an actuality.

In the context of Jeremiah 31:34, for God not to remember means that no action will need to be taken in the new age against sin. The forgiveness of which this verse speaks is so comprehensive that sin has been finally dealt with in the experience of the believer. In this verse we are not only pointing to the action of God in Christ, reconciling the world unto himself. We are also looking to the effects of the work of Christ in the final experience of the believer. In the eschatological age of which Jeremiah is speaking, sin will not be a factor; it will be foreign to all human experience. The point advanced here is not a contrast between the restrictions under which the old covenant labored and the freedom the Spirit gives in the new. In Jeremiah's new age, sin will not need to be confessed nor progressively forgiven. This verse points us beyond the course of present human experience to the perfected unfettered fellowship of the new creation, to the time when tensions with human experience have been finally overcome.

In short, the new covenant of Jeremiah points to God's final gift. It does not point to a new measure of forgiveness, since God's forgiveness is freely given within both Testaments. But it points to a new apprehension of that forgiveness within human experience, an apprehension which will mean perfected human service and response. Jeremiah 31:31–34 thus looks beyond the community of the New Testament age to the operation of life within the framework of a revealed new creation. Then the new heavens and the new earth will have arrived and the New Jerusalem descended, the dwelling of God will be with humankind, they will be his people, and he will be their God (Rev. 21:3–4). The book of consolation concludes with two chapters which promise the restoration of Judah's land (Jer. 32) and institutions (chap. 33).

Jeremiah 34 records matters relating to the prosecution of the final Babylonian siege of Jerusalem—a word to the vacillating Zedekiah (vv. 1–7) and the callous treatment of slaves during the conduct of the siege (vv. 8–22). As a final contrast to the catalog of disobedience in chapters 26–36, we have the pious example of the Rechabites, in an incident from what appears to have been Jehoiakim's time (chap. 35). Jeremiah 36 ends the sequence, underscoring the nation's rejection of the Word.

The Fall of Jerusalem and Its Implications (Jer. 37–52)

Matters relating to the fall of Jerusalem (Jer. 37–39), the aftermath of the fall (chaps. 40–45), oracles against the foreign nations (chaps. 46–51), and then an extended summary of the fall of Jerusalem (chap. 52) conclude the book. But the ministry of Jeremiah was not a failure. It was in fact a saving ministry, for it provided reasons for what happened in 587/586 B.C., and it was designed to prepare Israel for the great changes which would occur in her experience in exile. She would from now on be immersed in a sea of power structures.

While the material of the Book of Jeremiah is somewhat un-coordinated, its general tenor is clear: Israel is to become a community of faith, a status that the exile will make clear. The term *Israel* will not again be able to be used exclusively of the nation. Although the post-exilic writings witness disappointing attempts by the returned community to set back the historical clock, the course of the future people of God has been determined. A new exodus (accomplished, as we know, by the death of Christ) will be followed by the divine imposition of a new covenant. While the New Testament makes it clear that the death of Christ provides the platform on which the new covenant will rest, the full implementation of the detail of the new covenant awaits the ushering in of the final expression of the kingdom of God. In effect, the proclamation of a New Israel (it is to be noted that preponderantly Jeremiah uses "Israel" as a theological term), a new covenant, and thus a new age for the people of God is the message of the Book of Jeremiah, presented to national Israel when the "times of the Gentiles" had come.

12

Ezekiel

Controlling the prophecy of Ezekiel are three great visionary sequences (Ezek. 1–3, 8–11, 40–48), all of them dominated by temple
concerns. Such focus gives us an indication of the general purpose of the
book, since the temple suggests the theme of divine kingship, of Yahweh's sovereignty over Israel. That this theme indeed is the emphasis of
the book is confirmed on two fronts. The first is the recurring use of the
phrase "that you may know that I am Yahweh" in explanation of the divine action. The second is the fact that Ezekiel is one of the few prophetic books which state explicitly that Yahweh's kingship over Israel
must be the factor that determines the future of Israel (e.g., 20:33).

The overall structure of Ezekiel is not difficult to present in broad
terms. Chapters 1–24 are given over to the denunciation of Jerusalem, to
prophecies of exile for Jerusalem's leadership and her people, and to
prophecies relating to Jerusalem's destruction. Chapters 25–32 are oracles uttered against the surrounding foreign nations, that is, prophetical
judgments against Israel's world. Such oracles are employed by most of
Israel's prophets. While they can be understood as an assertion of Yah-

weh's authority over the world and function generally as a rebuke to nations that have mistreated Yahweh's elect people, perhaps their origin
lies in the notion of rebuke to vassals which rebelled from the former
Davidic empire (as the collection in Amos 1–2 may suggest). Finally,
chapters 33–48 deal with prophecies of restoration. There are inter-
actions within the book which permit such a classification to be a general one only. The time references range from 593 B.C. (Ezek. 1:1, on the
most probable interpretation) to 571 B.C. (29:17). The book thus covers
the ministry of Ezekiel to the exiles in Babylon prior to the fall of Jerusalem (587/586 B.C.) and during the period immediately thereafter. Again,
speaking broadly, chapters 1–24 deal with the foreshadowed destruction
of the city and temple, while chapters 33–48 culminate in the presentation of the new-temple complex, which is virtually identical with the
New Jerusalem. Of the fourteen dated references in the book, all but the
difficult 1:1 are directly correlated to King Jehoiachin's reign (exiled in
597 B.C. but still considered to be king in exile by the deportees). This
fact may seem to suggest that Ezekiel strikes a pronounced Davidic note.
We shall see, however, that this is not so. On the contrary, the Davidic
line is rarely referred to directly; and when it is, the reference is almost
always disparaging. The message of the book, indeed, is that the prior
political leadership has failed and the future of the people of God will be
guaranteed only by the imposition of divine leadership.

The Call of Ezekiel and the First Temple Vision (Ezek. 1:1–3:15)

The first vision of Ezekiel sets the tone for the entire book. The similarity of Ezekiel 1 in form and content to the call of Isaiah has often been
the subject of comment. Both Ezekiel 1 and Isaiah 6, after giving a date,
show how the prophet is overwhelmed by a vision of Yahweh. In each of
them the vision includes an ominous note of divine judgment. Each
chapter features winged creatures which have human qualities and are
associated with a divine throne (implied in Ezek. 1). Both prophetic calls
are received in a context of worship (Isaiah in the temple, Ezekiel perhaps at a "praying place" by the river Chebar), and both prophets (as Ezekiel's call develops in chapters 2–3) are sent to people who are unwilling
to hear (Zimmerli 1979, 108–10).

The five paragraphs of the vision of Ezekiel 1 (commencing in vv. 4, 7,
15, 22, and 26) are tied together by the use of the same idiom, "like the
gleam of" (see vv. 4, 7, 16, 22, and 27). The first and last paragraphs (1:4,
26–28) describe the figure who rides upon the chariot, while the intervening ones describe the living creatures (vv. 5–14) and their relationship to the wheels beside them (vv. 15–21) and to the platform or

firmament above them (vv. 22–25). Ezekiel 1:4 graphically introduces the vision with a general description of the divine manifestation, which is expanded in verses 26–28 by a repetition (in reverse order) of the three items seen in 1:4, namely, flashing fire, brightness, and storm (Parunak 1979, 124). These are not merely incidental details furnished by the prophet, but are the very characteristics of the Lord who appears. The description of the platform and what is above it (vv. 25–26) is reminiscent of the description of the enthroned Yahweh who was seen by the elders of Israel (Exod. 24:10). In this way continuity with the Sinai traditions is indicated. The last temple vision (chaps. 40–48) also promotes this connection (Parunak 1979, 72).

Heightening the majesty of the enthroned Lord is the extended description of the servant creatures (Ezek. 1). They are later identified in 10:15, 20, and 22 as cherubim and elsewhere as supporters of the ark throne (see 1 Sam. 4:4; 2 Sam. 6:2; Ps. 18:10). This identification increases the probability that it is Yahweh as both locally enthroned and yet omnipresently mobile who is encountered by Ezekiel. The attention given to the throne and the similarities to Isaiah 6 suggest not only association with the Zion traditions, but also Yahweh's movement in judgment against what is clearly the Jerusalem temple (see Ezek. 10). That the storm vision emanates from the north, the numinous area from which judgment at the time of the exile was expected to come (cf. the "foe from the north," the chaoslike irruption of judgment in the Book of Jeremiah), confirms this interpretation. As a preliminary hypothesis, therefore, we may imagine that Yahweh is depicted in Ezekiel 1 as enthroned, accompanied by ministrant attendants (though unlike the seraphim of Isa. 6 the cherubim—temple guardians, door deities in the ancient Near East—function only as bearers of the throne), and moving down in judgment from his heavenly palace against the Jerusalem temple, the earthly replica of Yahweh's heavenly seat of authority. If this suggestion is accepted, then the movement of the Book of Ezekiel is clear. Judgment is to begin at the household of God; the book thus commences with Jerusalem and her temple under imminent judgment. Yet the covenant faithfulness of Yahweh has led us to expect a movement beyond judgment, and so the Book of Ezekiel concludes with the magnificent conception of Yahweh as enthroned in what must be the New Jerusalem (though the city of chaps. 40–48 is unnamed), that is, as permanently located among his people in a new city from which, in Edenic terms, the waters of life flow.

Ezekiel 1 is thus glory-dominated, allusive in its description of the Yahweh encountered, and characterized (as is the prophecy as a whole) by an extreme emphasis upon Yahweh's transcendence. Before such an appearance the prophet is abased; nevertheless, he is addressed (2:1–2), sent to a rebellious people (vv. 3–5), and encouraged by divine assurances in a manner somewhat similar to the call of Jeremiah (2:6–3:3). He is then recommissioned, more specifically in 3:4–11, before being returned by the Spirit to his exilic location (vv. 12–15), conscious of Yahweh's exodus power and of the unique and ecstatic nature of his experience. (Note that "the hand of the LORD" is upon him [3:14]. A similar assertion is made in 8:1 and 40:1, thus bonding together the three visionary sections, chaps. 1–3, 8–11, and 40–48.)

Ezekiel's Role and Message (Ezek. 3:16–7:27)

Ezekiel's prophetic role is outlined in 3:16–23. He is to be a watchman set over the house of Israel, personally responsible for conveying the warning with which he has been charged, namely, the threat which comes from the enmity directed against Israel by Yahweh himself! Somewhat paradoxically, Ezekiel is then confined to his house and told that he is to be bound and rendered dumb (vv. 24–27), actions which seem to negate the charge he has just received. We are therefore to take the phrase "unable to reprove them" (v. 26), that is, to act as a mediator (the probable meaning in this context; see Wilson 1972, 98), as an interpretation of what will be meant by Ezekiel's dumbness. Until this dumbness is removed (by the fall of Jerusalem; see 33:22), the prophetic word to Israel is one of undeviating judgment relating to the destruction of city and temple. Any messages of hope in chapters 1–24 beyond this destruction do not weaken the stark character of the prophetic threat directed against Jerusalem and her temple in its historical context. The very symbols of the community's faith were marked out by the message for destruction, a message completely unacceptable to the Israel of Ezekiel's day.

Ezekiel's message then commences with two acts of paradigmatic symbolism graphically depicting the siege (Ezek. 4) and the fall (Ezek. 5) of Jerusalem. Ezekiel is frequently engaged in such acts, which, on the basis of answers from God to spectators who have inquired about the meaning of them, appear to have been public. It is important to note that prophetic symbolism, though always a component of prophetic ministry, was concentrated around the period of the exile (it abounds in Jeremiah and Ezekiel). Unlike sympathetic magic, whose purpose was to influence the deity, symbolic acts were seen by Old Testament prophets as self-effective proclamations of the divine Word pointing to a new divine intervention into Israel's history. While prophetic act was not identical with prophetic word, they were inseparable. The prophetic act provided the occasion for the prophetic announcement—the symbolic act could no more stand by itself than the history of Israel could stand by itself without a prophetic interpretation of its significance.

Ezekiel's message was not limited to Jerusalem. Jerusalem as a sacral center was merely the barometer for the land as a whole. The apostasy of the land is treated by reference to the "mountains" on which syncretistic acts of covenant disloyalty had occurred (Ezek. 6). Such behavior results in the virtual dismissal of the land as a promised land (chap. 7).

Departure of the Divine Glory (Ezek. 8–11)

The cycle of vision followed by prophetic ministry recommences in chapter 8. It is significant that the visionary experience of Ezekiel within chapters 8–11 is set in the context of the first point of contact between the prophet and the exilic elders, representative of the entire congregation of the deportees. The vision which follows is thus a response to their implicit inquiry (see 14:1–3, which tells of an approach by elders whose apostasy is reminiscent of that seen by Ezekiel at 8:11–13). Doubtless anticipating a question regarding the divine intent for the exilic community, Ezekiel's vision presents the actuality of judgment about to befall Jerusalem, which the vision of chapter 1 had foreshadowed. Unthinkably, Yahweh, resident in the temple since its dedication by Solomon, is about to depart from it by means of the heavenly chariot met in Ezekiel 1.

Ezekiel is transported by the Spirit to Jerusalem and is moved to four different locations in the temple. A detailed presentation of abominations proceeding in the Jerusalem temple with the knowledge and consent of Israel's elders appears in 8:5–17a. Then follows an indication of the judgment to be visited upon Jerusalem's inhabitants, though a remnant is to be marked off and spared (8:17b–9:11). Ezekiel 10, the central chapter of the vision, involves the divine abandonment of the temple. Ezekiel 10:1 recalls the appearance seen above the firmament in 1:26–28. The glory of Yahweh, which had previously consecrated the temple (Exod. 40; 1 Kings 8), now fills the temple destructively (Ezek. 10:2–7). The identification of the detail in Ezekiel 10 with the vision of chapter 1 is made clear by the extended description of cherubim and chariot in 10:8–17. In verses 18–19 the glory of Yahweh departs from the temple, Yahweh mounts the waiting chariot, and the house is forsaken. Verses 20–22 reinforce the connection between Ezekiel 1 and 10 (Parunak 1980, 68–69).

Ezekiel 11:1–21 then repeats the sequence of judgment upon the conspirators, this time by way of Ezekiel himself. The death of Pelatiah, a principal conspirator (v. 13), provides the occasion for a divine word regarding the future of the exilic congregation (vv. 14–21). Promises previously associated with covenant, Jerusalem, and temple are now transferred to a new temple (the "sanctuary" of v. 16), which Yahweh will convene in exile. A new beginning for Israel in exile is thus foreshadowed in terms of the new heart and new spirit which Yahweh will provide for his people. Verses 22–24 return the prophet to the scene of 8:1. The glory of the Lord departs from the east gate of the temple, to which it will return in the closing vision of the prophecy (43:1). The response to the inquiries of the elders is then shared with the exiles (11:25), completing the sequence of these chapters.

The Exile Symbolized (Ezek. 12–23)

As with the first visionary sequence, there now follow two symbolic actions (12:1–16, 17–20) depicting the imminent exile. This prospect of the reduction of the nation is carried forward, principally by reference to leadership within exile, until the dissolution of the nation is represented under the figure of the burned vine in Ezekiel 15.

Clearly unmoved by Ezekiel's acted parables, the Israelites who are still in the land disown prophecy (12:22). This disavowal is embedded in a section running from 12:21 to 13:23, which is an attack upon false prophecy of various descriptions as an ineffectual and apostate substitute for the real proclamation. Again the elders assemble and, like their compatriots condemned in Ezek. 8–11, are identified as idolatrous. There is no word for them unless they repent (14:1–11), nor would it be sufficient for the present generation to plead the merits of its ancestors (see the citation in vv. 12–23 of Noah, Daniel, and Job, whose piety was renowned), since Ezekiel is emphasizing the responsibility of individual Israelites. Israel is now only fit for burning (chap. 15).

The prophecy appears to take a new turn with the review of Judah's history and the role played by Jerusalem. There is a clear correspondence between the beginning and closing chapters of this section—chapter 16 is given over to the religious apostasy of the nation, while chapter 23 focuses on her political infidelity. Jerusalem throughout her history had proved herself an adulteress (16:1–43) more corrupt in fact than Sodom or Samaria (vv. 44–58). Yet divine fidelity to the covenant may be expected, and Israel will be reestablished (vv. 59–63; note that the language of this section [e.g., "everlasting covenant" in v. 60] is reminiscent of Isa. 54:10 and Jer. 31:31–34). Kingship, which had contributed to covenant breach (Ezek. 17), will cease, and the reigning king be removed to Babylon. Only a slender hope of messianic kingship is advanced at the end of this chapter (vv. 22–24).

Under the symbol of an individual the sin of the nation is surveyed in Ezekiel 18 in terms of the responsibility of each generation. Each individual is presented as responsible for his or her own sin. This doctrine of responsibility (which is not new with Ezekiel) is exhibited in verses 1–

20 by an examination proceeding through three generations. (Cf. the same three-generation span referred to in an examination of Israel's history in chap. 20.) It is made clear that present conduct is not determined by past associations. The message is clear to the nation. Yahweh desires its life, not its death. Ezekiel is not to be understood as denying the notion of corporate responsibility, an old biblical doctrine (see Exod. 20:5–6), but at this critical time in Israel's history is to be seen as providing a counterpoise or a complement to the older doctrine. Israel's attempt to disclaim responsibility for the exile is thus rejected. A review of kingship since Josiah is conducted (Ezek. 19), without prospect of its continuance, however, for the chapter ends on the note of lament.

Ezekiel 20 is a key chapter providing a review of the previous history of Israel. Her present history in the land (vv. 27–29) has been determined by attitudes developed in Egypt (vv. 5–10) and by the first (vv. 11–17) and second (vv. 18–26) generations in the wilderness. Her reaction to the divine word then has put Israel now into her wilderness situation in exile. There is no prophetic word for Israel (vv. 30–31), but God will impose a future on her (vv. 32–44). Her disposition to submerge herself among the nations and thus to withdraw from the Sinai covenant is attacked. Israel is still divine property, and God will assert his kingship over her (v. 33). In the manner of the first exodus redemption, he will gather her in a further exodus, bringing her through a wilderness situation in which she will be refined (note "pass under the rod" in v. 37). A further covenant (to be expected following an exodus) will be given to Israel, presumably the new covenant. On God's holy mountain (i.e., Zion) Israel will once again serve God in the land (vv. 40–44).

The aim of this review of history and its consequences for Israel and her future is that Israel might have knowledge of Yahweh (see 20:26, 38, 44, at the end of each section). The phrase "you will know that I am Yahweh" occurs in Ezekiel freely, chiefly to indicate the goal of a divine action. Such a knowledge of Yahweh is not arrived at by speculative insight, but by recognition of divine control over history. This realization comes through the prompting of Yahweh's agents (i.e., prophets), which in the final analysis is a demand for submission to divine sovereignty. Yahweh had promised Israel that he would be with her in the unfolding of her history (Exod. 3:13–15). The prophetic word indicates to Israel the presence of Yahweh in history, judging and saving. But this indication is not merely a notation of cause and effect, but a call for obedience and worship to a Yahweh who is already known by Israel and who can be described only in terms of encounter (Zimmerli 1982, 82–98).

Before the prospect sketched out by Ezekiel 20 can reach fruition, judgment must be passed on Israel and her leadership, which is to be replaced by that of Nebuchadrezzar. (The threat of Ezek. 20:45–49, judgment by fire, is developed in 21:1–27, where Jerusalem, the sanctuaries, and then the land are depicted as falling to Nebuchadrezzar's sword.) But not Israel alone, but also those who have afflicted her (Ammon is singled out in vv. 28–32) will suffer.

The people as well as the leaders must bear responsibility. Ezekiel 22 details the abominations of Jerusalem in covenant breach. She must be thoroughly purged from sin (with the barest hint offered in vv. 17–22 that a cleansed people would result). Chapter 23 resumes the adultery allegory of Ezekiel 16: Samaria and Jerusalem are separately and jointly arraigned for a political infidelity which goes back as far as Egypt and thus must be viewed as intrinsic to Israel's nature. More recently it has expressed itself in relationships with Assyria and Babylon. Samaria was judged but Jerusalem has not taken warning. Judah would certainly bear her own sin as an illustration of divine consistency and control over history (see v. 49, "you shall know that I am the Lord GOD"). Verses 11–35 detail Jerusalem's sin, as verses 5–10 do Samaria's. Ezekiel 23:1–4 identifies the two sisters, and verses 36–49 summarize the past apostasies and foreshadow further punishments to be inflicted.

Oracles Against Foreign Nations (Ezek. 24–33)

The chapters immediately preceding and following the oracles against the foreign nations (chaps. 24 and 33) deal with the siege of Jerusalem and its outcome. (The siege commenced in December-January 589/588 B.C., and the city fell in the summer of 587/586.) This structure offers some clue to the manner in which the oracles against foreign nations function in the Book of Ezekiel.

Jerusalem is presented in the parable of the cooking pot (24:3–14) as under siege. To the difficulties and sufferings of the period a mute reaction like Ezekiel's response to the death of his wife is demanded from the exiles (vv. 15–24). With the fall of Jerusalem (vv. 25–27) Ezekiel's dumbness will cease; that is, from that point onward prophecies of hope can be expected. There follow oracles against the nations that had sought to take advantage of Israel's distress. Such nations fall within the sphere of the Abrahamic curse on Israel's despisers (Gen. 12:3). Israel's restoration must be preceded by the judgment of her world. Ammon, Moab, Edom, and Philistia are summarily dealt with in Ezekiel 25. Tyre, which sees the removal of Jerusalem as opening the way for further commercial expansion, is singled out for special attention in view of her political importance and seeming impregnability in Ezekiel's day (chaps. 26–28). There is an extensive use in chapter 28 of Eden traditions: the prince of Tyre is cast into the role of the primeval man in the garden of God, the priest-king in the Garden of Eden. Sidon, as an adjunct to Tyre, is briefly dealt with in 28:20–24. Attention then switches to Egypt, which had survived the Assyrian period intact but will be broken by Babylon (chaps. 29–32). Egypt will share the fate of Assyria, which has entered Sheol.

These oracles against the foreign nations not only are Yahweh's claim to the wider world, but provide the link between judgment and hope in Ezekiel's prophecy. The harsh treatment of Israel must be requited; the divine intention for her must be carried out. Israel is suffering, but she will be returned to her land. The kingdom of God cannot be ushered in, however, until the enemies of the kingdom have been dealt with. Chapters 38–39 share this theme.

Repetition of the watchman theme in Ezekiel 33:1–22 begins a new phase in the prophecy with a return to Ezekiel's original commission. It is now noted that the judgment foreshadowed in the earlier announcement has been carried out (vv. 21–22); the capture of Jerusalem relieves Ezekiel's dumbness and permits him to begin the prophecies of hope in chapters 34–39. Six prophecies, all introduced with "the word of the LORD came to me" (33:23–33; chap. 34; 35:1–36:15; 36:16–37:14; 37:15–28; chaps. 38–39), follow in unbroken succession without any indication of a time lapse between them. They thus connect the fall of Jerusalem with the hope which must flow therefrom. By implication the first prophecy (33:23–33) explains the apparent discrepancy between the Abrahamic promises (note v. 24) and the judgment to be exercised upon Israel, which included loss of the land. The prophet replies that the physical enjoyment of the land was conditional upon obedience; quite naturally, the notion of the Promised Land figures prominently in the material which follows.

Divine Leadership and Restoration (Ezek. 34–36)

Ezekiel 34:1–6 reviews the problem of faulty leadership which had produced the exile. In a future age Yahweh himself will shepherd Israel (vv. 7–24), though in the reconstruction there is room for a Davidic undershepherd, but only as a minor figure (he is called "prince" in v. 24 and not "king"). As a result of divine leadership, conditions of paradise-like peace follow (vv. 25–31). Ezekiel 35:1–36:15 deals with the elimination of any threat to the Promised Land and thus the removal of all enmity, symbolized in chapter 35 by Israel's old enemy, Edom. Ezekiel 36:16–37:14 begins by reviewing the factors which led to the loss of the land (36:16–20). A restoration will come about only because it is God's clear intention to vindicate his holy name through Israel (vv. 21–23). In 36:24–38 the order by which restoration will be accomplished is given. People and land will be brought together by an exodus (v. 24). Israel will be ritually cleansed, that is, the covenant will be restored, and a new heart will be given to her (v. 26). The parallel gift of a new spirit (v. 27) will make obedience possible. We may cut the knot as to whether the divine or human spirit is meant here by suggesting that the passage refers to the activity of the divine Spirit upon the human spirit. Though the whole nation is in view, this ultimate gift of the Spirit, previously reserved in the Old Testament for Israel's rulers, democratizes leadership in this passage, so that presumably all become priests and kings in the new age. Unlike Jeremiah 31:31–34 it is not said here that the law will be placed in the heart, though in the theology of covenant renewal, familiar to the exilic prophets, this step would have been assumed, since the human heart was regarded as the volitional and emotional center of the person. Ezekiel 36:28–38 leads us to the consummation of the program, namely, the restoration of the land or, in Edenic terms, the renewal of creation.

The Valley of Dry Bones (Ezek. 37–39)

In Ezekiel 37:1–14 the process of restoration is looked at from another point of view. The prophet is taken to the valley of his call (cf. 3:22 with 37:1), where he witnesses the results of the prophetic ministry of judgment, namely, a charnel house of dry bones, what was once the house of Israel. By the divine power to re-create (note the allusion to Gen. 2:7 in Ezek. 37:5), a mighty national resurrection occurs. Which comes first in the Old Testament, personal resurrection or national resurrection, is still disputed. However, there does seem some warrant for suggesting that the hope of immortality is always present in the Old Testament. Yahweh is always seen as being able to kill or make alive (1 Sam. 2:6), and this belief issues into various statements about a personal resurrection (Isa. 26:19; and possibly Job 19:26). The doctrine of personal resurrection receives prominence, however, when the emphasis shifts from the state to the individual after the fall of Jerusalem.

The significance of the national resurrection is shown in the next address (37:15–28), where a New Israel is reconstituted from the previously warring factions, Judah and geographic Israel, with the entire nation once more in the Promised Land under Davidic leadership. In these new and changed circumstances a covenant of peace, an eternal covenant, is made with Israel. The Abrahamic (and creation) promises of being blessed and multiplied are then reinvoked (v. 26). God now indwells his people in this new relationship (v. 27). Among its results are a witness to divine sovereignty and confession thereof by the whole world.

The relationship of chapters 38–39 to what precedes and follows is somewhat difficult to gauge. They deal with an assault by Gog from Magog upon the reconstituted people of God dwelling in peace, the defeat of Gog, and his final elimination. On the one hand, they seem to operate as an apocalyptic commentary upon and as a restatement of the principles underlying the oracles against foreign nations (chaps. 25–32). On the other, they deal with threats to the newly restored people of God which must be overcome before the onset of direct divine rule through the establishment of the temple age, to which Ezekiel 40–48 points (Niditch 1986, 220–23).

The New Temple (Ezek. 40–48)

Finally, following the removal of all opposition to the people of God in the new age, the symbol of divine rule—the new temple—commands attention in Ezekiel 40–48. The cosmic character of this vision is underscored by its being presented on the world mountain, the "very high mountain" of Ezekiel 40:2, which is clearly identifiable as Mount Zion (Levenson 1976, 7). These chapters draw their particular theological stance from the remote past, particularly the period of the exodus and conquest. Since the vision represents a new beginning in these older terms, a possibility exists that Sinai characteristics are also to be associated with this mountain, and all the more so because the blueprint for the new temple emerges from heaven just as the pattern for the exodus tabernacle did (cf. Ezek. 43:10–12 with Exod. 25:9). There is thus probably a confluence here of the older sacral traditions of Sinai and Zion, both of which place the emphasis upon divine kingship. Just as the building of the tabernacle completed the exodus and was its logical conclusion, so the eschatology presented in Ezekiel 40–48 is dominated by the construction of the new temple. Also, just as the meaning of the exodus was proclaimed by the cultic response of Israel to divine kingship expressed through tabernacle and temple, so here the new temple functions as Yahweh's kingly setting in the holy city.

The vision begins with a detailed description emphasizing the writer's absorption with the temple. Moving from the outer wall (Ezek. 40:5–16) to the outer court (vv. 17–27) to the inner court (40:28–41:26) and back to the outer court (42:1–14), the tour finally concludes outside the wall (vv. 15–20). Standing at the center of the material is the structure of the house itself (40:48–41:26). Its elaborate symmetry, its continuity with and yet distinction from the temple of Solomon, and the emphasized use of symbolic numbers all serve to suggest that we are moving in these pictures from what has been historically experienced to an eschatology in which the central notion of worship will characterize the response of the perfected people of God. Thus the temple vision serves to state more emphatically the general tenor of Ezekiel's eschatology to this point.

The temple tour recommences with the reappearance of the divine presence (see Ezek. 43:2). We have here clear echoes of the older Sinai encounter. Summaries of that encounter (Deut. 33:2; Judg. 5:4–5; Ps. 68:8; Hab. 3:3–4) have two features which are emphasized in Ezekiel 43:1–5: the Lord approaches from the east, since Israel approached Sinai from the west (i.e., Egypt), and the manifestation of the divine presence is thunderously audible. Verses 3–4 take us back to the prophet's earlier visions recorded in chapters 1–2 and 9–10 (Parunak 1980, 72). We gather that the cumulative message of those visions has been realized in Israel's history to this point. In short, the apostate nation has been judged and then restored to the land under divine kingship. In the inner court two prophetic pronouncements are delivered concerning the temple (43:5–44:3) and its use in worship (44:4–46:24). In these chapters there is a careful removal of the temple from any former political associations (see 42:20; 44:6–9). It is now a purely priestly domain, which the prince may not enter (45:4–8). The stress is clear. Yahweh is the sole ruler in the new age (cf. 20:33), or to put it differently, the reality of the future throws the failures of the past into bold relief. The movements of the prince in regard to the sanctuary are quite circumscribed. The ideals of the Davidic period have been passed over in the interests of older sacral conventions, particularly of the exodus-conquest theology.

The influence of the building upon the land is then outlined in Ezekiel 47:1–12 in terms of its purifying and sanctifying effects (cf. Exod. 15:17–18). Waters of life flowing from the sanctuary heal the land and change it into a paradise, making it a garden of God. Trees of life (Ezek. 47:12) are planted on either side of the stream, which itself increases to an immeasurable degree (v. 5). These trees will be for food (v. 12), and unlike an earlier time, one may eat of their fruit without fear of judgment in this new age. The land, cleansed and renewed by divine possession of it, is then divided (vv. 13–23). No conquest is needed, merely purification. The division of the land is then undertaken with regard to the ideal borders of earlier periods (cf. Num. 34:1–12). Allotments are given to the seven tribes to be located in the north (Ezek. 48:1–7). Then, as in the case of the division of the land in the conquest period, the undertaking is interrupted in order to provide for the sanctuary (cf. Josh. 18:1; see Parunak 1980, 74). That is to say, our attention after the first allotments is directed to the holy site, which is set aside for the Zadokites, the purified priesthood (Ezek. 48:8–12). The Levites, the public, and the prince then receive attention (vv. 13–22). Finally, land is allotted to the five remaining tribes (vv. 23–29). The handmaid tribes (Gad, Asher,

Naphtali, and Dan) are furthest from the temple. The sacred shrine itself is surrounded by the tribe of Levi as a further protection from contamination. Judah is directly to the north of the shrine and Benjamin to the south, thus obliterating the old north-south division. The tribes probably share equally in the distribution of land. Thus the new society seeks to redress the economic and political imbalances of the past. The account concludes with the name of the city, Yĕhōwâ šāmmâ ("the LORD is there").

Having begun with a vision of judgment directly related to the temple, the Book of Ezekiel ends with a vision of a new society which is temple-controlled and theocratically centered. The fact that the shrine and the city are no longer in Judah and that Zion is referred to only obliquely in these chapters appears to be an explicit rejection of the Jerusalem royal theology. In short, what we have here is a symbolic presentation of a return to the patriarchal promises, land allotted to a new people of God. No pattern from Israel's history accounts for the order of the tribes, another fact which points to a new beginning. The tribal arrangement, foursquare around the sanctuary, is a reflection of the older exodus structure and its theology. That there are no Levitical cities also implies a preconquest structure. In short, Ezekiel has gone back behind the monarchical period. In so strongly criticizing this period and holding it responsible for the political and religious breaches described within the book, Ezekiel implicitly rejects any doctrine of the inviolability of Jerusalem and the Solomonic temple.

The emerging new-temple theology in Ezekiel is clearly not a blueprint for a postexilic restoration. Rather, if Israel is to have a future, Yahweh himself will bring about a new beginning with himself at the center. He alone will be responsible for the future of the people of God. He alone will erect the new temple. Ezekiel's role has simply been to warn Israel of what impends and, once it has happened (587/586 B.C.), to relay to Israel the shape of the future (40:4; 43:10–11). The perfect symmetry we have seen in chapters 40–48, the holy city removed from direct tribal contact and thus from any political tensions, and the centrality of worship in the new age all point to the exalted doctrine of the presence of Yahweh offered in the Book of Ezekiel. From the divine palace there now flow forth never-ending blessings, the product of perfect divine rule. The holy city has become the world center, the navel of the universe, and thus Yahweh's ultimate control over history has been demonstrated to his people. In the way that their faith had led them to expect, they finally know indeed that "he is Yahweh."

Ezekiel 40–48 makes no provision for Davidic kingship. Indeed, instead of *king* the term *prince* is used for the political ruler of the future age (see 44:3; 45:7–8, 16–17; 46:2; 48:21–22). This terminology is consistent with the diminished role assigned to David and to kingship generally in this book, as we have noted, and with the clear theocratic aims of Ezekiel. In a grand panorama the book has taken us from the picture of Jerusalem's temple under judgment to the heavenly temple from which that judgment emerged and which has now become the world center around which the new society will be constructed.

The Book of Ezekiel moves from the temple of Jerusalem under judgment (chaps. 1–3, 8–11) to the restoration of the people of God (chaps. 34–36), the defeat of the final opposition directed against the reconstituted Israel (chaps. 37–39), and a description of the new temple in the end-time Zion (chaps. 40–48). We have viewed the necessary process of renewal which must come upon the people of God, their vindication, and their final occupancy of the Promised Land. Ezekiel thus presents the hope of the people of God and the issue of God's final indwelling presence among his people, the theme to which Revelation 21–22 is devoted.

13

Hosea

The dating of the prophecies of Hosea is fairly well defined by the introduction to the book (1:1), which refers to activities from Jeroboam II of Israel (Hosea seems to refer to the turbulence in the north which followed his death in 747 B.C.) until Hezekiah (probably a reference to his coregency with Ahaz, which began in about 727). Thus they span the period of decline in the north to shortly before its exile, which Hosea anticipates but does not mention. The book is divisible into two broad sections, chapters 1–3 and 4–14. Attempts to unravel the puzzle that chapters 4–14 pose in terms of thematic presentation have been unsuccessful. Further attempts to subdivide Hosea 4–14 (e.g., chaps. 4–11, the dynamic of God's struggle with Israel; chaps. 12–14, the prospective fall of the north), or to see the book as originally addressed to the north but then overlaid with Judean material, or to view it as promise superimposed onto earlier judgment oracles (as well as other possibilities) do not fully explain the difficulties of this book, whose broad thrust is, however, clear. For our purposes the book may be dissected as follows:

Chapters 1–3 are a general indictment of Israel under the image of a marriage relationship; to this indictment has been added conditional promise. These three chapters are not easy to interpret, and details are often baffling. This opening section of the prophecy is characterized (as is the book as a whole) by the bold adoption of Canaanite Baal imagery and language, appropriated in the interests of condemning the syncretistic fertility cults. Hosea presents Yahweh as the bestower of the blessings previously associated with the cults. In general terms the book ends (Hos. 14) on the note of a covenant return which is presented in terms of abounding fertility. Thus the book moves from covenant breach to covenant renewal, while exposing the full range of national sins along the way, showing itself to be covenant-centered and in contact with the Sinai traditions. Allusions to Israel's past—the patriarchs, exodus, and conquest—abound in the book. In sum, it is a recall to Israel's beginnings and to covenant fidelity. Unlike Amos, a near contemporary who devotes little actual space to the question of idolatry (though implications are clearly there), Hosea majors on Israel's religious deviation. Social sins are mentioned only in passing. The aberrant worship structure and its need for correction (not for thorough removal, as in Amos) are main concerns of this book. It is covenant-centered, and most of the mainstream covenant themes (loyal love, knowledge, and fidelity) occur frequently.

The Unfaithful Wife (Hos. 1–3)

The opening material of Hosea most naturally divides itself into two elements, each introduced by "Yahweh said" (1:2; 3:1). The command to Hosea to marry an adulterous woman (1:2) is offensive to modern readers, but probably anticipates what will happen within the marriage relationship rather than defines the current status of the woman, Gomer. Between 1:2 and 2:1 three oracles relating to the children of the marriage offer a progressive review of the history of Israel. The birth of Jezreel ("God sows") is an indication of divine sowing, that is, of judgment to come, to be followed by an expected harvest (1:3–5). This judgment is consequent upon the sin of Jehu (either his dynasty, ca. 841–752 B.C., or his realm, Israel). The birth of a second child, "Not pitied," spells the end of the northern kingdom; the future hope lies with Judah (vv. 6–7). But the birth of the third child, "Not my people," spells the end of the covenant (1:8–9).

After these three oracles dealing with the dissolution of the nation, a citation of the Abrahamic promise (Hos. 1:10–2:1) heralds a new exodus (in v. 10 Israel is again called "sons"), an Israel formed by the unification of the two kingdoms, the constant prophetic dream (v. 11). The name *Jezreel* is here used positively to represent the ingathering which these promises foreshadow. Such ambiguity is characteristic of Hosea.

Hosea 2 presents an allegory of covenant renewal under the traditional prophetic imagery of marriage. It is contested whether there is consistency in the use of the imagery. The children, who seem to be divided Israel, are introduced in verse 1 only to be dismissed and to reappear in the eschatological restoration of verses 22–23. The wife seems to be identified alternately with Israel and her land (Andersen and Freedman 1980, 124). Perhaps this personification of the land at various stages of the address is intended to heighten the implied comparisons and contrasts with the Canaanite Baal (i.e., fertility) worship which underlie the passage.

Hosea 2:2–5 deals with the conduct of mother Israel, who is to be rebuked by her children (the current generation of Israelites?). A separation from her husband has taken place, though divorce is not in view. The attempt to make vivid the enormity of her cultic apostasy through the intimate series of images in verses 2–5, which in itself suggests the closeness of the covenant relationship and its personal nature, ends only in a declaration of self-interest by Israel (v. 5b) to pursue the fertility deities. A sentence of judgment follows in three parts, each introduced by the word *therefore* (vv. 6, 9, 14). Yahweh will prevent Israel from pursuing the Baals, and the shallow determination of Israel to return to Yahweh will founder on lack of knowledge of the Yahweh who is to be sought (vv. 6–8). The series of deprivations which follow (vv. 9–12) are a visitation of the covenant curse for the reasons described in verse 13, namely, her commitment to Canaanite syncretism.

The judgment theme appears to continue with a further *therefore,* but with an unexpected twist. Without any motivation for a change of lifestyle within Israel, the subject turns to covenant renewal. The theological idealism with which the Israel of the Sinai period was surrounded appears in verses 14–15, evoked by the unmerited free will of Yahweh, who has remarkably turned Israel from depravity to dependence. We are to understand that these effects have been produced by the impending separation from the land, which is the clear punishment for covenant breach.

Only after this restoration, which is reported in detail in a series of oracles in 2:16–23, does Yahweh directly address Israel. The threats of the earlier part of the chapter are now removed, and the marriage metaphors are boldly resumed. God brings the mother into the wilderness now to allure her, to create a new covenant in which the harmony between God and Israel will be reflected by the harmony to be found within creation itself (v. 18). There will be a new marriage (vv. 19–20; cf. v. 16), and Israel will now "know" Yahweh (v. 20), just as she did previously. This declaration of the renewed relationship forms the climax of the chapter, while the variety of covenant terms in verses 19–20 (righteousness, justice, steadfast love, mercy, faithfulness) indicates the depth of the renewal. Courtship, betrothal, covenant making, exchange of vows, and giving of new names are the renewal components in verses 14–23. The reversal in meaning of the names of the children is now brought into play (vv. 21–23) as Israel, with blessing viewed from many perspectives, is presented as the people of the new covenant (see Andersen and Freedman 1980, 284–86).

In Hosea 3:1–3 Israel's history of infidelity is again reviewed in a chapter which seems to be a continuation of chapter 1 (3:1 seems to command continued love of a wayward woman, not remarriage). But this time it is told in the first person, as opposed to the third-person account of Hosea 1. A total suspension of married life for a defined period is required (3:3), which verse 4 interprets as a suspension of cultic life, making it clear that the cultic apostasy is the great deviation with which these first three chapters are dealing. Hosea 3:5 contemplates an exile, after which a new era corresponding to the mood of 1:10–2:1 (and to the renewal of 2:14–23) commences.

Thus, through the sustained play on the marriage metaphor, the covenant relationship between Yahweh and Israel has been reviewed in Hosea 1–3. Hosea is the first to use this highly personal metaphor, which thereafter becomes a frequent one in the Old Testament prophets. His book reviews Israel's history, institutions, and religion by employing language which draws attention to the initiation, development, and present state of the covenant relationship. He takes pains to contrast the idealistic beginnings (or the sinful beginnings in the case of the northern kingship) with what is now the empirical reality. Marriage is thus the vehicle used to illustrate the nature and the continuance of the Sinai covenant relationship. Its suitability is obvious. At Sinai, as in marriage, two parties not naturally related were yoked. The relationship was initiated by the husband, Yahweh. In this relationship there could, by its very nature, be no divorce. At the same time there were contractual notes about it which gave the relationship a legal status and made it inviolate. A wide range of terms was employed to depict its deep intimacy and highly personalized nature.

Clearly, then, the message of this prophecy will underline Yahweh's unfailing constancy and adherence to the Sinai relationship in spite of constant provocations by the human partner. Israel will ever be in breach, but Yahweh will not give her up. He will give her over to temporary punishment through exile, a result reached by a great struggle within himself between his compassion and his sense of justice. But beyond that there will be a new creation. There will be the fulfilment of the commitment dating back, as Hosea understands it, to the patriarchal promise and the Sinai relationship in which Yahweh gave himself in free choice to Israel. A love that will not let Israel go finally brings us from covenant breach to a covenant renewal (Hos. 14) involving both Israel and her world.

Covenant Breach (Hos. 4–12)

Hosea 4 begins with the general indictment against Israel. Covenantal values, expressed in three important terms, are lacking (v. 1). The absence of "faithfulness," "kindness," and "knowledge of God" (this last term actually comprehends the whole relationship; cf. 2:20) has resulted in the sorry condition of the nation. In particular this absence threatens the gift of the covenant, life in the land. This is the note on which the indictment begins and ends (vv. 1–3). Yahweh's lawsuit against Israel rests on this statement of the disarray of the relationship. (The word *rîb*, "controversy" in v. 1, is frequently used by the prophets as a technical term for an arraignment of Israel on the grounds of covenant breach.)

The three terms in 4:1 have been carefully chosen and move progressively. "Faithfulness" is solidity and firmness, adherence to what has been established as normative. The covenant relationship is in view here, and faithfulness in this connection is virtually a synonym for righteousness—the maintenance of an accepted form of the relationship. Faithfulness therefore is not a propositional but a personal exercise, not an active searching for what is consistent, but a fidelity to norms which have been given.

Especially covenantal is the Hebrew word *ḥesed*. "Kindness" provides a good rendering. In a human context the word refers to a specific action taken by one party in behalf of another on the basis of a close personal relationship. Such action, motivated by *ḥesed* and designed to respond to a need, is undertaken in a spirit of faithfulness to a prior obligation. If performed, this act does not arise from a sense of mere obligation (i.e., from the legality of a commitment), but from a sense of personal loyalty which the relationship involves. *Ḥesed* does not apply to the establishment of a relationship, but reflects fidelity and loyalty to an existing relationship. Its aim is to preserve the tenor of a relationship which already exists. When used of Israel in the Old Testament, it means faithfulness to the spirit of the covenant, not merely to the letter. When used of Yahweh, it speaks of his willingness to go beyond the strict legalities of the relationship and to preserve it in spite of the fault of the erring partner (Sakenfeld 1975, 324).

Emphasis is placed on the final term, "knowledge of God." Again we have a deeply personal term. It points to the manner in which God reveals himself—in Israel's case, through covenant. (Usually in the context of covenant the wording "knowledge of Yahweh" appears.) "Knowledge of God" (*'ĕlōhîm* is a general word for Deity) will, in the context of Hosea's prophecy, mean trust in the general providential superintendence of Yahweh. That such trust does not exist in Israel means covenant breach in the specific terms of rejection of the covenant commandments, notably the Decalog of Exodus 20, which seems to be alluded to in the five Hebrew infinitives used in Hosea 4:2. In its turn this rejection means the withdrawal of the Abrahamic benefits (v. 3a), which inevitably affects the very structure of creation itself (v. 3b).

We cannot present the material of this prophecy in detail, but what follows are specific illustrations of the summary statement of 4:1–3. Verses 4–10 are an indictment of the priests who have exchanged Yahweh for Baal. The priests will suffer as do the people, since by verse 9 they are virtually deconsecrated. Their misuse of the sacrificial system will bring them no satisfaction. Verses 11–19 turn to the implications for Israel of this apostasy of their sacral leadership. Israel has given itself over to fertility practices which will be counterproductive. In Hosea 5:1–7 Israel's leadership—priests and kings—are summoned, arraigned with all Israel, and then condemned—a complete generation of non-Israelites has been born! What looks like a reference to the Syro-Ephraimite war of approximately 733 occurs in verses 8–15, where there are alternating references to Ephraim and Judah, both of whom appeal to Assyria. This reflects the historical position of the times, with disastrous results since Assyria is in fact Yahweh's lion!

Hosea 6:1–3, a famous passage, reflects a belief in the ability of Yahweh to resurrect the life of the nation. This passage, which is similar to and anticipatory of Ezekiel 37, may also reflect national repentance following the disaster previously reported (Hos. 5:12–15). More fanciful theories of contact with dying and rising cults are to be rejected, since the covenant nuances of the passage (6:2–3) are clear. Yahweh's reply (vv. 4–6), however, points out that the popular responses to the demand of the prophetic word have been cultic and not ethical. Hosea 6:7–7:2 details the crimes of Israel by reference to anticovenant activities (indulged in since the crossing of the Jordan and thus since the occupancy of the land—in v. 7 "Adam" appears to refer to the fording of the Jordan in Josh. 3:16) at Israel's principal sanctuaries, again prompted by the priests. Even when Yahweh seeks to restore his people, he is still faced with covenant infidelity (7:1–2).

At this point the prophecy becomes more decidedly political, with successive oracles being directed against Israel's kingship and the international politics in which Israel has been involved by its rulers. Kings rise and fall (Hos. 7:3–7), reflecting perhaps the instability of the northern kingship following the death of Jeroboam II in approximately 747 B.C., as the nation gives vent to its political passion. (The puzzling image of the baker's oven in vv. 6–7 may refer to the political passion which the successive regnal changes in the closing years of Israel's history engendered.) Although foreign alliances constitute the death knell of Israel (7:8–16), yet the people in their extremity fail to turn to Yahweh and continue to indulge in fertility practices (vv. 13–16). Reversal of the exodus will be the result (v. 16).

Thus the fall of Israel is traced to Israel's inability to understand her covenant mandate. Israel had been run merely as a political state, but this approach ignored the Sinai commitment by which Yahweh's kingship had been recognized. The role of prophecy in all this was to point Israel back to her covenant obligation as the sole source of her life. Like his successors, Hosea brings no new demands, simply a call to be faithful to the platform by which Israel's national life in the Promised Land could be secured.

This basic message is repeated on a different level in Hosea 8. Yahweh has now declared war because of covenant breach (vv. 1–3), evident at the political level (the people had set up their own form of kingship, v. 4a) as well as at the religious level (vv. 4b–6). Thus the agricultural success which the cults were to provide will fail to materialize (v. 7). International alliances (vv. 8–10) and the misuse of the sacrificial system (vv. 11–13) have resulted in the cardinal sin of which the Book of Deuteronomy had warned—Israel had forgotten her Maker (v. 14)! Hosea 9:1–7a seems to reflect upon the fall festival, the most important of the three annual Israelite festivals. It should have drawn Israel's attention to Yahweh as provider. This emphasis upon the land as Yahweh's is interspersed with references to Israel's inevitable exile. In verses 7b–9 the prophet reflects upon the ineffectiveness of his office. Set up as an offset to kingship, it had been locked in combat with kingship since the inception of that office ("days of Gibeah" in v. 9 is probably a reference to Saul's election; cf. 1 Sam. 11:4).

Hosea in turn reflects upon the fact that Israel had defected ever since the wilderness days (9:10–14); Baal-peor serves as the model of that defection (Num. 25). What then happened at Baal-peor is now happening at Gilgal, which will necessitate a return to the wilderness situation (Hos. 9:15–17). Every significant institution in the north (altars, high places, king, the bull image of Samaria, and the cult associated with it) will be dealt with as the land becomes desolated by Assyrian aggression (Hos.

10:1–8). Kingship wrongly used ("days of Gibeah" in vv. 9–10) has led Israel astray. At this point the agricultural imagery of which Hosea is so fond is brought into play to depict Israel's vocation (vv. 11–13). Trained to use the land while in the wilderness, she has misused it and will thus have to return to the wilderness. This punishment will be effected by Assyrian aggression, apparently by Shalman (v. 14), a reference to the campaign of Shalmaneser V against Samaria in 724–722 B.C.

In chapter 11 Hosea again recalls Israel to her past. Verses 1–4 proclaim God's care exercised through the exodus and Israel's subsequent and longstanding refractoriness. Disaster in the form of a reversal of the exodus is now about to break upon them (vv. 5–7). This is not a prospect, however, in which Yahweh takes delight; verses 8–9 indicate the inner disposition of Israel's God, who struggles with the necessity to punish the object of his love. Yet wrath will not be the last word. It cannot be, given Yahweh's nature. Reversing the lion image, Yahweh will roar for Israel (i.e., dramatically redeem Israel from exile), and there will be a new exodus (vv. 10–11). Like the exodus generation (Exod. 4:22), those who return will be "sons," having prefigured in exile a radical new movement, though no further details are advanced.

Hosea 11:12–12:1 takes up a new reproach against Israel and Judah as unrepentant of their policy of foreign alliances. The prophetic propensity for comparing present conditions with past history is brought into play again in 12:2–14, where the patriarchal conduct of Jacob is compared to the conduct of present Israel and Judah. Even the inveterate deceiver Jacob had turned at Bethel to Yahweh; would not they also (v. 6)? However, later in the passage, after a biting reproach has been delivered to the north for identifying with the inhabitants of the land (12:7–11), there is a derogative reference to Jacob, who left the land (v. 12) to serve for a wife, not to serve Yahweh. In spite of such behavior, Yahweh did not give up on Jacob's descendants; for by the prophetic ministry of Moses (v. 13) Israel came up out of Egypt, and by the ministry of a subsequent prophet (Elijah?) Israel was preserved. There are enough details in this narrative to indicate that Hosea was cognizant of the patriarchal traditions. If there has been a somewhat free use of them, it is not an inconsistent use, simply an insistence that Israel was always saved from herself by means beyond herself. Basically Ephraim has remained a facsimile of his ancestor, although his state of life ought to have been determined by the character of Yahweh's interventions.

Covenant Renewal (Hos. 13–14)

Finally, chapters 13 and 14 present negative and positive assessments of the future. Hosea 13 ranges over the past, present, and future of Israel.

Baal worship was characteristic of their early history (v. 1) and has continued (v. 2), but it will be removed (v. 3). In verses 4–8 Israel is again referred to her past (cf. Exod. 20:1). Shepherd Yahweh, who has led them through the wilderness, will now make Israel a prey. Israel is thus beyond rescue, a condition that her political institutions—especially kingship—have produced (13:9–11). Like an unborn child who refuses to break out of the womb and thus perishes, Ephraim refuses now the opportunity to repent (vv. 12–13). Hosea 13:14–16 is to be taken as the ultimate threat. Yahweh, who has power to protect from death and hell, will deliver Ephraim and Samaria over. Although Samaria may look prosperous, Yahweh's "east wind" (i.e., Assyria) will destroy it (v. 15).

The destruction of the state and the demolition of the political fabric of the north are necessary precursors to renewal. Israel, north and south, was a nonpolitical concept stemming from Yahweh's election. Her history is a record of the failures which come from relying on institutions and of the degeneration of religion into formality and syncretism. Since the major emphasis in Hosea is on the land and the means by which it is to be retained, it comes as no surprise to find that the prophecies of return in Hosea 14 are couched in terms of abundant fertility and fruitfulness. In verses 1–3 Hosea invites Israel to turn back to Yahweh ("return" is a familiar Old Testament idiom for covenant renewal). She is to take along words provided by Yahweh himself (v. 2)! Yahweh will respond and heal the relationship. The pronounced use of fertility images in this section (vv. 4–8) indicates the degree of congruity which will then exist between Israel and her land. Finally, in verse 9 an editorial note has been introduced summoning the reader to observe how Yahweh acts in regard to his gifts. Adherence to covenant—that is, acceptance of the right way—should be the result.

The first three chapters of Hosea pivot around chapter 2, an allegorical interpretation of Israel's whole history from the exodus to the coming exile and pending restoration. Hosea conceives of Israel as living between two eras. The first stretches from the exodus to the exile. The second, beginning with a new captivity, will climax with a second entry into the Promised Land by way of a new exodus. The restoration of the covenant relationship will make the land an Eden and will bring Israel into harmony not only with her land but with her world.

The problems which Hosea sees clearly as having put Israel into the disastrous position in which she now finds herself are cult and kingship, false worship and reliance upon political leadership which has invariably proved to be inept and faithless. Israel has mixed with her world, and she will be destroyed by her world, in particular, by the major power of the day, Assyria. Much of the book, as we have seen, is given over, somewhat repetitively, to an examination of Israel's malaise. The cult has become Baal-infected. Yahweh has been separated from nature and has become the God of convenience, to be called upon only when difficulties become unmanageable. Much of the blame for these conditions must be laid at the feet of the priests (4:4–10; 5:1–7). In the new era Hosea looks for a complete transformation of the cult. Thus the offerings of the new community will not be the material gifts and sacrifices by which Yahweh has previously been placated (14:1–3). New words are needed, confessional words, words of love and of gratitude acknowledging Yahweh's sovereignty over Israel and all creation.

The moral problems of the community do not engage Hosea in the way in which other preexilic prophets take up the questions of social reform. Hosea sees clearly that it is Israel's spiritual adultery, her harlotry, which has undermined and drained the nation's moral fiber. Israel is self-judged, and exile will be the occasion for purging and reflection and the basis on which Yahweh can begin again with her.

The dominant motifs in Hosea are bound up with the land, its gifts, its productivity, and yet its misuse. What ought to have been the good life in the land is the essential theme of the book. This good life is clearly the great covenantal blessing to which the Book of Deuteronomy points, a book bearing a marked relationship to Hosea. By Hosea's time the land by which Israel was virtually identified was about to become desolate. How could it be recovered? Hosea's answer is that it will be recovered only by a fresh initiative from Yahweh, who made it available in the first place. Yahweh will not desert his people. With that hope the faithful in Israel must be satisfied. Hope for the future can be built upon the unchanging faithfulness of Israel's Redeemer. In the tenderest of terms employing the richest imagery, Hosea has stated the intentions of the covenant, the manner in which they ought to have been implemented, and the punishment which must result from failure in this area. But the marriage which began at Sinai will continue, for in the ideal depiction of this relationship Yahweh permits no divorce.

14

Joel

Joel is not a difficult book to analyze. Its overriding theme of the day of the Lord and what that day will mean for Israel and Israel's enemies structures the book into its two halves (1:2–2:27 and 2:28–3:21). The outline of the book may be presented as follows:

1:1	Superscription
1:2–14	The locust plague
1:15–20	Foreshadowing of the day of the Lord
2:1–11	The day of the Lord
2:12–27	The call to repentance
2:28–32	The gift of the Spirit
3	The last judgment

The Plague of Locusts and the Day of the Lord (Joel 1:1–2:27)

The first half of the Book of Joel deals with what is best understood as an actual plague of locusts pictured in the form of an approaching army.

151

Presented as a literal plague in Joel 1:2–14, it is then seen in 1:15–20 and 2:1–11 as indicative of a much deeper reality than the opening description seems to suggest. In short, we are faced with a natural evil in chapter 1 which is then theologized in 2:1–11 in terms of "the day of the Lord."

In Joel 1 the approach and significance of the plague are described in verses 2–12, and its effect upon various groups of the community is gauged: on the unresponsive, the "drunkards" (vv. 5–7); on Zion (vv. 8–10), who is called upon to lament for the cultic dislocation and the deprivation of offerings which the plague will cause; and on the farming community, whose holdings and livelihoods will be threatened (vv. 11–12). The priests (vv. 15–20), being responsible for the spiritual welfare of the nation, are then to proclaim a public lament for the coming day. (Priests are addressed directly in vv. 13–14, while vv. 15–18 may be their response as in a communal lament they recognize that the locust plague indicates "the day" of a divine visitation.) A brief prayer from the prophet sums up the magnitude of the disaster (vv. 19–20). Human being and beast, fields and brooks, animate and inanimate have been exposed to the devastating effects of the locust onset. It is clearly a major disaster which then causes the prophet to look further at the underlying reality of what has been involved in this attack upon the land.

Joel makes his examination in 2:1–11, a unit which is encased by the ancient and theologically pervasive notion of the day of the Lord, which is reflected in the natural disaster experienced. This is not an independent description of a disassociated event, for Joel senses that the plague contains features of, and is a precursor to, Yahweh's final, decisive visitation upon Judah. Traditional "day of the Lord" language is used here (e.g., the day is a day of darkness [v. 2]; cf. Amos 5:20; Zeph. 1:15). The approaching day is to be signaled by the sound of the trumpet, indicating that it is a type of countertheophany, since its chief features (gloom and darkness, mountains, fire, terror-struck populace) are typical of the Old Testament theophanic presentation from Exodus 19 onward. This fearsome army marches on Jerusalem, reducing the land to a wilderness in its wake (vv. 3–9). The sobering reality underlying all this destruction is that Yahweh's hand is turned against Judah. This visitation is his coming in judgment (vv. 10–11); the reason for this divine action against Jerusalem, which figures prominently in Joel 1 and 2, seems to be the cultic degeneracy of the community. We gain no more than hints in this regard—certainly social and ethical issues are not detailed by Joel—but we are told that previous cultic repentance (see 2:13) may have been superficial (cf. the demand in 1:13–14 to repent thoroughly).

The phrase "day of the Lord" is found about twenty times in the Old

Testament prophets. In evaluating its significance in Joel, much depends upon the date we assign to the book. (The older expositors suggested a ninth-century date, early in the reign of the boy-king Joash, ca. 835–796 B.C. The book seems to fit most naturally, however, into the period covered by the ministry of Jeremiah, 626–582 B.C.) The first usage of the term is found in Amos 5:18, where it is clearly a well-known popular concept, a day which is to be desired. It thus seems to be in harmony with Amos's concern to clarify the covenant expectations which the northern community of Israel cherished. Earlier opinion traced the term to a prebiblical mythological concept that divided the world into fixed ages. To this concept was attached the notion of a day on which the older order passed away, the new age was ushered in, and the cyclic process continued, eon giving way to eon. Were this theory of its origin true, the Old Testament use of the term would be directly eschatological, yet not all of the Old Testament references bear this thrust. Concentrating upon Isaiah 13, Ezekiel 7, and Joel 2, some commentators have emphasized a holy-war component as providing the background for the term, but again not all of the Old Testament references fit. In particular, Amos 5:18, which is usually taken as the starting point for discussion, seems not to refer to holy war. Still others have linked the term to a divine intervention to exact covenant curses upon Israel for breach of treaty. But this interpretation likewise suits some references but not all. The common factor in all is Yahweh's presence, but the manner of that presence is ambivalent. In Joel 2 and 3 it is certainly a day on which Yahweh will do battle with his enemies, as it is in Zephaniah 1:1–2:3. Amos 5:18 appears to indicate, however, that in the popular conception the day was a manifestation of Yahweh in some theophanic way for Israel's benefit, while the context of Amos generally suggests that there is some connection between this day and the cult. Perhaps we may postulate that while the term initially denoted the presentation of Yahweh's kingship through some cultic association, with Amos it assumed a connotation of God's decisive visitation in judgment either against Israel or, as it is later developed, against Israel's foes.

Following Joel 2:1–11 and perhaps arising out of it (Prinsloo 1985, 49–61), verses 12–17 issue a clear call from Yahweh to repent on the basis of his long-suffering character; the priests are then urged to translate this call into national action. It seems to have had its effect, for Yahweh responds by driving back the fearful northern army (vv. 18–20). Blessings from the land ensue (vv. 21–23), betokening harmony once again between Israel and her world, and thus covenant restoration. Barns are now full and vats overflow as the land responds in superabundant productivity which reverses the ravages of the locust-ridden years (vv. 24–27) and thus the disaster of 1:2–14. Israel views all this as a manifestation of covenant fidelity (see v. 27, where the note of "your God" and "my people" dominates).

The Outpouring of the Spirit (Joel 2:28–32)

The famous passage on the outpouring of the Spirit, taken up by Peter in Acts 2, forms the centerpiece of the prophecy. It draws to a conclusion the theme of covenant renewal, effected after judgment, which 2:1–11 and 12–27 have taken up. Its eschatological tenor, however, indicates that it too has moved beyond a position of particular judgment to one of final judgment upon the people of God. As the centerpiece of the prophecy, Joel 2:28–32 operates as a fulcrum connecting both halves. It takes its rise from reflection upon the act of particular judgment effected through the locust plague, yet it has in view the final judgment upon the people of God, which is effected by the last great assault (this will be the subject of Joel 3).

The outpouring of the Spirit upon all flesh (Joel 2:28) clearly has immediate reference to the fortunes of Judah, but equally clearly, Peter's use of Joel in Acts 2 gives the passage a much wider dimension. Spirit and flesh (divine nature and potential; human limitation) bring opposites together in a great anticipation of the new creation. Like the last Adam (1 Cor. 15:45), all flesh become partakers of the life-giving Spirit. What is natural gives way to what is thereafter spiritual. As an immediate consequence of this transformation, and with all social divisions and social barriers removed, all become recipients of the divine mind through the Spirit, all will be in immediate communication with Yahweh, and all will directly reflect the Word (i.e., will prophesy). This complete renewal, this regeneration of the people of God, brings into force Moses' wish for Israel (Num. 11:29) and fits her vocationally to become the community she has been marked out to be (Exod. 19:3–6). The description of the intervention to occur on the day of the Lord—"portents . . . blood and fire and columns of smoke" (Joel 2:30–31)—has undeniable exodus connotations. The transformation of the heavens (sun and moon in eclipse) points to the cosmic upheaval by which the final "day" will be preceded. The community of salvation to emerge is identified with the remnant (v. 32).

Judgment and Blessing (Joel 3)

After the preliminary announcement of final salvation for Judah and Jerusalem (Joel 3:1), the unit which follows is encased by judgment features, with a satirical invitation offered to the nations to prepare for holy war, using whatever implements may be pressed into service

(vv. 2–12). Judgment, which began earlier in the book with the household of God, now extends to the whole world. With the oscillation between eschatology and particular application which we have noted so far, Joel switches in verses 3–8 to offer paradigmatic examples (Tyre, Sidon, and Philistia) of tyrannical oppression inflicted on the people of God in his own time, an oppression which will be requited. In harvest terminology, verses 13–21 describe the fate of the Gentiles, thus returning to the locust-plague language of 1:13–20. Joel 3:15 repeats 2:10, confirming that the locust plague is an anticipation of the final "day." God the Warrior (note the image of divine involvement in holy war—v. 16) intervenes in judgment in both episodes.

After considering the nature of the divine intervention by which the Gentile world will be judged (3:15–17), the prophecy concludes with the promise of a restored paradise for God's people. Jerusalem, as the world center and font of blessing, dispenses fertility (v. 18). Nothing is said about world pilgrimage and thus about world submission in all this. The message concerns only world judgment (vv. 19–21) and thus divine vindication of Judah's (and Israel's) election.

Cleansing and restoration, comfort for God's people, is the theme of the last passage in Joel. If the prophecy was written in or around the exilic period, the theme binding the book together—the desolation of Judah followed by restoration and covenant blessing—echoes the new-covenant theology of the exilic period. Joel is more particularistic than Isaiah 40–66, but this is simply to say that the centrality of Jerusalem in Joel echoes the typical emphasis of southern prophecy, which Isaiah 40–66 transcends. Yet with his note of God's redemptive act for the people of God, followed by a world judgment which ushers in paradise regained, Joel is at one with typical prophetic eschatology.

15

Amos

Amos seems to have been written about 750 B.C., since
(1) Jeroboam II of Israel is still reigning, (2) there is no hint of the disruption which characterized the end of his reign, and (3) only general prophecies concerning the exile of the north are advanced. The prophet's introduction to his mission occurs in 1:1–2. Oracles against the foreign nations are found in 1:3–2:3, against Judah in 2:4–5, and against Israel in verses 6–16. Conclusions are then drawn in Amos 3 for the current history of Israel. Chapters 4–6 compose the central section of the book, especially chapter 5, where it is noted that the lack of true worship in the north is the problem to which the Book of Amos is directed. Amos 7:1–9:6 is a cycle of five visions in which Amos's theology is progressively unfolded and a narrative concerning his call is embedded. Amos 9:7–10 returns to 3:1–2, namely, to the election of Israel and its consequences, while 9:11–15 takes up the themes of chapters 1–2, namely, the relationship of Israel and Judah to the nations and to Yahweh's eschatological purposes. We have, therefore, in the book as a whole the following:

Introduction to Amos's Mission (Amos 1:1–2)

Amos describes himself as a shepherd (1:1). This term may designate a status higher than an ordinary shepherd, perhaps an estate manager. Perhaps he engaged in mixed farming, since in 7:14 he describes himself as a dresser of sycamore (fig) trees. The important feature of these initial verses is their Zion orientation, which stamps Amos's prophecy. The roaring of Yahweh from Zion indicates that some problem relating to the northern kingdom's stance toward Jerusalem requires attention (cf. the roaring lion on the move in 3:4). Since Zion and the Jerusalem temple are the prophetic symbols of divine government, Israel's failure to acknowledge Zion's position constitutes a basic flaw in their doctrine of God, in effect, a denial of Yahweh's sovereignty. It is suggestive that a reference to Carmel is associated with the introduction, for that name is evocative of the contest over the question of divine sovereignty which had been fought by Elijah in 1 Kings 18. This reference raises suspicion that the north may have reverted to a position of syncretism somewhat similar to that which Elijah had challenged. Zion and Carmel represent cultic confrontation, and indeed the contents of Amos depict him as declaring war upon the northern sanctuaries and proclaiming implicitly the sacrosanct character of Jerusalem. Moreover, the fact that the book ends on the note of a restoration which is Zion-oriented, presenting Jerusalem as the divine mountain with implications for the wider world, causes us to conclude that by Amos's time the contours of Zion theology had been fully developed, even if the expanded expression of them occurs in the south slightly later (in Isaiah). We may surmise from the Jerusalem concentration of Amos 1:2 and 9:11–15 that Yahweh is moving from Zion in judgment against the north on the probable grounds of false cultic stances, postures that, because of their assertions of sovereignty, are a denial of his rule.

Oracles Against the Foreign Nations (Amos 1:3–2:3)

The oracles against the foreign nations can be placed in no one historical context, but may be a review of relationships between Israel,

Judah, and their neighbors extending over some hundreds of years. Not all of the oracles have reference to Israel (or Judah), since the crime of Moab does not concern Israel and that of the Philistines may not. This fact lessens the possibility often raised that the nations are censured in these oracles as members of the former Davidic empire for crimes committed against that kingdom.

The order of the oracles is not merely geographical. Some scholars have suggested connections with an order in the earlier (nineteenth and eighteenth centuries B.C.) Egyptian execration texts—south, north, west, and then Egypt itself, reflecting Egypt's Nile orientation—but the correspondences are not exact. Moreover, the curses from the execration texts were designed to have a magical effect, while Amos's strictures stem from ethical and theological considerations. It has been proposed that in Amos's oracles we have an alternative listing of the enemies of Israel and Judah. But it is doubtful whether the interest Amos displays in them is purely national. More to the point in terms of the interrelationship of the oracles is the suggestion that the link between the oracles is literary (Paul 1971, 399). Commencing with Aram, Israel's principal enemy, there is a link with the oracles against Philistia in terms of the punishment envisaged (1:4, 7), while Aram and Philistia are also linked in Amos 9:7. Philistia and Tyre are linked at Joel 3:4–8, Jeremiah 47:4, Ezekiel 25:16–17, and here in Amos 1 by a leveling of the identical accusation (vv. 6, 9). Edom, Ammon, and Moab are frequently linked (e.g., Deut. 23:3–8; Isa. 11:14; Jer. 48–49). In Amos 1 the notion of brotherly attitudes connects Tyre and Edom (vv. 9, 11), while the three southern states complete the list with appropriate linkages. Edom and Ammon are linked by the nature of the offense (both presumably wrought with the sword; see vv. 11, 13), and then Ammon and Moab by the nature of the punishment (by fire; see 1:14; 2:2).

Oracles Against Judah and Israel (Amos 2:4–16)

Judah and Israel are then surveyed. These two oracles break with the literary pattern which controls the previous six. Judah is reproached for a general covenant breach (2:4–5), but Israel is treated at length, and clearly this oracle forms the climax to the sequence. Amos's audience may have listened approvingly to this point, even to the oracle directed against Judah, but punishment for themselves would have come as a surprise. The logic of the climactic denunciation presumes that Israel would have conceded the connection between sin and punishment— even upon Judah for a covenant breach in which Israel did not feel involved! However, a particular *covenantal* basis for the denunciation against Israel could stand only if Israel saw the foreign nations as involved or included in Yahweh's Sinai covenant with her—but clearly they were not! Since Judah is denounced for covenant breach, it may well have been Amos's assumption that Israel and the nations *were* included in a wider concept of a universal covenant. The application of covenant promises to Israel (and Judah) in any case exacted more in responsibility from her.

The final oracle against Israel (2:6–16) is the longest of the series. It shares many features with the others. Thus Israel is placed on the same level as the surrounding nations, but for different reasons. It is noteworthy that there is no mention of a national covenant. (The word *covenant* occurs in Amos only in 1:9, where it is used in another connection.) Perhaps the concept of covenant had become so distorted that the word was best avoided. But Amos sees the north as having rejected the covenant, which he indicates by using the more formal language of justice and righteousness. Covenant in Amos is everywhere presupposed as the relationship binding Yahweh and Israel, for the mere fact that a prophet raised the issues of social abuses, class distinctions, judicial partiality, and oppression of the poor meant that he acknowledged a covenant ethic which did not permit such offenses. The new focus of the prophets was the judgment message directed against Israel (e.g., about a holy war organized against the nation), but they were not theological innovators. Prophetic theology came from the history of Yahweh's dealings with Israel, and on that basis the prophets called Israel to account.

In claiming that the personal will of Israel's God is binding upon Israel and should govern her moral response in just the same way that the nations should recognize a principle of universal morality operating in Yahweh's world, Amos is, however, advancing to new ground (Barton 1980, 49). He expands the covenant concept to indicate that the special privilege accorded to Israel under covenant is a particularization of a more general posture of response which should control the created order. This accounts for the novel twist that Amos gives to the doctrine of election. Israel is not indemnified by it but is made all the more culpable. How much worse, then, is the sin of Israel as elect! How logical is the "therefore" in Amos 3:2!

In the climactic oracle against Israel, it is noteworthy that the expulsion of the Amorites comes first in the review of Israel's history (v. 9, after her pressing social sins have been exposed [vv. 6–8]). Only then does mention of the exodus follow (v. 10), while the third item in the review is the prophetic ministry by means of which the Sinai covenant was to have been preserved (vv. 11–12). Amos's thrust is thus directed against Israel's possession of the land, with the implication that exile (vv. 13–16) must result.

Witnesses Summoned Against Israel (Amos 3)

After presenting the responsibilities of election (3:1–2), Amos by deft use of rhetorical questions (vv. 3–6) compels his listeners to pay attention and to frame a reply. The sequence of thought seems broken by the prose verse 7 (as opposed to the poetry of vv. 3–6), but this simply serves to throw verse 7 into clear relief as the dominant verse of the chapter, revealing to the audience that Amos's ministry is one of compulsion. The language of Amos 3:7 also points to Amos's prophetic authority as an auditor of proceedings whereby the history of Israel has been determined and thus lays the basis for his claim to prophetic integrity. (In v. 7 note the use of *sôd*, "secret," which by extension points to the prophetic membership of the heavenly council, the royal body with which Yahweh surrounds himself; cf. Jer. 23:18; Isa. 6.) The roar of the lion (Amos 3:8) points to the inevitability of punishment (cf. 1:2), though the tenor of 3:8 indicates that Amos did not approach his task with particular relish. In a somewhat mocking reversal of the holy-war motif, the two great powers of the day, Egypt and Assyria, are then called upon to witness the inner corruption of Israel (vv. 9–10). They are to assent to her punishment, vindicating its fairness, even when viewed from the basis of their lesser ethical connection to Yahweh. Exile will result and great devastation (vv. 11–12). Verses 13–15 provide an epilog ("punish" in v. 14 returns us to 3:2) reinforcing the message of the chapter (Gitay 1980, 295). Election must, if disregarded, lead to exile (v. 15), and all asylum will be denied to Israel (v. 14). Amos 3 thus provides the basic message of the prophecy, building upon the careful argumentation of chapters 1–2 and directing us to the inevitable consequences in store for the north.

Israel's Impending Judgment (Amos 4–6)

Amos 4 begins somewhat strangely as exposition of the outline of Amos 3, with an attack upon the indulgent behavior of the noble women of Samaria (vv. 1–3), who will be prominent in the march into exile. In commencing with them, Amos is referring to the reversal of relationships in public order which their lead in sinfulness has helped to bring about (cf. Isa. 3:18–26). In Amos 4:4–5 the inner reason for this public collapse is given, namely, the mechanical approach by Israel to the cult, the heart of the nation. Notably, in Amos the cult is referred to disparagingly as "your cult" ("your sacrifices," "your tithes," etc.). Amos 4:6–11 then deals with the covenant curses which have been operating and have as yet been unperceived (hunger, drought, crop failure, etc.). The blessings of Leviticus 26:3–13 (the chapter to which Amos seems to be referring in this material, though undertones of Deut. 28 are also present) have been reversed. The key verse Amos 4:12 is therefore most likely a warning and not an invitation. A fragment of a hymn brings the chapter to a close, emphasizing by its content Yahweh as Creator and then Judge. (Amos 4:13; 5:8–9; and 9:5–6 all seem related hymnic fragments used by Amos to sum up or to focus his argument.)

Amos 5 has a clearly perceptible structure (de Waard 1977, 176). The two sections—verses 1–17 and 18–27—are connected by the thought patterning of the chapter. The theme of verses 18–27 is that ritual substituted for right worship will lead to ruin, a subject that builds upon verses 1–17, where correct worship is defined. The dirge of verses 1–2 has the prophet looking into the coffin of virgin Israel, her promising life cut short, fallen on the Promised Land! The measure of destruction foreshadowed in verse 3 grounds the lament of verses 1–2. The reason for all of this disaster seems provided in verses 4–6, in which Israel is urged to seek Yahweh and not the northern sanctuaries. (The message "seek the LORD and live" seems ironic, since the sanctuaries are condemned in v. 5; see Hunter 1980, 70–71). Verse 7 turns the argument to social injustice, the outward demonstration of the inward malaise, while verses 8–9 (the hymnic fragment) form the midpoint of the chapter. Verses 10–13 return to the theme of verse 7, while verses 14–15 echo the thought of verses 4–6. Finally, verses 16–17 take up the lament of verses 1–2.

The midpoint of verses 8–9, and perhaps the key phrase of the prophecy, is the note on which verse 8 concludes: "Yahweh is his name." In the context this statement is not an assertion about Yahweh's person or nature, but a reminder that this name had been given to enable Israel to call upon God (Exod. 3:13–15). By rejecting this name in worship, Israel has invited Yahweh's judgment! Yahweh as Creator and Judge threatens (vv. 8–9, perhaps with a reference to the flood in v. 9)! In short, the central demand that the Book of Amos makes is that the Israelites in the north put the character of Yahweh and their response to him in worship at the very center of their national life.

Given this background, it is difficult not to imagine that the reference to the day of the Lord in 5:18–20 has cultic connections. Perhaps, as some have suggested, it is a reply by Amos to a popular expectation of Yahweh's manifestation (theophany) cherished by the north and bound up with some northern cultic celebration, perhaps some New Year festival. While the connection between the "day" and Yahweh's intervention in holy war is often made in the Old Testament, this is not a necessary or universal connection. The common element in all the references to this day is the dramatic appearance of Yahweh to bless or to judge. If the reference in 5:18–20 has cultic connections and responds to popular expectation, then the material of verses 21–27 follows quite naturally. It is hardly likely that these verses operate as a complete rejection of sacrifice, but this section makes it clear that Israel's idolatrous worship will lead her into exile (v. 27).

In Amos 6 the prosperity of Israel as a whole is reviewed. In verses 1–2 complacent people are invited to draw an object lesson from the Assyrian treatment of Israel's neighbors; the moral and religious reasons for this warning are given in verses 3–6. Verses 7–11 foreshadow exile as a judgment, just as 4:1–3 did when the same question was discussed. Amos 6:12–13 points to the lack of reality which characterizes Israel's political life. They have had minor political successes, but an Assyrian exile is pending (vv. 13–14).

Amos's Five Visions (Amos 7:1–9:6)

The last major section of Amos runs from 7:1 to 9:6. The five visions perhaps review Amos's ministry. They are interrupted by the clash between Amaziah, priest of Bethel, and Amos (7:10–17). All of the five visions have a somewhat similar form; they consist of two pairs (7:1–3 and 7:4–6; 7:7–8 and 8:1–2) and a fifth vision (9:1–4) to complete the sequence. The first two visions emphasize the effectiveness of Amos as a mediator, while the following pair speak of God's decision to judge. The final vision exhibits the nature of that judgment. The first three visions also form an introduction to the confrontation between Amos and Amaziah, which leads to Amos's expulsion from Bethel. The fourth adds nothing new but reinforces the third. The juxtaposition of visions and the biographical note of 7:10–17 seem to indicate that Amos's preaching caused his expulsion.

The first two visions portray a dramatic action. In each case the prophetic response to the divine threat is to plead the smallness of Jacob. As Walter Brueggemann (1969, 386–89) has noted, the word *small* is used in the Jacob traditions (particularly in Genesis—see, e.g., 32:10–12) and in covenant traditions in the Old Testament to underscore Israel's election—she has no rights or credentials when called and thus is unable to help herself. In the appeal to Jacob as small, then, there is contained a covenant plea to restore helpless Israel.

The movement to the third vision brings us into difficulty, for the word usually translated "plumb line" (v. 7) seems not to fit. The Hebrew phrase is, literally, "wall of tin, with tin in his hand"—plumb lines in antiquity were made of lead! The fourth vision, which is directly related in type to the third, is based on a wordplay. One might thus expect wordplay in the third vision as well. With a slight rearrangement of the Hebrew consonants we may read verse 8 as "I am setting you in the midst of my people Israel" (instead of "I am setting a plumb line in the midst of my people Israel"). That is, the prophet himself is the "wall of tin," the impenetrable wall, of verse 7 (see Peterson 1977, 77–78).

Verse 9 is a transition linking the third vision to the dialog of 7:10–17. The point at issue in this section is Amos's authority to operate in the north. The content of his message (v. 11) is improperly labeled by Amaziah as conspiracy. (The Hebrew term Amaziah uses normally refers to sedition by a person legally subordinate to the country and its ruler—as Amos was not.) After Amaziah's report to Jeroboam, there is the exchange between Amaziah and Amos. (Note the interconnections between vv. 9, 11, and 17, which seam the passage together.)

Perhaps in the use of the word *seer* (7:12) Amaziah is raising the question of the legitimacy of Amos's ministry as a Judean in the north, since it is claimed that "seer" is a term normally associated with prophetic connections at the royal court (Paul 1972, 1155). Amaziah's demand that Amos "eat bread" in the south would therefore seem to be a call to exercise his ministry gainfully in his own recognized domain. The hypothetical character of these two suggestions, however, must be recognized, for "eat bread" occurs nowhere else in the Old Testament in the sense of "earn a living," and the terms *seer* and *prophet* are broadly interchangeable. In Amos 7:14 it is uncertain whether the verb to be supplied should be present or past. If a present tense is supplied ("I am no prophet"), then a denial of official connection with the professional guilds may be here advanced by Amos. Yet such a general denial seems to contradict the connections with the prophetic movement which Amos implicitly claims in 2:11. In view of the clear commission appealed to in 7:15, it seems better to supply a verb in the past tense in verse 14: "I was neither a prophet, nor a prophet's son."

In any case Amos supports his right to minister (as Old Testament prophecy always supports its rights) by an appeal to Yahweh's direct intervention in his life (7:15). His ministry is a clear threat to the establishment in the north, as Amaziah recognizes. Amos not only defends his ministry, but pronounces the same judgment upon Amaziah (v. 17) as he has pronounced upon Israel and the house of Jeroboam.

The fourth vision (Amos 8:1–2) offers a clear message. Israel looks secure and in full bloom, but is really ready for dissolution; she is ripe and about to decay. Amos 8:4–6 returns to the question of social justice to draw a direct connection between the way of life of the exploiters and their judgment (vv. 7–8). Some commentators have referred verses 9–10 to a theophany presented through a New Year's festival conducted in the north, but such a view is difficult in view of the same material in the judgment context of 9:5–6. The verses seem best taken as a mourning ritual for some natural disturbance. Verses 11–14 foreshadow a peril to come upon the north which even the more virile will not be able to endure.

The vision of Amos 9:1–4 differs from the previous four in that Yahweh himself reports it. By its size and position this vision seems the climax of the five. The fourth vision (8:1–2) announced the end; the fifth tells us how it will come. Cosmic upheaval (perhaps figurative language) directed at the (Bethel?) sanctuary will attend the end (9:1). Verses 2–4a consist of a series of five conditional sentences growing in the intensity of the divine resolve to judge. The announcement of the fixed divine intent occurs at verse 4b ("I will set my eyes upon them for evil and not for good"), while in the hymnic conclusion of verses 5–6 the order of Yahweh as Judge and then Creator lays greater emphasis upon the fact of pending judgment.

The Future Hope (Amos 9:7–15)

Amos 9:7–8 deals with Israel's election and the responsibilities which stem from it. Other peoples such as the Philistines and the Syrians have had their own exodus, for God has dealt with them historically in a way appropriate to each. This fact does not in itself imply that Israel is reduced to their level, but simply that God acts sovereignly in the history of nations. But Israel is now a "sinful kingdom" and thus has negated the concept of a kingdom of priests, the vocation to which God had called her (Exod. 19:6). Judgment must therefore come (Amos 9:9–10).

Finally, Amos 9:11–15 deals with restoration after judgment. These verses do not come as an afterthought but complete the Zion eschatology implicit at Amos 1:2. The "booth of David" to be repaired is best taken as Jerusalem (cf. Isa. 1:8). The genders of the Hebrew suffixes in verse 11 must be closely noted; perhaps all the eschatological components—Jerusalem, temple, and Davidic dynasty—are being alluded to. ("Its breaches" is feminine plural, and "it" in "rebuild it" is feminine singular; these could be references to Jerusalem and the temple respectively. "Its ruins" is masculine plural and thus seems to refer to the Davidic dynasty.) Edom (v. 12) seems to be a paradigm for the repentant Gentiles, who will finally share in the covenant promises. To complete the book, verses 13–15 display the themes of a second exodus and Eden recaptured.

The Book of Amos moves from the Lord "roaring" from Zion to the restoration of Zion. It is thoroughly Jerusalem- and temple-oriented. Its major plea is for right worship which reflects a right doctrine of God.

The north had developed a syncretistic Yahwism which was reflected at its shrines and in its feasts. The cult of the people thus had become theirs and theirs alone, since it failed to put Yahweh at the center. Amos calls on them to remember Yahweh, to hallow his name (see 5:8), to offer right worship, and thus to reject the mechanistic approach to the cult which has sapped the strength of the north. To heed that call would rebuild the kingdom of God (9:11–15). But we know that, received without honor, the somber predictions of Amos were fulfilled within thirty years in the final destruction of the north.

16

Obadiah

The dating of this small book is uncertain. Historical references to a disaster confronting Jerusalem occur in verses 11–14. Some connect this passage with 2 Kings 8:20–22 and 2 Chronicles 21:8–10, and thus with the ninth century B.C. But Edom remained a problem for Judah throughout the biblical period (cf. Mal. 1:3). Most would agree that to date the book shortly after the fall of Jerusalem in 587/586 B.C. is more natural. It is clear from the eschatological stance of the conclusion of the prophecy—Edom will be judged in a process which emanates from Zion—that Edom has assumed the features of the exilic paradigm of the enemies of the people of God. In typical Old Testament presentation, a historical incident is seen in terms of wider eschatological dimensions.

Verse 1a forms an introduction to the book, which begins, as it concludes, with a threat directed toward Edom. Obadiah 1b–4, in which the pride of Edom and her confidence in her remoteness are repudiated, is very similar to Jeremiah 49:14–16 and thus indicates the use of traditional material. The message is clear: seemingly impregnable arrogance will be brought down! The thoroughness of this judgment is then illus-

166

trated by the analogy of the pillagers offered in Obadiah 5–6. Edom in the day of her distress may expect no help from outside friends, and even her famed wisdom will not avail her (vv. 7–9). In verse 8 the hint of divine intervention serves to heighten the mounting tension of the passage. Edom will receive what she has meted out to Jerusalem (vv. 10–14).

But Edom's punishment will merely be an example of Yahweh's typical holy-war intervention, of his "day" (vv. 15–16). The movement toward eschatology grows more direct with the mention of the day of the Lord, and the prophecy now turns from history to final prospect for the people of God. When that day comes, the remnant of the people of God will be gathered on Mount Zion (vv. 17–21), acting as an arm of God's judgment on Edom, Israel's initial (and typical) enemy. The return of the Promised Land, particularly that portion affected by Edomite predations, and the gathering of the scattered people of God are the themes of verses 19–20. Verse 21 by its terminology harks back to the premonarchical period ("saviours" who will "judge," KJV), underscoring the final theocratic rule of the kingdom of God to which the conclusion of the verse points. Thus the program of the restoration of Israel, the judgment upon the Gentiles, the return to the Promised Land, and the endtime divine rule demonstrate Obadiah to be a carrier of mainstream prophetic eschatology.

Despite the destruction of Jerusalem and the exile, the future for the people of God is secure. Edom is to know this truth. This is the burden of Obadiah, who, in addressing historical reality, typically sees in the events of his time the foreshadowing of the inbreaking of the kingdom.

17

Jonah

Perhaps no other book in the Old Testament has proved so difficult to classify as has the Book of Jonah—and doubtless the argument will continue. The forms of prophetic narrative appear at the beginning of the book and then again at the beginning of the second half of the book (3:1–3). The prophetic tone continues with an allusion to Elijah in 4:3, 8, and to the nature of his ministry, with which Jonah's can be compared. (Note the clear parallelisms between Jonah and Elijah: both flee, both are faced with death, both fall into a deep sleep, both sit under a tree and ask to die, and both are associated with a forty-day activity.) If the book is a parable, its point is not clear. It seems not to be an allegory, since none of the available details which might have been exploited is pressed. There seems no reason to deny its prophetic status, though consideration of its purpose must be deferred until the details have been considered. On the whole, however, its message is clear. The word of God, once announced to a prophet of God, will not return void. It will move from Israel to Nineveh despite the reluctance of the messenger, and it will break him if he opposes it. Finally, the identification of the hero with the court prophet of 2 Kings 14:25 seems secure. We do not enter into the difficult question of the dating of the book. The matter must be left open. The content of the Book of Jonah is arranged as follows:

1 The flight
2 The psalm
3 The mission
4 The angry prophet

Jonah's Flight (Jonah 1)

The Book of Jonah is characterized by the frequent repetition of key words and phrases as well as by its wealth of allusions to Old Testament contexts. The book is divisible into two clear halves, chapters 1–2 and 3–4, with fine parallelism obtaining between (and within) the two sections. Jonah 1 focuses on Jonah's flight from the presence of the divine word (cf. Gen. 4:16), not simply a desire to quit Palestine. His flight is a wish to sever any connection with his prophetic office and to move to an area beyond the present reach of God's word, Tarshish. (Isa. 66:19 lists Tarshish as a point to which, as one of the ends of the earth, Yahweh's fame must be made known.) Jonah 1:4–16 has been shown to be a chiastic presentation (see fig. 2) centering around Jonah's statement on fearing in verses 9–10a and concluding with verse 16b as the resolution of the difficulty (Cohn 1969, 51).

Figure 2 **Chiastic Structure of Jonah 1:4–16a**

A (4–5a) Narrative, and sailors' response of fear
  B (5b) The sailors' prayer
    C (5c–6a) Narrative, with sailors at center
      D (6b) Captain's speech
        E (7a) Sailors' speech
          F (7b) Narrative displaying sailors' mood
            G (8) Sailors' question
              H (9–10a) Narrative on "fearing"
            G' (10b) Sailors' question
          F' (10c) Narrative displaying sailors' mood
        E' (11) Sailors' speech
      D' (12) Jonah's speech
    C' (13) Narrative, with sailors at center
  B' (14) The sailors' prayer
A' (15–16a) Narrative, and sailors' response of fear

We may note that as Jonah moves away from the divine presence—into the boat (1:3), down to the hold of the boat and into sleep (v. 5), and presumably into death (v. 12)—the mariners, who are first simply depersonalized sailors (v. 5), move closer to Jonah's God. In 1:5 the vague term *'ĕlōhîm*, "deity," is used; in verse 6 the captain calls to the universal deity, *the* God *(hā 'ĕlōhîm)*; verse 10 reports the sailors' recognition that Jonah was fleeing from Yahweh; and finally verse 16 includes a confession of Yahweh.

The sailors are represented as typical Gentiles, generally god-fearing (on the basis of an intuitive knowledge) and compassionate. Jonah, by contrast, flees before the knowledge of God which he has through direct revelation; and he displays throughout the book a total lack of compassion. Through prompting by the sailors (representing the pagan world) Jonah is, in effect, forced to consider his commission (v. 8). The sailors' questions elicit from Jonah a statement of faith as a "Hebrew" in avowedly Abrahamic terms (cf. Gen. 14:13) which has at its center a basic confession of fear before Yahweh, who is now identified as the Creator.

Thus the theme of the first chapter is the unconscious success of Jonah as the embodied word. The Gentiles' general factual awareness of God is gradually transformed into a reverential awe as they move from a deistic conception of God to a particular faith in Yahweh (Jonah 1:16). Their "fear" moves from an elemental fear in verse 5 to a fear of the divine messenger (v. 10) and finally to a fear of Jonah's God (v. 16). This emphasis through the sailors sets the tone for a major theme of the book—the reaction to the word by the Gentiles.

Jonah's Psalm of Thanksgiving (Jonah 2)

The psalm of Jonah 2 underscores Yahweh as the reverser of circumstances and functions rhetorically as a kind of musical pause. It is to be divided into (1) an introduction (v. 2); (2) an initial stanza lamenting Jonah's banishment from Yahweh's presence, his temple (vv. 3–4); (3) a second stanza (vv. 5–7) where the theme is descent into Sheol and prayer from there to the heavenly sanctuary; and (4) a conclusion (vv. 8–9) in which Jonah expresses confidence of being heard (a customary ingredient in the thanksgiving psalms), rejects idolatry, and vows to renew his relationship with Yahweh and (presumably) thus to fulfil his commission (Walsh 1982, 219–29). The centrality of Yahweh is indicated by the position of that divine name at the beginning and conclusion of the psalm, with Jonah's experiences being concentrated into the middle section (the divine name or an allusion to it occurs in every line of the psalm except for vv. 5–6a). By this confessional psalm of thanksgiving Jonah is moved from storm to calm, as the sailors in Jonah 1 have been moved from calm to storm to calm (Cohn 1969, 78–83). The purpose of the psalm is to fit Jonah by forgiveness for the mission to Nineveh. The psalm recalls the episode of the fish as now past, Jonah presumably having been returned to Palestine. It is thus preparatory to and anticipatory of the new beginning of Jonah 3.

Jonah's Renewed Commission (Jonah 3)

The commission is renewed in Jonah 3:1–3. There is no thrust or parry by Jonah this time, but mere obedience. Commissioned to go to Nineveh, he arrives and announces the sole words of prophecy in the book, "Yet forty days, and Nineveh shall be overthrown!" As elsewhere in the book, there are echoes of definite biblical contexts which import an element of ambiguity into the statement (here by the verb *overthrow*). "Forty days" and "overthrow" in verse 4 connote, respectively, the flood and the fate of Sodom and Gomorrah. Yet the verb *overthrow*, which reminds us of the fate of the cities of the plain, is essentially neutral, pointing simply to a change in the condition of a person or object. Ironically, in this prophetic announcement of doom there is thus the nuance of repentance as a possibility; this is confirmed by the later movement in the chapter. As in chapter 1, Jonah is the unconscious catalyst who, in contact with pagans, brings them to repentance. In both instances their situation is reversed by the pronouncement of the divine word (cf. 1:9). Led by the king of Nineveh, the city repents (vv. 5–10), accepting that its future is bound up with God's free grace (see 3:9–"Who knows, God may yet repent and turn from his fierce anger, so that we perish not?"). Clearly this reversal is a key to the book, for the divine response is promptly recorded by the narrator in verse 10.

Jonah's Anger (Jonah 4)

We have in chapter 4 somewhat of a parallel to Jonah 2. The prophet is again in a crisis situation (4:1; cf. 2:1) leading him to pray (4:2a; 2:6a). He refers back to a distressing situation in Palestine, his own premonition of Nineveh saved by Yahweh's graciousness (4:2b–3; cf. 2:6b–7, where he had been saved by the same grace from the depths of Sheol itself). The freedom of God, expressed in salvation here, creates for Jonah an intolerable situation to which verses 4–11 respond. The salvation of Nineveh provides an indication that Yahweh's extension of grace cannot be predicted or manipulated, and it certainly cannot be confined to Israel. This reflection (v. 2) upon the old credal formula of Exodus 34:6 (Magonet 1983, 36), restricted there to the covenant relationship, provokes a personal crisis for Jonah. He is not able to live with such a concept of Yahweh's grace, and he begs Yahweh for death (Jonah 4:3).

Jonah 4:4–11 provides the resolution of the book. Questioned by Yahweh as to the grounds for his anger (v. 4), Jonah retires to watch, under the shade of a gourd, whether or not Nineveh will fall (note the repetition of the question of v. 4 in v. 9). Jonah, unrepentant, cherishes the hope that Nineveh will still be overthrown. The change of divine name within this chapter bears noting. As used by Jonah here, Yahweh is to be associated with covenant compassion, 'ĕlōhîm with punishment and discipline.

The withdrawal of the protective gourd which God had created for Jonah is followed by the divine word which spares Nineveh (4:11). God points out that Jonah has no grounds for anger in the matter of the gourd which God had given and taken; much less so, then, should he be angry over Nineveh. Jonah had no claim on the plant and thus no right to talk about justice or injustice (Fretheim 1978, 234). The book concludes where it begins—with Yahweh's word.

Some have pointed to divine freedom as the major issue in the Book of Jonah. Indeed, the emphasis in the last verse of the book is on God's sovereignty and his ability (as opposed to human inability) to make the best choices. The Book of Jonah could also be read as a condemnation of Israelite particularism. Such a theme, however, is nowhere pronounced, and it detracts from the more general issues to which we have referred. Equally the book is not intended to resolve the difficult problems of the exilic period (i.e., mixed marriages and collaboration within the land with foreigners), for these matters are not taken up. Nor was it written to demonstrate the possibility of repentance in the most unlikely of circumstances, for repentance as a possibility is the presupposition with which the book commences. God is the initiator of crises in human experience, and God resolves them. We are dependent upon a grace which cannot be anticipated or expounded, just as it cannot be measured. On that note, as a fitting summary of the whole, the book concludes.

18

Micah

Micah was a stirring preacher of judgment; indeed, his book begins and ends on that strong note (1:2–4; 7:7–20). He preached in the last third of the eighth century B.C. (during the reigns of Jotham, Ahaz, and Hezekiah), slightly later than Isaiah but generally overlapping with him chronologically and sharing most of his basic concerns, probably witnessing also the fall of Samaria and the Assyrian visitation of 701 B.C. upon Jerusalem. The book is clearly divided into three sections; each begins with "Hear" (1:2; 3:1; 6:1), and each, following the design of Isaiah 1–12, alternates prophecies of doom (1:2–2:11; chap. 3; 6:1–7:6) and hope (2:12–13; chaps. 4–5; 7:7–20; see Willis 1969, 5–42). The book begins with an international summons to judgment, a proclamation of the descent of Yahweh from his holy temple in heaven to the world (1:2–3). It concludes with this mission accomplished (7:14–17); the final doxology, however, relates to the immeasurable nature of divine forgiveness and a restatement of the Abrahamic promises (7:18–20). The book proceeds with a stern indictment of Jerusalem and Samaria. The social corruption which was rife in Micah's time is constantly referred to; leaders of north and south are accused. At the same time the book, like Isaiah, exhibits a strong confidence in the future associated with Yahweh's kingship to be exercised from Zion; and much of the prophecy is given over in the hope sections to the exposition of traditional Zion eschatology.

In view of the rejection of contemporary society and yet the espousal of a future for the people of God, it is not surprising that, like Isaiah, Micah has a strong emphasis upon the place and purpose of the remnant. Both in Isaiah and Micah, virtually for the first time in Old Testament theology, a distinction is made between the nation, which is roundly condemned, and the faithful within it, who will endure the fires of purification and form the nucleus of the future people of God. Thus the concept of an Israel within Israel, incipient from Sinai onward, is given clear expression in both of these prophetic books, and by this presentation arises the clear concept of a people of God that survives the demise of the northern and southern kingdoms. We consider now in order the three broad divisions of the Book of Micah.

1:1	Introduction
1:2–2:13	First cycle
1:2–2:11	Judgment
2:12–13	Salvation
3–5	Second cycle
3	Judgment
4–5	Salvation
6–7	Third cycle
6:1–7:6	Judgment
7:7–20	Salvation

Judgment and Salvation: First Cycle (Mic. 1:2–2:13)

The descent of Yahweh in judgment is universally announced as affecting the whole earth (1:2–4). The particular reason for this coming is the failure of both north and south, Samaria and Jerusalem, to be centers of right worship (v. 5) and thus to be points of witness to the wider world. The doom of Samaria for idolatry is then pronounced (vv. 6–7). The lament which follows anticipates by its geographical references the approach of Assyria to Jerusalem in 701 B.C. and thus the devastation of the land of Judah (vv. 8–16). Also, the similarity of this material to David's lament over Saul and Jonathan (2 Sam. 1:19–27) underscores the poignancy with which the prophet views the approaching disaster, which he is powerless to avert. The judgment thus beginning with the people of God is, in the opinion of Micah, paradigmatic of what will happen to the wider world.

The activities of monopolistic landowners are the subject of the prophetic lament in Micah 2:1–5 (cf. Isa. 5:8). Punishment appropriate to their crime on the principle of requital is anticipated: they will be bereft of the land which they have filched! Verses 6–11 continue the dialog with the landowners (or with false prophets speaking on their behalf, as some suggest). Micah then parodies their false assumptions (v. 6). With a slight revocalization of the received Hebrew text (suggested by van der Woude 1969, 247), verse 7 would read, "He [Yahweh] affirmed [what has been undertaken by] the house of Jacob"—a prophetic appeal to the covenant affirmation of Yahweh (cf. Deut. 26:17–18). In this case the false appeal of Micah's opponents to a popular doctrine of election is rejected. For having made women and children their victims (vv. 8–9), they themselves will be denied the enjoyment of the Promised Land (v. 10). While his opponents say, "Do not preach" (v. 6), to a prophet of God, they are willing to listen to a charlatan (v. 11). A message of hope in verses 12–13 confirms the election promises of God to Israel, the continued existence of a remnant. Yahweh as their King will bring his sheep into safety. This promise of the restoration of Israel, in view of the connection between shepherd and Zion imagery at 4:6–8, is perhaps an allusion to the vindication of Zion/Jerusalem, from which Yahweh's world leadership will issue.

Judgment and Salvation: Second Cycle (Mic. 3–5)

Micah 3 is dominated by the theme of justice, the key word appearing in all three oracles. Unjust leaders who viciously prey on the people will receive their deserts (vv. 1–4). Prophets who expect fees will be denied spiritual gifts—unlike Micah, who points to the power resident in him (vv. 5–8). Leadership based upon bloodshed and corruption will be the ruin of Jerusalem and the temple (vv. 9–12).

Micah 4 begins a long section of hope which embraces also chapter 5. These two chapters have in view the eschatological divine rule from Zion over a restored people. Each of the seven oracles in the section takes its rise in doom and passes on quickly to hope. While they lack formal connection to each other, by repetition their message is clear. Jerusalem and the people of God will be vindicated! Micah 4:1–5 strikes the note familiar from Isaiah 2:2–5. Jerusalem will be the world center to which all nations will flow in pilgrimage. Yahweh's law *(tôrâ)* will thereafter regulate the affairs of nations. In Micah 4:6–8 shepherd imagery is used to depict the final state of the remnant people of God—they will be shepherded by Yahweh after having been abused by corrupt Jerusalem leadership. Jerusalem's predicament (vv. 9–10) will be resolved only after a Babylonian exile. Micah 4:11–13 appears to depict the conditions of

701 B.C. Nations are gathered around Jerusalem, whose situation is hopeless, but Yahweh intervenes. In 5:1–6 the city is again besieged and without hope. The reigning king will be smitten and then replaced by a new David. Perhaps this message refers to the advent of Hezekiah and the Assyrian threat of the late eighth century. What is certain is that the Davidic rule depicted in this section is ideal, and 5:2 seems to refer to a dramatic new beginning as in David's time. The overthrow of Assyria ends this section, suggesting that the solution for political difficulties is the ideal rule described here (and contemplated in 1 Sam. 16:1–13 and 2 Sam. 7). In Micah 5:7–9 only a remnant exists. But in exile it will become as plentiful as dew or heavy rain and thus a life-giving blessing in this situation. Finally, in 5:10–15 Israel is under threat from powerful foes. She takes refuge in her defenses, which Yahweh will destroy as well as the idols which stand behind them. He will then become Israel's strength, turning his power against the nations. Each of these carefully compiled episodes in Micah 4–5 has in view some threat to Zion and the eventual removal of that peril.

Judgment and Salvation: Third Cycle (Mic. 6–7)

Micah 6:1–7:6 forms the third "doom" section. In the famous passage of 6:1–8 the issue at stake is the conduct of the people of God within the covenant. The case against Israel is presented in lawsuit fashion in verses 1–5. Israel asks what will avert the judgment (vv. 6–7). Micah responds with what is already known, namely, that obedience is better than sacrifice (v. 8). Verses 9–12 take up the reasons for the indictment: the familiar social sins, commercial exactions, and extortion. The sentence follows in verses 13–15: the economy will be stricken (a punishment that again fits the crime). A summary of and reasons for the punishment complete the chapter (v. 16). Judah and her leadership are likened to the days of Omri and Ahab in the northern kingdom and may expect similar punishments.

The prophet speaks in lament tones in 7:1–6. The harvest is past, and Israel is not saved (v. 1)! Again on review are the calamitous moral situation of Micah's day and its deleterious effect upon personal relationships (vv. 2–6). Finally, the book ends with a long hymnic expression of hope (vv. 7–20). Verse 7 is a transition, but in verses 8–10 Jerusalem addresses her enemy and expresses confidence in Yahweh. The prophet then addresses Jerusalem, rejoicing in the expectations which await Zion (vv. 11–13). Walls and city will be rebuilt, and the land that has been desolated will be recovered. In verses 14–17 Israel is in difficulties, and Micah appeals for an exodus intervention to end the humiliation imposed by the nations. The ground of this prophetic appeal to Yahweh is the immeasurable capacity of God to forgive and his steadfast adherence to the Abrahamic covenant (vv. 18–20).

This prophecy of Micah, the elder from Moresheth (note Jer. 26:17–18), breathes the passionate conviction of a man who, in his own town gates of Judah, has witnessed much of the social inequities and the partialities in leadership to which he refers. He offers no new solutions for them, and his message is still the unpalatable prophetic conviction that offenses against the covenant will be responded to with appropriate punishment. He relies greatly, however, upon the character of Yahweh, recognizing that Yahweh will preserve Israel in spite of herself. Yahweh's commitment, given to Israel's forefather Abraham, will finally be translated into the reality of Yahweh's rule over a purified remnant people from Zion, and the whole order of creation will be affected.

19

Nahum

The subject matter of this superbly artistic book, whose wealth of imagery must not be entirely reduced to historical specifics, is narrowly directed to the impending fall of the Assyrian capital, Nineveh. Like Obadiah, Nahum singles out a Gentile power as the incarnation of world evil. Nahum 1 is largely given over to a theological explanation of divine intervention in history as demanded by Yahweh's character (v. 2). This intervention issues concretely in judgment to be exercised upon Assyria, which in turn means consolation for Judah. Chapters 2–3 carefully link transgression and punishment. That the world Judge punishes aggression is a theme the book progressively underscores and graphically illustrates. The overall outline of Nahum is as follows:

1:1–14   Judgment on Judah's enemies; salvation for the people of God
1:15–2:13 Announcement of the fall of Assyria
3   The fall of Nineveh

Judgment and Salvation (Nah. 1:1–14)

After the superscription, verses 2–8 offer a broken alphabetic poem (acrostic) which is a theological reminder to Judah of Yahweh's character as Judge of his world. The controlling word in verses 2–3a, which depict the attributes of the Divine Warrior who is about to arrive with universal judgment (vv. 3b–8), is "avenging." While the word *jealous* (v. 2) indicates the disposition of Yahweh to brook no rivals, to demand recognition of his universal sovereignty, "avenging" indicates the practical implications of Yahweh's jealousy. "To avenge" is used in biblical contexts where the sense demanded is "punish" or "vindicate," depending upon the subject referred to. (In Josh. 10:13 "punish" is required, while "vindication" for Yahweh's people is intended in Judg. 11:36; 2 Sam. 22:48. The "day of vengeance of our God" in Isa. 61:1–4 is the day on which Yahweh intervenes to rescue the elect and to bring them salvation.)

After the manifestation of the divine character, expressed in terms of the older cultic confessions (cf. Nah. 1:3a and Exod. 34:6; Num. 14:18, etc.), world judgment by the Divine Warrior occurs (Nah. 1:3b–8). The effects of this judgment are expressed in typical poetic imagery as a reversal of the creation victory: the sea is rebuked, sterility replaces fertility, and the world and its inhabitants are convulsed and unable to face the fury of Yahweh's wrath (vv. 4–6). This act of judgment (vv. 7–8) is viewed from the two perspectives involved in our earlier representation of Yahweh as destroyer of the wicked and vindicator of the faithful.

The judgment oracle in 1:9–11 becomes a particular application of these eschatological and general truths as it tells the senselessness of Assyria's pitting herself against the controller of history. A divine pronouncement follows in verses 12–14, apparently foreshadowing salvation for Judah (in vv. 12–13 the Hebrew pronouns are feminine) but burial for mighty Assyria.

Announcement of Assyria's Fall (Nah. 1:15–2:13)

Nahum 1:15–2:2 reflects what has been predicted in Nahum 1 by commencing with a heraldic announcement of the fall of Assyria (1:15), the return of the exiles (perhaps the dispersed north—the difficult v. 2 is not a parenthesis, nor should it be joined to v. 3, but more probably refers to the return of the northern exiles following the Assyrian collapse), and the restoration of the glory of Israel, the people of God.

This summary is then developed in the remainder of Nahum 2. The attack by the divine army, the defense of the Assyrian capital Nineveh, and its final ruin are the subject of 2:3–10. The lionlike Assyria is then depicted as desolate in the taunting poem with which the chapter concludes (vv. 11–13).

The Fall of Nineveh (Nah. 3)

In 3:1–7 the fate of Nineveh is detailed. Verses 1–3 survey the city as attacked and then reduced. The reason is advanced in verse 4: the international harlotry of Assyria has enticed her world to ruin. Verses 5–7 discuss the public exposure of Nineveh by Yahweh and the revelation of her inner corruptness. The principle of divine requital is emphasized in verses 8–10—Assyria will now stand as desolated as Thebes, the capital of Egypt, which had been sacked by Assyria in 663 B.C. Nineveh will stagger helplessly, mocked by Yahweh's prophet! She is invited to prepare for the siege (vv. 11–17). Prepare as she may (v. 14), the fire of divine judgment will engulf her, as will the traditionally associated judgment of sword and plague (v. 15). Her vaunted resources (v. 16) and her organizational leadership (v. 17) will all be swept away.

Nahum considers Assyria's epitaph as the prophecy concludes (3:18–19). Her kings are dead, her armies scattered. Assyria's passage from the scene of history provides the occasion for universal rejoicing.

The narrow range of this book seems particularly nationalistic, but it is not merely so. Nahum is painting a very broad scenario of history for us. His concerns are not the state of Judean religious health, nor even the ultimate future of the people of God. Thus no social problems nor Zion theology is aired by this book. Rather, Nahum is drawing our attention to the ultimate security for the people of God which divine control over history affords. That this truth is particularly applied to a problem manifest in his own day does not lessen its generality. God, the righteous Judge, surveys human affairs. This fact alone ensures the comfort of his people. Nahum (whose name means "comfort") is the conveyor of this truth.

20

Habakkuk

The prophecy of Habakkuk is set between the rise of the Babylonian power (626 B.C.) and the fall of Jerusalem. The key to understanding the book appears to be the psalm of chapter 3, in which Habakkuk is encouraged to see the events of his own day through the perspective that a survey of the history of salvation offers. This will provide an attestation for divine fidelity, the major theme of Habakkuk 2. We may divide, then, the book as follows:

1:1–2:4 Question and answer, Habakkuk and Yahweh
2:5–20 A fivefold condemnation of the oppressor
3 Habakkuk's expectation

Dialog Between Habakkuk and Yahweh (Hab. 1:1–2:4)

The first chapter is structured around two prophetic laments (1:2–4, 12–17) to which divine responses are given (1:5–11; 2:1–4). Habakkuk's plea for divine endorsement of his ministry as he struggles against Judean social corruption has so far gone unheard. His complaint centers upon the apparently ineffective character of the prophetic proclamation of Torah. His burden is that the divine Word has exercised little effect upon his hearers (Janzen 1982, 399).

The divine reply occurs in 1:5–11. The efficacy of the divine Word will be seen in the impending world change by which Judean conduct will be rebuked. Babylon is about to move to the center of the political stage, replacing the oppressing Assyrian, a fact which will produce incredulity among the Judean population (v. 5). The further prophetic inquiry of verses 12–17 commences with a confession of the eternality of God (for v. 12 we are adopting the textual reading of the rabbinic editors, "thou shalt not die"), who has ordained the Babylonian oppression. Why then, in the light of this admitted divine control over history, is evil still tolerated (v. 13)? Will not Yahweh exercise control over his own creation (v. 14)? Attention then seems to turn to the Babylonians again (vv. 15–17), who, limited and unaware of the role they play, worship the implements of war by which they impose their might.

The divine reply (2:1–4) indicates that the time for which the prophet seeks has been appointed, and he needs only to watch (v. 1) for the turn of events. Verse 2 is somewhat enigmatic, but perhaps the meaning is that this prophetic message will refresh the weary. The sudden coming of what is projected is underscored in verse 3. The meaning of the crucial verse 4 continues to be in dispute. The probable intent is that the righteous of the period will live by the fidelity which Habakkuk's vision attests. (This view takes the possessive attached to the word *faith* as a reference to the vision. Even if we take it as referring to the believer, the vision is still an attestation of divine faithfulness to prior promises; see Janzen 1982, 404.) The faith on view here, as is often the case in the Old Testament, has a passive quality, for the divine trustworthiness in relationships has already been established.

Fivefold "Woe Oracles" (Hab. 2:5–20)

A series of five woes follows in verses 5–20. Verses 5–8 present the insatiable lust of some oppressor (Assyria? or perhaps the enemy in general?). Verses 9–11 show that the attempt by the exploiters to insulate themselves against disaster will not avail, and verses 12–14 describe as illusory the labor of the vaunted city-builder who ignores the real purpose of creation. Next, those who seek to seduce companions for their debauchery are condemned (vv. 15–17), as is idolatry, that form of human pride which refuses to acknowledge the lordship of the Creator (vv. 18–19). The divine reality—Yahweh's rule over all creation as he sits enthroned in his holy temple (v. 20)—provides the guarantee that abuses of power, political and social, will not go unpunished.

Habakkuk's Prayer (Hab. 3)

The psalm of chapter 3 provides the vision for which Habakkuk was bidden to wait. By its survey of the past history of Israel's salvation, it furnishes demonstration of divine fidelity which assures the future of the righteous. A series of elements—superscription (v. 1), prophetic petition (v. 2), the manifestation of the Divine Warrior (vv. 3–7), the battle report, the purpose for which he has come (vv. 8–15)—celebrates again the basic victory of the exodus, by which Israel's place within history was established. Yahweh's coming from Sinai as Lord of creation (v. 3), as the Divine Warrior who is armed with supernatural weapons and will intercede for his people (v. 4), convulses animate and inanimate creation (vv. 6–7). Poetic artistry and fact are mingled (perhaps there are allusions to the plagues in v. 5 and to the wilderness march in v. 6; cf. the crossing of the sea and the Jordan in vv. 8–10 and the conquest's long day in v. 11), but it is typical for descriptions of divine appearance to have mythological touches.

The purpose for which Yahweh had come (and is coming) is then explicated in 3:8–15. He is coming to defeat the primordial enemies—the river, the sea, the floods—which are to be riven (read v. 9b as "thou didst cleave the rivers of the earth"), as the chaos dragon (Tiamat in the Babylonian epic Enuma Elish) was split asunder in the creation battle and is now personified in some new historical encounter. Creation (the mountains, sun, and moon in vv. 10–11) stands appalled at the prospect of this intervention, which recalls the primordial battles but which is directed to the present threat facing Judah. The threat is personified in sea-dragon terms (read "tail to neck" in v. 13). This is the earth-shattering vision for which Habakkuk has waited. It does no more than simply insist that Yahweh is consistent; as he dealt with one threat in one crucial era of history, so he will meet another now in a similar world struggle in this present era.

After this vision we read of the response of the prophet. Awe (v. 16) turns to quiet commitment (v. 17), irrespective of events, to patience and confidence in God's strength (vv. 18–19). The life in which one must patiently wait has now been received through the vision delivered.

The Book of Habakkuk reveals to us the spiritual pilgrimage of this prophet. Cast into the form of an autobiographical movement, it takes us from the prophetic complaint about divine inactivity in history to the firm resolution to exercise patience (3:16–19) even though history seems to offer no new indication of divine involvement. To this anguished prophet God gave a fresh vision of himself. The dialog of chapters 1–2 is replaced by experience in Habakkuk 3. He is finally moved to his position of 3:16–19 by the promptings of inner conviction in response to prayer; Habakkuk can now see that the power in Israel's past history is available to the righteous who shall live by faith. This book reveals a genuine sharing of a doubt which assails all believers, a feeling that God stands aside from the moral struggle of the believer. This doubt is removed not by the addition of new facts, but simply by the addition of a new perspective; not new revelation, but new insight into old revelation. The key verse Habakkuk 2:4 is taken up repeatedly in the New Testament, admittedly in different contexts than the present, but nowhere more significantly than in Romans 1:17. There the righteousness of God, which in that context appears to be divine fidelity to the patriarchal promises, is responded to by trust in the gospel which reveals that righteousness, a gospel providing further attestation of the unchanging character of God in salvation and judgment. Habakkuk needed this reassurance, as did his times. Doubtless, having ascended to the heights (3:19), his ministry provided the confidence needed for the faithful in his day to capture his sense of vision.

21

Zephaniah

Zephaniah prophesied concurrently with the early ministry of Jeremiah, but seemingly before the Josianic reforms of 621 B.C., since there are abundant references to syncretism. The universal turn which this seventh-century prophecy assumes gives it its interest. The content of this very deliberate prophecy of judgment is as follows:

1:1–2:3 War declared by Yahweh on Judah
2:4–15 War declared on Judah's enemies
3 The judgment of Jerusalem and its aftermath

Yahweh's Declaration of War on Judah
(Zeph. 1:1–2:3)

After the superscription the book opens with a threat from Yahweh to destroy everything upon the face of the earth (Zeph 1:2–3). This introduction sets the tone both for prophecies of sweeping judgment under the broad orbit of the advent of the day of Yahweh upon Judah and the nations thereafter mentioned, and for the note on which the book concludes—the expected eschatology of Zion's world significance.

False worship, a typical prophetic theme, is the reason advanced for the initial attack upon Judah and Jerusalem (1:4–6). The cultic overtones of the day-of-the-Lord theme which follows are thus clear (1:7–2:3), but there is a transmutation of the concept of the day into the imagery of holy war (implicit in Amos). Yahweh will attack Jerusalem for its assimilation of foreign customs (v. 8) manifested particularly in the adoption of pagan religious practices by Jerusalem's leaders (v. 9), which is naturally associated with social injustice. Ominously, Yahweh will enter from the north, the area of numinous threat (v. 10). Jerusalem's entrepreneurs and the economy which supports them will be removed (v. 11). In Jeremianic fashion, Yahweh will search Jerusalem with candles to expose the offenders (vv. 12–13; cf. Jer. 5:1)! In this great day when the cultic acts are to be reversed (Judeans are to be Yahweh's sacrificial lambs; see v. 7), no offense will escape divine scrutiny. Conditions at Bethel in Amos's time have been duplicated in Jerusalem (cf. Amos 6:1). Men are at ease, theoretically holding a doctrine of Yahweh, but in practice denying his reality (Zeph. 1:12).

Verses 14–18 turn more narrowly to the theme of the day of Yahweh. The dependency upon Amos 5:20 is clear. It is a day on which Yahweh will roar against Zion, a day of darkness (i.e., a day when the universe is plunged back into primeval chaos). Warrior Yahweh advances upon his creation, beginning with his own household! Desolation, distress, and a terrible end await Jerusalem (Zeph. 1:15–18). Prominent in this first chapter is the divine word directly spoken by Yahweh himself (1:2–6, 8–13, 17)—it is punctuated only by prophetic asides that add a graphic and vivid note to the nature of the divine threat. The nation is then called to an assembly of repentance (2:1–3; there are adumbrations of Joel here). However, the only hope advanced is that by heeding such a call the humble (i.e., the remnant, a notion which receives prominent attention later in the prophecy) will be delivered (v. 3).

Yahweh's Declaration of War on Judah's Enemies (Zeph. 2:4–15)

The remainder of chapter 2 is given over to oracles delivered against foreign nations (vv. 4–15). Unlike the situation confronting Amos, who needed to establish plausibility before turning to Judah and Israel, Judah at this point in history needs no convincing of the reality of the threat, and Zephaniah thus begins the chapter with her. The world-shattering character of her judgment has a ripple effect upon the surrounding nations, the traditional enemies of Judah to the west (Philistia; see

vv. 4–7) and east (Moab and Ammon; see vv. 8–11). After their judgment the remnant of Israel will possess the territory of the enemy. Brief oracles against Ethiopia, a power to the south (2:12), and, in language reminiscent of Nahum, against Assyria in the north (vv. 13–15) conclude the chapter.

Jerusalem's Destruction and Her Future (Zeph. 3)

Jerusalem becomes the subject of the lament in 3:1–5. Again the problem is corrupt leadership. Princes, judges, prophets, and priests have all perverted their roles, while the ideal leadership of Yahweh, available continually to the community, has been ignored (v. 5). Verses 6–8 are difficult to classify but are a direct address by Yahweh heralding a world conflagration in which all nations (including Israel and Judah?) will be engulfed. There is a call (to Jerusalem? or to the remnant addressed in vv. 9–13?) to fear and wait for Yahweh and for the day on which he will gather the world together for judgment.

This prophecy ends on a note of great hope. The judgment of Babel will be reversed (v. 9), and the foundation of human unity will be Yahweh. The centrality of Jerusalem is implied in verse 10. The return of the scattered people of God, whose tongues will demonstrate the new gift of pure lips, will characterize this New Jerusalem (vv. 11–13).

A song of praise concludes the prophecy. Zion is now called upon to rejoice in the salvation which has come (vv. 14–16), namely, Yahweh as King in her midst (v. 17). All "sorrows" (NIV) will be excluded from this new city (v. 18). The prophecy finishes on an Abrahamic note: salvation is depicted in terms of the achieving of a name for the gathered, an event which has world significance. All this will occur as a result of Yahweh's decisive intervention (v. 20).

On the eve of the exile, Zephaniah brings to the south the Isaianic message of the security of the faithful under the kingship of Yahweh, the fidelity of Yahweh to his Abrahamic promises, and the dominant centrality of Jerusalem/Zion, where Yahweh's throne will be established. The prophecy has thus moved from universal judgment to the universality of salvation in a judged world where the Abrahamic promise of a great name for his descendants has been realized in the gathered remnant through whom the world at large is to be blessed.

22

Haggai

Haggai's four oracles are dated within the book as ranging between August and December 520 B.C. After a period of uncertainty within the Persian Empire, Darius I had recently come to power. The aim of this brief prophecy is clear: to persuade the returned exiles in Jerusalem and what remained of Judah to rebuild the temple. There is some superficial difficulty in reconciling the accounts of Ezra, Haggai, and Zechariah as to the date of the commencement of work on the second temple and the identity of the temple builder. Ezra 3:8 suggests that the work was begun by Zerubbabel, which is supported by Haggai 1:12–14 and Zechariah 4:9. Ezra 1:8 and 5:14–16 indicate that it was Sheshbazzar, the prince of Judah and Persian-appointed governor. We note that Zerubbabel's name is mentioned when the religious implications of the building operations are in view (Ezra 3), and Sheshbazzar's when the secular. If we accept the further suggestion that the verb underlying the somewhat puzzling phrase "lay the foundation" (Ezra 3:6, 10; 5:16; Hag. 2:18; Zech. 4:9) is more generally used to refer to progressive stages in the building operations (Andersen 1958, 1–35), then the problem is solved. In Haggai's day the statement that "this house lies in ruins" (Hag. 1:4) would then mean that the building was partially reconstructed but not frequented by worshipers (i.e., that it was desolate). The book contains four major divisions:

1	The sin, judgment, and repentance of the people of God
2:1–9	The place of the rebuilt temple in the economy of salvation
2:10–19	Who may rebuild the temple
2:20–23	The address to the temple builder

Israel's Repentance (Hag. 1)

The political situation in the Persian Empire may have contributed to the lethargy which Haggai addresses. Cyrus, the conqueror of Babylon, died in 530/529 B.C. and was succeeded by his son Cambyses, who later died by his own hand in 522. After several revolts, he in turn was followed by Darius I Hystaspes, whose position was not fully secure until 520 B.C., about the period when Haggai writes. Haggai 1:1–2 identifies the prophet, the people, and the problem he will address. Speaking on the first day of the month, perhaps on the occasion of a festival or holy day, Haggai addresses his first charge to the community leaders Zerubbabel and Joshua, Davidic representative and high priest respectively. Although the returnees have been restored in their land (v. 4), they continue to insist that conditions are not yet conducive to the rebuilding of the temple.

The ground of difficulty between the prophet and the community is quickly established in Haggai 1:4–11. Although work had apparently begun upon the temple in the initial period of the return (538 B.C.), it had not been undertaken with any degree of thoroughness. Though the temple was seemingly standing in Haggai's time (the comparison in 1:4 between the state of the temple and the manner in which the people are housed, i.e., in "paneled houses," suggests that the temple is nearly completed but requires roofing), it was not the focus of public attention. The site, as a worship center, seems to have been deserted (we are taking the Hebrew word ḥārēb, "desolate," in the sense of "unfrequented"). Haggai's argument in 1:4–11 may be reduced to the community's need to "seek first the kingdom of God." The difficulties of the times to which the people have referred have been caused by the community's dispiritedness and lack of commitment. If they put the building of the temple first, the difficulties of the period (depicted in v. 11 in the familiar terms of Deut. 28 as the operation of the covenant curses) would vanish. This lack of obedience to the primary requirement of the return, this lack of recognition of Yahweh's sovereignty over the returned community by building the temple as the emblem of his sovereignty, Haggai correctly construes as covenant defection.

Haggai's message has its intended effects: in 1:12–14 the community's attitude changes. An appropriate covenant response (v. 12—the people "obeyed the voice of the LORD their God, and . . . feared before the LORD") is greeted by the prophet with words of encouragement and covenant renewal, "I am with you" (v. 13; cf. Exod. 19:3–8—note that in 2 Kings 17:7–23 and 2 Chron. 36:15–16 the reason for the fall of the north and the south is given as the failure to hear the prophetic word). The pattern of Haggai 1 has thus been (1) the traditional presentation of the people's sin (vv. 2–5); (2) prophetic preaching in response, with attention drawn to the covenant curses which have been operant because of national failure (vv. 6, 9–11); (3) the repentance of the people in reaction to the prophetic word (v. 12); and (4) covenant reaffirmation (v. 13; see Beuken 1967, 27–49). The substance of Haggai 1:14–15 resembles the commissioning of Moses to build the tabernacle (Exod. 35:29; 36:2). Thus the rebuilding of the temple will stamp the returnees as the people of God.

Rebuilding of the Temple (Hag. 2)

The address of 2:1–9 occurs a little over one month later (in Sept. 520 B.C.) and is designed to meet the derogatory comparisons which have been drawn between the first temple and what is being erected (v. 3). Verses 4–5 are reminiscent of the older charge to Joshua to be strong and of good courage (the charge here is to Zerubbabel and a different Joshua; cf. Deut. 31:7; Josh. 1:6). The returned community, like the community of the conquest period, are to take heart in the provision of the divine Spirit, who had operated in the exodus community (Isa. 63:14) and would similarly overcome all obstacles arising in the present period. The account continues with the eschatological promise that would be attached to the rebuilding of the temple. The depiction of pilgrimage to Zion in verses 6–9 and the double entendre in verse 9 bound up with the word *place* (indicating both temple and Promised Land) make clear the benefits that Haggai expects to accrue to the returned people of God as a result of the temple building. The building of the temple would bring peace to the Promised Land by its placement, and Haggai sees its erection as a necessary preamble to the ushering in of the eschatological age, which for postexilic prophecy was a matter of imminent expectation (cf. the New Testament view of the second coming). Since what is being built is, in the mind of the prophet, the eschatological temple, its glory will surpass the Solomonic temple (v. 9). God himself will rule from it, not merely dwell in it, drawing the wealth and submission of the world to Jerusalem.

After the conversion call of Haggai 1 and the tenor of 2:1–9, it is difficult to feel that the people addressed in 2:10–14 (on the twenty-fourth day of the ninth month, 520 B.C.) are the returnees. Of course, these verses may provide a general warning to the population that repentance without performance has no significance, yet the change in tone seems abrupt. All the people spoken of in this passage are "unclean." This fact seems to rule out the return community as being in view, as does the pejorative use of "nation" in verse 14 (such a use of the word only rarely applies to Old Testament Israel). It is better to suppose that the people addressed are the opponents to the temple building of whom we hear in Ezra 4:4 (where "the people of the land" appear to have been the occupants of Palestine who had not been exiled; their request to participate in temple building with the returnees was rejected by Zerubbabel, presumably on the grounds of their cultic defilement). Accordingly, the "work of their hands" (Hag. 2:14) would be not what they offered in sacrifice, but participation in temple building. Verses 15–19 are best seen as offering encouragement to the returned community, in spite of opposition of the character we have noted, to continue to carry out the charge to build. They are to remind themselves of how they have been blessed since the decision was taken to recommence the work (vv. 18–19). There were intervening difficulties, to be sure, but they have been overcome.

The oracles of this prophecy display a balanced character. The first and third oracles refer to the condition of the returnees and the need to take positive steps to rebuild the temple, while the second and fourth detail the eschatological consequences which will flow from the rebuilding of the temple. The fourth oracle (2:20–23), which was given on the same day as the third, is addressed to Zerubbabel as temple builder. It is no accident that this address immediately follows the rejection of semipagan participation in temple building. The language used of Zerubbabel in this section ("servant," "signet ring," "chosen") was used earlier to express rejection of Jehoiachin, a preexilic member of the house of David (Jer. 22:24). General continuity with Davidic tradition is thus being expressed here, but in the absence of more definite historical evidence than we have, it would be too much to suggest that Zerubbabel is being addressed messianically or that the prospect is being entertained of a Davidic restoration. Zerubbabel is a continuity figure only and is addressed primarily as the Persian-appointed governor (Hag. 2:21). However, his role as temple builder does stress Davidic continuity, a theologically important detail.

Certainly Haggai is in continuity with the program of Ezekiel and with the general message of restoration that Ezekiel offered (Ezek. 40–48). But his prophecy is no mere return to preexilic nationalism, nor is it given over to petty or cultic concerns. If it were, prophecy would be in its demise. But, on the contrary, Haggai argues that from the small and disillusioned postexilic community there will arise the eschatological people of God. God has not forgotten his promises delivered through Moses and David, and they will be honored by the ushering in of his kingdom.

23

Zechariah

Zechariah exhibits much the same range of concerns as does Haggai, namely, the rebuilding of the temple and thus the return of Yahweh to Jerusalem and the role of that city as world center. His prophecies were delivered over a period of slightly more than two years—from October 520 B.C. (Zech. 1:1) to December 518 (7:1). Normally the book is divided into two (or three) sections, chapters 1–8 and 9–14 (or 9–11 and 12–14), and questions of authorship and connection between the sections are then raised. In view of the clear theological connections between the components of the book, however, there is no good reason why theories of multiple authorship should be raised. Zechariah 1–8 is oriented toward the rebuilding of the temple and the subsequent role of Jerusalem. Zechariah 9–14 is more enigmatic and difficult to interpret, but it is noteworthy that these chapters begin where chapter 1 does, namely, with the return of Yahweh to Jerusalem and the temple (9:1–8), while they conclude with the role of Jerusalem as the world center (14:16–21), as does chapter 8. It is possible, therefore, that Zechariah 9–14 offers a theological commentary upon the more historically oriented first section, and all the more so since the material of chapters 9–14 is often considered to be what later came to be called apocalyptic or protoapocalyptic literature. Summarily, we may present the contents of Zechariah as follows:

1:1–6   Introduction
1:7–6:8   The visions of Zechariah
6:9–15   The coronation of the high priest
7–8   Moral and social issues facing the returned community
9   Yahweh's march on Jerusalem
10   Judgment on false leadership and the return of the exiles
11   The rejection of the shepherd
12–14   End-time conflict and the emergence of the New Jerusalem

Covenant Renewal (Zech. 1:1–6)

Zechariah 1:1–6 introduces the Book of Zechariah on a sustained note of covenant renewal as a precursor to temple building—a theme which we have observed in Haggai. Note the emphasized use of "return" (vv. 3–4), a term often used theologically in covenant contexts in the Old Testament to signify "repent" (cf. v. 6). The returnees in this section are carefully separated from their fathers (v. 4), so that the issue of a new beginning after the return from exile becomes clear. The exile had atoned for the past, and the vista of a new beginning is now offered through the series of visions which follow.

The Visions of Zechariah (Zech. 1:7–6:8)

Zechariah 1–8 contains a series of seven visions (we are excluding Zech. 3 on account of its style and content). These visions are largely temple-oriented (Halpern 1978, 180), with the fourth vision (4:1–4) forming the centerpiece. Visions are quite a normal component of prophetic literature, but this formal arrangement of seven (or eight, if Zech. 3 is included), together with the bizarre imagery, points toward the emergence of apocalyptic visions as part of the thought of this period, though in Zechariah 1–8 we are still formally in the domain of Old Testament prophecy.

Accompanying each vision are interpretation by an angelic presence and commentary. (That no interpretation is supplied in Zech. 3 reinforces the opinion that this chapter stands outside of the sequence.) In the first vision (1:7–17) four patrolling horsemen emerge from "the myrtle trees in the glen" (an uncertain reference—perhaps the entrance of heaven is in view). Having patrolled the earth, they report, disturbingly (since the prophet is looking for the shaking of the nations), that all is quiet. In the ensuing heavenly council the prophet is commissioned to carry a message of consolation to Jerusalem (vv. 14–17). To the previously raised question as to when the exile will really end (v. 12), the divine response is anger to be vented against the nations and comfort extended to Jerusalem. Verse 16 makes it clear that Yahweh's return to Jerusalem will alone guarantee its security. Therefore, what needs to happen now is that the temple, the emblem of divine protection and government, be built.

The second vision (1:18–21) is of four horns which four craftsmen are to cast down. Although horns are usually suggestive of an altar, here they are symbols of power. No succession of world empires seems in view, simply the more general message that world authority will not prevail against the kingdom of God. The degree to which world power is to be kept in check is seen in the third vision (2:1–5), which speaks of a measuring line to be cast around measureless Jerusalem (cf. Ezek. 40:3). Yahweh himself will provide a wall of fire around Jerusalem, suggesting the flaming sword of Eden (Gen. 3:24). There may also be notes of the new exodus here (cf. Exod. 13:20–22; Isa. 4:5–6). Following this vision is a call to return from exile (Zech. 2:6–7), since the rebuilt Jerusalem will provide warrant for the return. (One may conjecture either that a series of returns following 538 B.C. has taken place or, more probably, that this vision offers a theological interpretation of the nature of the return from exile.) Verses 8–9 are difficult but may mean that after having been commissioned by Yahweh (i.e., after having seen the glory), the prophet is certain that his ministry will be vindicated by events. Zechariah 2:10–13 completes the theological presentation by announcing the coming of Yahweh as world King to Jerusalem, to which the nations will now come in pilgrimage.

Zechariah 3 is concerned with the purification of the high priesthood and thus the recommissioning of the postexilic priesthood with the new age in view. In what seems to be a heavenly council Satan, as a kind of prosecuting attorney, accuses Joshua (v. 1). But God has decided for Jerusalem (v. 2) and has plucked Joshua from the fires of exile, purified and refined, thus rebutting Satan's charge. Being clad with new garments suggests a change of fortunes, and thus Joshua is a symbol of the new age (vv. 3–4), while the placing of the turban on Joshua's head indicates the last act relating to his investiture. Additionally, the gold plate on the high priest's miter signified Israel's holiness (Exod. 28:36–38). The prophet's personal notation on the importance of the turban (Zech. 3:5), which in Exodus is the vestment signifying the high priest's representative character, is designed to underscore the reconstitution of Israel as the people of God in the person of the high priest. Verses 6–7 express the thought that Joshua's having access to the heavenly council would de-

pend upon right worship in Jerusalem, while verses 8–10 make the restored priesthood a guarantee of the future, a sign of the effective word of
the prophet. Probably the stone of seven facets (v. 9) is to be connected
with the ancient Near Eastern practice of ceremonially engraving the
foundation stone of the temple. The building of the temple will achieve
the Solomonic concept of rest, for now all Israelites (v. 10) will sit under
their own vine and fig tree (cf. 1 Kings 4:25).

Zechariah 4 offers the central vision of the seven. This chapter is concerned with the blessing of God to come through the leadership of the
community in the new age. The meaning of the lampstand with its
seven lamps is not clear (vv. 2–3), though it seems to symbolize Yahweh's
worldwide dominion. The lampstand is flanked by two olive trees
(vv. 3, 11–14) or two "sons of oil" (not, as mistranslated in v. 14,
"anointed ones," since the word used for oil in this context is not otherwise used in the Old Testament for anointing). Joshua and Zerubbabel
are symbols here of community blessing. The two are, in their own
ways, representatives who usher in the new postexilic age. Verses 6–7
seem to point to the removal of a stone from the ruins of the former temple, the site of which is cleared. This stone is then laid as the first stone
(vv. 8–10), the foundation stone of the new temple, thus signifying continuity between the ages.

The fifth and sixth visions both denote the removal of wickedness
from the land and are thus cultic and purificatory in their tenor. In 5:1–4
the scroll on which the curse is written has the dimensions of the porch
of Solomon's temple, probably an indication that the building of the new
temple will remove the curse which the scroll contains. In the sixth vision (vv. 5–11) wickedness in the form of a woman in a measuring basket
(an ephah) is removed from the land and fittingly consigned to Shinar
(i.e., Babylon), where an antitemple, the house of verse 11, is built for it.
The seventh vision (6:1–8) is clearly parallel to the first; the four chariots
come out this time from between the pillars which provide the gateway
to the heavenly palace (the "mountains" of v. 1). The combat wagons sent
out toward the north presage judgment upon the area from which any
threats to the people of God in the postexilic period were thought to
impend.

All seven visions take place on the same evening. The structure of
each of the seven visions is identical: introduction, what is seen, prophetic questioning, and communication from the interpreting angel. Visions one and seven are clearly related as expectation and result and in
their details. Vision three follows upon the political liberation which vision two foreshadows. Vision four is central, while five and six are interrelated by the factor of the cleansed land as a prerequisite for temple
rebuilding.

Coronation and Deliberation (Zech. 6:9–8:23)

Zechariah 6:9–15 deals with the crowning of Joshua. Two crowns, however, appear in the text (vv. 11, 14). Is Joshua to be crowned twice, once for himself and once for the absent Zerubbabel? More likely, verse 13 is to be taken as a complementary address by Zechariah to the two leaders (Ackroyd 1968, 198–99). The prophet alternately addresses Zerubbabel and Joshua, telling the former to build the temple and rule, and the latter to put on splendor and be priest. Perhaps Zechariah is thus signifying the dual control of the postexilic period. Verses 12–13 probably signify a ceremonial coronation of Joshua which looked forward to an ideal age of the new temple and messianic fulfilment. Since the rebuilding of the temple by Zerubbabel was by this time well advanced, verse 12 can hardly refer to it. Moreover, the association of branch with ideal messiahship (Isa. 11:1) looks beyond human kingship to the age of fulfilment, of which the return from exile was a foreshadowing.

Chapters 7–8 are largely given over to a discussion of moral and social issues facing the returned community. A question about the validity of exilic fasting (7:1–6) leads to a traditional prophetic summarization of the righteousness God requires of his people (vv. 7–14). Messages of hope presented in 8:1–8—the return of Yahweh to Zion, its repopulation, and then covenant renewal—are followed by encouragement to the people on the basis of the future for Jerusalem (vv. 9–17). Verses 18–23 conclude the first section of the prophecy, indicating that the previous fasts will now be replaced with festivals directed toward the prospect of Jerusalem reestablished as the world center. Zechariah 8 ends with the note of the Gentiles' reaction to all these developments: in the new age they will repeat the old confession made by the Philistine Abimelech to Abraham, "God is with you" (Gen. 21:22), summing up the blessing to be extended to the world through this New Jerusalem.

Theological Commentary (Zech. 9–14)

The details of these chapters are extremely complex and will be referred to only briefly in this survey. The historical references in 9:1–7 have proved particularly difficult to interpret; it is best to regard the geographical references as typifying the traditional foes of Israel (Hanson 1975, 292–324). This passage deals with the march by Yahweh from the northern borders of the Promised Land to Jerusalem and the temple. There Yahweh will reign through the eschatological king (vv. 8–10), a reign which induces the release of the captives (vv. 11–13) and the theophanic appearance of Yahweh as the Divine Warrior (v. 14) by whom the restoration has been accomplished. The chapter closes with an assurance of Yahweh's protection and a reference to the fertility of the new order (vv. 15–17).

Zechariah 10:1–2 is a critique of false leadership, which can turn fertility into drought. The rest of the chapter continues this attack but concludes with the imposition of Yahweh's leadership. Verses 3–5 speak of judgment for the false shepherds but salvation for the misled flock. Verses 6–10 pledge Yahweh's restoration of the northern and southern kingdoms, including the return of the scattered exiles. Processional notes referring to the second exodus conclude the chapter.

Zechariah 11:1–3 is a taunt song against proud leadership, continuing the theme of chapter 10. In verses 4–17 the prophet is commissioned to fatten the community for slaughter, since nothing can be expected of them (vv. 4–6). Verses 7–10 reverse the tenor of the restoration program for north and south reported in Ezekiel 37:15–28. The flock is slain, and the kingdoms are again divided. (V. 8 is admittedly difficult. Does it mean the elimination of all false leadership, with three as a symbolic number?) In verses 11–13 the prophet is given his hire, but contemptuously designates it for temple use. In verses 14–17 the prophet represents false leadership and indicates its eventual destruction. The message of the chapter is clear: Yahweh has offered good leadership to bring about covenant renewal and unity between north and south. This leadership has been spurned, and the results of this rejection must now be accepted by the community.

Chapters 12–14 now concentrate our attention upon the end-time conflict, from which Jerusalem will emerge as the new-creation center. Zechariah 12:1–9 describes the conflict which engulfs Jerusalem. The nations attack (vv. 1–3), divine victory comes through Judah (vv. 4–7), Jerusalem is delivered (v. 8), and the enemy destroyed (v. 9). The reception of the Spirit and the work of regeneration in the people of God are then noted, including the national weeping which betokens heartfelt repentance (vv. 10–14). (The phrase "him whom they have pierced" in v. 10 may open the way for seeing a note of vicarious, servant-type suffering in this passage. The text reads "me whom they have pierced," but is commonly amended to "him whom they have pierced." In this case it is Yahweh who has been "pierced," but perhaps *through* his servant representative. At any rate the christological application of this text in the New Testament makes the point clear; see Rev. 1:7.) The lamentation which was part of annual fertility rites has now been replaced with national repentance (Zech. 12:11–14), its scope indicating that the whole community had been involved in idolatry, which has now been completely removed. All community leadership—royal, prophetic, and priestly—is now cleansed.

Eschatological cleansing together with the removal of all idolatry is again the emphasis of 13:1–6, a reinforcement of the previous passage. Verses 7–9 resume the imagery of Zechariah 11. God's own shepherd has been smitten, and the sheep scattered. It is difficult to determine the context for these verses, but they may review the suffering which preceded the repentance of 13:1–6. In the New Testament, Jesus applies to himself this theme of the smitten shepherd by whom the remnant is preserved (Matt. 26:31).

Finally, Zechariah 14 presents a symbolic picture of the eschatological day (Hanson 1975, 369–401). Impelled by Yahweh, nations fight against Jerusalem (vv. 1–2), and only a remnant of the people are to be saved. Victory is divinely given (vv. 3–5). Mountains are leveled as Yahweh comes with his holy ones, the remnant in processional return (cf. Isa. 40:3–5). A new created order results (vv. 6–8), with the transformation of the earth by living waters flowing from Jerusalem (cf. Ezek. 47:1–12). Verses 9–10 proclaim the universal reign of God from Jerusalem (the geographical description is remarkably similar to Jer. 31:38—a foreshadowing of the operation of the new covenant?). Surrounding territory is then flattened and Jerusalem is elevated, thus throwing her into clear relief as a world symbol. Jerusalem's security is sure (vv. 11–15), but covenant curses will afflict her enemies. In verses 16–21 the nations come yearly as pilgrims to Jerusalem, under the threat of withheld fertility. Jerusalem now becomes totally identified with the temple as a sacred site. Temple and city now merge (vv. 20–21).

Like the Book of Haggai, the prophecy of Zechariah lays heavy stress upon God's purposes for temple rebuilding and the eschatological era which is expected to result. Chapters 1–8 interweave these expectations together with the history of the postexilic return. Chapters 9–14 seem to lift the note of the prophecy to a higher pitch, with chapters 9–11 reflecting upon the quality of Judean leadership, while Zechariah 12–14 poses the end-time threat to Jerusalem and describes the manner of its removal. We conclude with the presentation of Jerusalem as the center of the new creation, the royal city from which Yahweh reigns. Revelation 21–22 brings us the same picture in the New Testament as the biblical canon closes.

24

Malachi

Underlining the content of the Book of Malachi is the covenant note at the conclusion: the return of the Elijah figure. Malachi is devoted to the task of covenant renewal (McKenzie and Wallace 1983, 549). The book raises what it sees as the inhibiting factor for the community of its own period, namely, their wilful approach to covenant observance. It concludes on the note of covenant recall through an Elijah, which can only be an eschatological possibility. The book is set within the Persian period and must be later than 516 B.C., since the temple is presupposed as built. It probably could be viewed as the precursor to the Ezra-Nehemiah reforms, since by its series of indictments it seems to prepare the community for them.

The book falls into six clearly defined sections, all of them with a bearing on some covenant ultimately traceable to the Abrahamic covenant. In each section the prophet or Yahweh makes an assertion to which the people then voice objections. The prophet then gives a short response. The name of the prophet himself, Malachi, which means "my messenger," may be a veiled reference to the figure expected in 3:1, or it could be an abbreviation for "messenger of Yahweh." The structure of the book is as follows:

1:1	Introduction
1:2–5	God's constancy
1:6–2:9	Condemnation of the priesthood
2:10–16	The infidelity of the people
2:17–3:5	The messenger of judgment
3:6–12	The call to repentance and condemnation of ritual offenses
3:13–4:3	Judgment for the community but the salvation of the elect
4:4–6	Epilog—Remember the law of Moses

God's Constancy (Mal. 1:2–5)

The opening dialog, which revolves around the choice of Israel and the exclusion of Edom, takes up the old patriarchal basis of election, as the personalized language of the section (Jacob and Esau) suggests. Whether this theme was prompted by some incident of the time (perhaps a gradual incursion by Edom from the south) or whether Edom is universalized here to represent nations outside of the framework of covenant, the point is clear. The covenant with the fathers, since it was based upon the elective concept to which Malachi appeals, is still operative.

Condemnation of the Priesthood (Mal. 1:6–2:9)

The following section begins with language recalling the covenant relationship—father and son, master and servant (see also "great King" in v. 14). Indifferent worship sanctioned by priests is the major consideration of this section. Such worship denies the specific nature of divine rule over Judah, and the prophet counters by pointing to the day when divine rule will be universally acknowledged (v. 11, where future verbs should be supplied). A covenant emphasis emerges in 2:1–9: priestly conduct is seen to contravene directly the covenant with Levi (referred to in Jer. 33:20–26 and Neh. 13:29; Num. 25:11–13 and Deut. 33:10–11, where the covenant referred to is wider than merely the tribe of Levi, are not in view). Perhaps there is implied here a reference to the reestablishment of the priesthood under Joshua after the exile (Zech. 3). We cannot be sure from the context of verse 4 whether the priesthood is being rejected by Malachi in favor of a more general covenant with Levi. Certainly the Ezra-Nehemiah reforms, which challenged priestly authority, sought to cut across narrow priestly privilege.

Infidelity of Israel (Mal. 2:10–16)

Malachi 2:10–16 raises covenant issues of a different character. The message turns this time to the people as a whole and their infidelity to the Abrahamic relationship. The "one father" to whom appeal is made in 2:10 seems to be Abraham; the people are related to God by a covenant which he instituted with their father Abraham. The spiritual nature of that relationship is under review here, and the language now turns fairly naturally to the marriage relationship which Judah has profaned. The Sinai covenant is often, as we know, depicted by the prophets in marriage terms, and the reference here in verse 11 may be to Judean apostasy (as it may be to intermarriage with aliens, a pressing matter of the times). The subject matter of the prophetic rebuke of verses 13–16 is difficult to determine. The text of verse 16 is uncertain, and the use of the Hebrew verb "to put away" for "divorce" is most unusual. It is unclear, then, whether divorce is actually in the prophet's view here, or he is simply making a further attack upon idolatry. In any case, the people's covenant breach of the Sinai arrangement is clearly in mind.

Messenger of Judgment (Mal. 2:17–3:5)

Such covenant breach invites response. God himself will come to judge those who ridicule the absence of his judgment (Mal. 2:17). The identity of the messenger of Malachi 3:1, who is seemingly to be equated with the messenger of the covenant in the same verse, is difficult. The verse contains references to Isaiah 40:3 and also to Exodus 23:20, both positively indicating divine direction to the Promised Land. Malachi 3:1 points to the land's retention, though this messenger is the deliverer of a threat to the existence of the community in the land. There is a hint that the messenger of 3:1 is to be identified with someone already on the scene, though his role will clearly be taken up in the Elijah figure of 4:4–6. The Lord of the verse is clearly Yahweh, who is about to visit his house in judgment (3:2). This passage may include an allusion to the ministry of Ezra, who, as a covenant-renewal figure (Neh. 8), would then anticipate the Elijah of chapter 4. Since the offerings of Judah and Jerusalem will be acceptable only when cleansed, the social malpractices to which 3:5 refers must be judged.

Call to Repentance (Mal. 3:6–12)

If 3:6 is taken (as is most natural) with what follows, then the section refers to God's covenant constancy despite the continued defection of his people (v. 7). Judah is now invited to repent, to adopt a proper attitude to the worship structure, and to support the system of tithes and offerings, in regard to which they have been particularly negligent (vv. 7–9). In a situation similar to that of Haggai 1:6–11, they are promised, if they repent, covenant blessings in the form of renewed fertility in the land (Mal. 3:10–11). The section ends appropriately with an allusion to the Abrahamic promises: "all nations will call you blessed, for you will be a land of delight" (v. 12).

Judgment and Salvation (Mal. 3:13–4:3)

No response to the previous call seems to have been made. The basic charges are therefore repeated in this section, namely, abuse of the temple and sacrificial system, and concentration upon materialism and its fruits (Mal. 3:13–15). But now a response occurs from "those who feared the LORD" (v. 16), perhaps a remnant group, and to them the promises of Exodus 19:3–6 are virtually repeated in Malachi 3:17. Perhaps verse 18 recognizes that right worship (the word *serve* is often used cultically in the Old Testament) is the object of election. The contrast between judgment upon the community and salvation for the elect in terms of the day of Yahweh is then made in 4:1–2, with the final and absolute destruction of the wicked promised in verse 3.

Faithful Obedience Required (Mal. 4:4–6)

The point of the book is thoroughly brought out in this appendix. Yahweh is faithful to his covenant, but he requires a response from the community of the day. Before the final day of the Lord comes, there will be an Elijah-type prophet who will declare the real issues set before the people of God. The coming of this Elijah (in terms of 1 Kings 18–19) will mean a restating of the covenant demands. After this Elijah, the day of the Lord or the coming of God will occur. If the Elijah initiative should fail, then the final covenant curses will fall upon Israel for covenant breach. Of course, these closing verses were fulfilled in the ministry of John the Baptist, which was followed by the day of the Lord, coming in the person of Jesus.

Malachi concludes the prophetic corpus and closes the Greek (and thus our English) Old Testament canon on this fitting note of the cleansing required by the community as a prelude to covenant renewal. Israel is potentially under a curse, for her assent to the covenant only in name will destroy her. This has been the essential message of Israelite prophecy from Samuel onward. Under Malachi, the prophetic movement concludes (through the coming Elijah figure) its witness to Israel on the high note of pronounced covenant emphasis on which it had, with the inauguration of the monarchy, begun.

Part **4**

The Books of the Writings

25

Psalms

The third and final division of the Old Testament canon contains miscellaneous material (poetry, wisdom literature, and history). Some of these works contain undoubtedly old material, and some of them (e.g., Psalms and Proverbs) are anthologies. Liturgical influences account for the presence of certain books within this division of the Hebrew canon. Each of the five Megilloth ("scrolls") is associated with a specific Jewish festival: Ruth with Pentecost, the Song of Solomon with Passover, Ecclesiastes with the Feast of Tabernacles, Lamentations with commemoration of the fall of Jerusalem, and Esther with Purim. Books such as Daniel, Ezra-Nehemiah, and Chronicles owe their presence in the group either to the date of their emergence (after the canonical process of history and prophecy had been completed) or to their form (Daniel). The collection is headed by the Book of Psalms, to which we now turn. The canonical order of the Masoretic text will be followed in the remainder of our Old Testament presentation.

The Structure of the Psalms

The Book of Psalms is an anthology whose movement or structural unity cannot be analyzed precisely. (The title is from Greek *psalmos*, "song, hymn." Originally the book appears to have lacked a title; later the Heb. word *těhillîm*, "praises," was applied.) Psalmody in Israel was, of course, much older than this collection; indeed, some of the most theologically significant literature in Israel appears early in poetic form (e.g., the "Song of the Sea" of Exod. 15). Whatever the origin of the various individual psalms may have been, they finally all became cultic in the sense that Psalms now represents in its final form the hymnbook of the second temple. This fact alone cautions us from relying too much upon historical-critical approaches as we endeavor to understand the meaning of particular psalms. The function of many individual psalms within the cult may, however, be inferred from their form. Any analysis of particular psalms or of the book as a whole must, of course, emphasize function. It is equally clear that the Book of Psalms reflects the experience of believers and thus the household of faith. It may therefore be expected not to initiate particular theological themes or emphases, but rather to seek to preserve them. Caution must be exercised when liturgical material of the Psalter is used to postulate an emphasis (such as a theology of kingship) which differs from, or is nowhere else attested in, the rest of the Old Testament.

Psalms is divided into five books (Pss. 1–41, 42–72, 73–89, 90–106, and 107–50). The first four conclude with a doxology, while Psalm 150 is a doxology which concludes the entire Psalter. Perhaps this division is as old as the time of the chronicler, for 1 Chronicles 16 draws upon Psalm 106 and follows with what amounts to a doxology, a reflection of the use of that psalm in the Psalter. The age of this fivefold division and the reasons for it are disputed. Perhaps it reflects the Pentateuch, a suggestion which is supported by the fact that the Pentateuch was divided into 153 sections for synagogue reading. Certainly, however, this somewhat artificial division indicates the anthological character of the whole and its gradual compilation.

Hints as to the way the whole book came into being are offered principally by the psalm titles (Wilson 1985, 155–62). Authorship seems to have been a predominating concern in the arrangement of books 1–3. Almost every psalm in book 1 is either expressly or implicitly ascribed to David (this is known from the superscription or, in the case of Pss. 10 and 33, by their relationship to the preceding psalm); here the preponderating divine name is Yahweh. Book 2 opens with Korah psalms (Pss. 42/43–49), while the transition to the additional Davidic psalms which follow is heralded by the intrusion of an Asaph psalm (Ps. 50). Psalms

51–65 are Davidic, as are 68–70, with which the untitled Psalm 71 seems closely connected. The transition between the two small Davidic collections is made by the repeated use of the title *choirmaster* in the psalm headings (Pss. 64–70). Book 2 ends with Psalm 72, which is dedicated to Solomon and concludes with a doxology. Noticeable also in book 2 is the preponderance of the divine name Elohim.

Book 3 also heavily features authorship. It begins with an Asaph collection (Pss. 73–83), while the subsequent Korah collection (Pss. 84–85 and 87–88) is split by a solitary Davidic psalm (86). The book concludes with a single psalm ascribed to Ethan (Ps. 89), but this one is similar in type to Psalm 88. In books 4 and 5 authorship is less prominent (only nineteen are credited, seventeen of them to David). Small collections within these books may be detected: the Psalms of Ascents (Pss. 120–34), functionally related also by their apparent use during Israel's major festivals; Psalms 113–18, traditionally associated with the Passover; and the fivefold conclusion to the book, the Hallel Psalms (146–50). More than this we cannot safely say, but the statement at the end of Psalm 72 that "the prayers of David, the son of Jesse, are ended" indicates a collection earlier than our fivefold division and suggests that the present book was formed chronologically, not liturgically. We may infer from 1 Chronicles 16:4 that Levites were preparing hymn collections in David's time, and from 2 Chronicles 29:30 that Asaph and Davidic collections existed by Hezekiah's time. No satisfactory account of our present numbering can be advanced; indeed, the Hebrew and Greek texts differ on the numbering.

Titles of the Psalms

Only a small minority of the psalms are without a title or some descriptive information. Many of the titles appear to describe function (e.g., *mizmôr*, "psalm," more than fifty times; *šîr*, "song," thirty times), some are clearly musical directions (e.g., *lamĕnaṣṣēaḥ*, "to the choirmaster," some fifty-five times), some refer directly to cultic use (e.g., Ps. 92, "for the Sabbath"), some advance historical information on the setting of the psalm (Pss. 3, 7, 18, 34, 51–52, 54, 56–57, 59–60, 63, 142), while still others ascribe authorship or indicate relationship. This matter of relationship is difficult, since the Hebrew preposition *lĕ-* can have several meanings. The phrase *lĕdāwid*, for example, can be translated "for David," "belonging to David," "by David," or "concerning David." In the last analysis we are dependent upon the content of the psalm, the particular type of Hebrew poetry, and probability. If the titles are not original, they are at least a useful aid as to how the Jewish community interpreted individual psalms.

Interpretation of the Psalms

Up until the middle of the nineteenth century, the psalms were classified by their titles or by their content. At the end of that century Hermann Gunkel classified them by what he judged to have been their relationship to the cult, that is, their intended use in a recurrent social or liturgical context. He defined five major types: hymns of praise, thanksgiving psalms, community laments, individual laments, and royal psalms. Minor types included songs of Yahweh's enthronement, wisdom psalms, pilgrim psalms, victory songs, community psalms of thanksgiving, and prophetic Torah psalms. For the most part Gunkel's classification has been adhered to. In particular, many Scandinavian scholars (led by Sigmund Mowinckel) have insisted upon a cultic origin for psalmody. The problem with such views is the distinction which must be drawn between origin and function. Undoubtedly, many of the psalms were of individual composition. Such psalms eventually acquired a liturgical function which provided the occasion for their collection. In the last analysis, similarity of psalm types refers to the similar way in which certain psalms were used in worship.

Attempts by other scholars to find a major cultic connection such as a fall festival or a royal Zion feast to provide a basis for most or much of the content of the Book of Psalms are called into question by the special pleading that such attempts intrinsically contain. In the case of Hans-Joachim Kraus (1966, 203–5), for example, the supposition is that Israel's confession of divine kingship could not have been early, even though the acknowledgment of the divine kingship of a deity was fairly universal in the ancient Near East.

Some note should be taken of the major modifications which Claus Westermann has made to Gunkel's thesis, again with general acceptance. Westermann has shown that Gunkel's division between the hymn of praise and the thanksgiving psalm is too forced, since the basic character of the thanksgiving psalm is praise, a report of what God has done and a reaction to it. Westermann rightly points out that the *Sitz im Leben* of the hymn of praise and the thanksgiving psalm (for which his own terms are descriptive praise and declarative praise, respectively) is not the cult, as Gunkel had argued, but Yahweh's intervention in the form of national or individual salvation. The backbone of the Psalter, suggests Westermann, is the lament. This type of psalm is a petition and thus a prayer for a change of the condition described. The design of the lament is therefore to secure God's intervention. Understood this way, the lament is a powerful witness to God's activity and thus anticipates psalms of praise for deliverance from the adversity described.

Admitting that there are various subtypes, Westermann in the main

divides the ingredients of Gunkel's classification into two ways of praying: plea (lament) and praise (hymn and thanksgiving). Thus he retains
classification but with the important difference that he emphasizes the
function of a psalm in liturgical use rather than its formal literary type.

Hebrew Poetry

A brief word must be offered on the subject of Hebrew poetry. It is generally held that the two ingredients which separate Hebrew poetry from
prose are parallelism and meter. There are various types of parallelism,
which usually operates between two lines:
1. *Synonymous*—a close similarity exists between the two lines.
2. *Synthetic*—the second line develops the thought of the first.
3. *Emblematic*—the second line illustrates the thought of the first.
4. *Climactic*—the second line repeats, with emphasis, the thought
   of the first.
5. *Antithetical*—the second line reverses the thought of the first.

It must be remarked, however, that the definition of Hebrew poetry is
a matter of some considerable dispute and doubt. The concepts of parallelism and meter as determinative have recently been challenged in the
interests of a classification based upon "line form," that is, upon the
grammatical and syntactical similarity between lines. The difficulty
with this approach is that it blurs the distinction between poetry and
prose. This recent challenge has not yet seriously threatened the older
appeal to parallelism. Finally, it must be said that, to date, all attempts to
analyze satisfactorily the metric patterns of Hebrew poetry have failed.

The Major Emphasis of the Psalms

The Book of Psalms is a compendium of biblical theology, and issues
touching every aspect of Old Testament thought and life are taken up
within it. There is, however, an overriding emphasis, which is broadly
suggested by the introduction and conclusion.

It is agreed that Psalm 1 provides a formal introduction to the book.
The concern of this carefully structured psalm is the two basic ways to
live. The right way is the way that delights in Yahweh's *tôrâ*; it will ensure that "blessedness," the note on which the Psalter opens, will be realized in one's personal life. The psalm first puts this idea negatively, that
there can be no happiness for those who walk in the way of sin. The truly
happy are those who find their center for living in a meditation upon
God's will for life, namely *tôrâ*. The Book of Psalms thus places before us
the theme of how life is to be lived. When we consider further that the
Hebrew title of the book is "Praises" *(těhillîm)*, we are left with the con-

viction that Psalms provides praise to Yahweh for having left us an indication of the correct way in which life is to proceed, no matter what
our circumstances. This concept of the book as praise is reinforced by
the fact that the Psalter, divided editorially into five books, concludes
with a fivefold flourish of Hallelujah Psalms (Pss. 146–50), introduced
and concluded by "Praise the LORD!" The final psalm is a litany of praise
to Yahweh as Creator and Redeemer. Psalms, a book written by men to
God, has become canonized through its use in general worship to depict
the experiences of life.

The Psalter is thus a book of praise proclaiming that God, as Creator
and Redeemer, has given to Israel through the Torah, through the revelation of himself in history, the possibility of new life and a complete indication of how it is to be lived. By this witness of Old Testament saints
and the presentation of their experiences in all facets of life, we are encouraged to trust Yahweh for the future as others have trusted him in the
past. Of course not all the psalms have reference to what God has done;
many of them are eschatological, referring to what God will finally do.
But here again, Old Testament eschatology rests upon the character of
Yahweh and his interventions in history.

Enthronement Psalms

Gunkel suggested that psalms such as 47, 93, 96–97, and 99 were
composed to celebrate the annual enthronement festival of Yahweh as
universal King. Mowinckel translated *yĕhowâ mālāk*, the liturgical formula occurring in these psalms (though *'ĕlōhîm* is the divine name in
the phrase in Ps. 47), as "Yahweh has *become* king," and postulated analogies with the Babylonian New Year festival, which celebrated the victory of the city-god of Babylon, Marduk, over the elements of chaos, a
victory which had brought creation into being. Mowinckel concluded
that the New Year festival was the occasion on which Yahweh's control
over the universe was reasserted. In addition to Gunkel's enthronement
psalms, Mowinckel associated approximately another forty with the
group.

There is in principle no objection to the notion of an enthronement
festival, if a liturgical presentation of something which had happened in
the past is in view. Two points, however, deserve attention. The first is
that the contested phrase *yĕhowâ mālāk*, which gave rise to the hypothesis, ought to be translated "Yahweh *is* king." We have thus an acclamation formula celebrating Yahweh's eternal kingship, clear from his
lordship over creation (to which the core psalms in this group, 47, 93,
96–97, and 99, all refer). Second, there is a pattern in these psalms which
points to Yahweh's eternal kingship: (1) through mythic analogies crea-

tion is presented as a cosmic victory, and (2) there are references to the history of salvation or to deductions to be drawn from it. Creation and history are thus narrowly tied together in all of these psalms. It is therefore invalid to refer to such psalms as enthronement psalms, since such a notion suggests the loss of authority and then its renewal. The eternal kingship of God was an Old Testament postulate and a major focus of worship. It would be strange indeed if liturgy did not reflect this emphasis.

Royal Psalms

Gunkel also pointed out that many psalms give prominence to the place of the Israelite king (Pss. 2, 18, 20–21, 45, 72, 101, 110, 132, 144:1–11). He argued that such psalms were used on important occasions in the life of the king. (This point has been so developed that some scholars take many, if not most, psalms to be royal.) Indeed, without any corroborative evidence in the Old Testament beyond the Psalms, the involvement of the Israelite king as Yahweh's representative in an assumed New Year festival was suggested. Here he combated and was overcome by the forces of chaos, which were an ever-present threat to Israel's stability. In a process of ritual humiliation he was delivered over to and then rescued from Sheol, betokening, as representative of Israel, the nation's passage through this threat. But this postulation of an annual dramatization makes too much of kingship, which arrived relatively late upon Israel's historical scene.

It is possible to hold a view of "sacral kingship" which sees the Israelite king—in common with his ancient Near Eastern counterparts—as the regulator and dispenser of blessing for Israel, as its corporate head (see Pss. 22, 28, 61, 63, 71, 89, 144, all of which probably refer to the king). It is clear that he is regarded as a divine appointee assured of divine protection and blessings (Ps. 2:6; 18:50; 21:3; 78:70; 89:18). The thought of several of the psalms, however, goes well beyond historical kingship and is clearly messianic. In such psalms the king's role as an adopted son, his spectacular victories, his priestly prerogatives, and other messianic motifs are extravagantly presented (e.g., Pss. 2, 45, 72, 89, 110, 132). These avowedly messianic psalms explain the extreme interest in historical kingship which the Psalms betray, providing a religious understanding of the king as an ideal figure which ran quite contrary to historical experience.

Finally, we note briefly that many theories have gathered around such terms in the Psalms as "wicked," "righteous," "poor," and "I." These terms have been variously interpreted as corporate or individual, as lay or royal designations. But the Psalter is a comprehensive book of Israel's experience, an anthology drawn from her religious history. Further, there can be little doubt that earlier psalm settings have been changed by liturgical function. Thus it may well be unwarranted to assume that such terms are applied consistently or unequivocally.

Creation, exodus, Zion theology, the law as God's light to the redeemed, God in various roles (Warrior, Judge, Shepherd), Sinaitic and Davidic covenant, and eschatological expectation all find their place within the compendium of the Psalms. But most of all, the Book of Psalms provides the great description of the life of faith, its blessings, its struggles, and its prospect. As Westermann has pointed out, the various types of psalms point us to a circle of faith. Descriptive praise for what God has done leads to the lament, in which attention is drawn to the condition of the psalmist, which is contrary to what the history of salvation might suggest for a member of the people of God. Lament changes to plea and then to the certainty of being heard—a typical movement in the lament psalms. Answered prayer in turn leads us into the declarative praise of thanksgiving, which gives expression to our experience of the character of God, to whom all praise is due.

26

Job

Wisdom Literature

Unlike the prophetic books, which assume special revelation, the wisdom literature is general and almost universal in its pronouncements. Most of the events of salvation history (exodus, conquest, etc.) are absent from this material, which concentrates upon the regular rather than the unique. There are hardly any national references beyond those which pertain to the king. The absence of these themes is occasioned by the fact that the wisdom literature relates people to their world more generally than do the books of salvation history. In short, the wisdom movement is operating within a wider framework than that of redemption. It is finally concerned with that harmony of orders which the created structure, animate and inanimate, must exhibit. We have drawn attention to a series of biblical covenants operative between God and his world since creation, covenants in which God's purposes for his world are revealed. The wisdom literature of the Old Testament is a broad call for individuals to operate within the limits which a theology of creation itself provides.

215

The books of Job, Proverbs, and Ecclesiastes account for more than half of the use of such terms as "wise" and "wisdom" in the Old Testament. They all share an interest in the development of pithy sayings, and all concern themselves with common intellectual problems relating to people and their world. While the difference between such books is great, they do seek to observe human character on the widest plane and to study its consequences. Since the interest in these books is anthropological, the neglect of the concerns of salvation history is understandable.

However, the integration of wisdom and salvation history is easily effected since both stand within the broad horizons of creation theology. In the wisdom books, creation is presupposed rather than expounded, as the search for order and regularity within the world goes on in a manner which displays the necessity of such a presupposition. And as for salvation history, we know that those who have been redeemed were created by God and are living in his world. They are challenged to live out their life in this world as part of God's order of creation. God has made the same universe available to believer and nonbeliever. The facts do not change, but there are differences in the construction which the particular world-view places on the facts. Challenged by one's world, each individual is confronted with personal limitations, the element of unpredictability which must characterize it as divinely created, and one's own misuse of it. But it is not the case that no distinction is drawn between the secular and the sacred in these books. For it is made clear in Job, Proverbs, and Ecclesiastes that the fear of Yahweh provides the context within which wisdom will operate. As such it is the beginning of wisdom.

The Nature and Structure of Job

The atmosphere of the Book of Job is non-Israelite and patriarchal. Its dating is unsure—certainly no criteria for dating are afforded by the fairly widespread use of Aramaic forms within the book, since these could point equally to an early as well as to a late date. The book exhibits the epic form, in which prose and poetry may naturally be intermingled.

To regard Job as an epic may well do justice to the form of the complete book, though the word *epic* must be used cautiously, for Job betrays an intensity of personal feeling which is foreign to the detachment of the earlier epic. To see the book as offering a parallel to the laments of the Psalms speaks only to the form of the dialog of the book. It ignores the fact that the poetic dialogs of the Book of Job do not function as the lament psalms do, to engender confidence and praise, and it ignores the place of the epilog and prolog as providing the key to the book. The category of drama has often been adduced for the book, but this is to apply a literary anachronism, since Jewish drama appears much later as a form. To apply the term *comedy* to Job is to misunderstand its theological purpose. None of the comparable materials of the ancient Near East offer proper parallels for this stimulating Old Testament book. Certain judicial features are present, but to regard it as an extended legal dispute is to account for only a fraction of its material.

Most of the prose in the book is found in the introduction (chaps. 1–2) and conclusion (42:7–17). A lament from Job (chap. 3) connects the prose introduction to the ensuing dialogs of chapters 4–26, in which Job's three friends (Eliphaz, Bildad, and Zophar) speak in turn and, with the exception of the last round of the debate (in which no speech by Zophar is offered and thus no answer from Job given), are in turn answered by Job. Job 27–28 appears to be a new movement by Job, a presentation of his own theological credentials kept intact during the heat of controversy. In chapters 29–31 Job reviews his case, appealing for a divine verdict. This is followed, however, by the judgment of Elihu, a final human summation from a detached onlooker (chaps. 32–37). The divine speeches of Job 38–41 then introduce Job's response in 42:1–6. The book thus offers the following outline:

1–2	Prolog—in the heavenly council
3–26	Job versus the friends; the three cycles of addresses
27–28	Job's impeccable orthodoxy maintained
29–31	Job rests his case
32–37	Elihu's solution to Job's problem
38–41	God's solution
42:1–6	Job's joyful response
42:7–17	Epilog—The restoration of Job

The Prolog and Epilog (Job 1–2; 42:7–17)

Since the prolog and epilog provide the understanding for the book, we first consider their content. Job 1:1–5 introduces us to this revered patriarchal figure, prosperous and yet righteous. We are then moved to the scenario of the heavenly council, where the Satan, who seems to be more than merely a roving advocate of the council, indeed a cynical accuser of the brethren in this parable (see Andersen 1976, 79), issues a challenge to God regarding the basis upon which Job's righteousness rests (vv. 6–12). The fact that two conflicting opinions exist in heaven underlies the issue which will be debated in this book. The Satan (the prosecuting attorney in the heavenly council) asserts that Job is righteous because he is blessed; God counters with the insistence that Job has been blessed because he is righteous. We shall see that the friends put forward the Satan's case, while Job argues the divine case. The stage is now set for the contest that will work itself out in the dialog. The issue is whether God will be vindicated in his judgment of Job, whom he has declared to be righteous and blameless (1:8). Will the divine reputation which has been hazarded on Job be preserved? Of course, we know it will, and we know now that in the dialogs which follow, even though Job is overthrown by calamity, he will retain his uprightness.

The challenge to Job is progressively sharpened by the loss of his property and family (1:13–22) and then, after the Satan's more cynical assertion that Job would recant if he was smitten physically, by his being afflicted with terrible adversity to his body (2:7). The reader now clearly sees the issues. This suffering of Job is unmerited. It is not retributive; there is no connection here between an antecedent offense and its consequence. We have been led to expect that the dialogs which follow will reflect not only Job's innocence, but also the fact that, under remarkable adversity such as Job has now experienced, he will not break. At once we are led also to see that the book is not concerned about suffering as such (since the basic issues are raised in 1:9–10, a point before Job's suffering begins), though faith upheld under adversity is a major theme. A still broader theme broached by Job is the existence of evil in our world and proper reactions to it.

The prose epilog in 42:7–17 completes the book. The Satan does not appear, since the test has been concluded. And indeed his place in the epilog (as in the dialogs) has been taken by the "friends," who occupy as disputants the place that the Satan had occupied in the prolog. We are told that the friends stand condemned but that Job is right. We are not told in detail how these judgments have been worked out, but we guess that by Job 42:6 he has come up with an appropriate personal response to his difficulties. We gather, judging from the Satan's cause-and-effect view that righteousness follows blessing, that in the dialogs the friends have largely taken a position of self-interest, and they are thus clearly wrong.

Job is then restored, as an act of grace, to a position twice as prosperous as he had been before God exposed him to testing. And what is more, the narrative elevates Job at the end to one who as intercessor influences the councils of heaven by which he himself has been affected. Job 42:10–17, which conveys the act of restoration, does not offer a doctrine of reward. Rather, what is being affirmed is the generosity of God.

Three Cyclic Addresses (Job 3–26)

The point of Job's lament in Job 3 is not to curse God's part in creation, nor is it a call for the destruction of creation. Job has already declared that he is prepared to accept good or evil from the hand of God—in effect, to trust, though he be slain. In chapter 3 he merely calls for release from the life in which he has ceased to see further opportunity. Sheol now has become the place of rest and repose for Job and offers a new threshold of hope (v. 17). Three cycles of addresses follow in which Job's friends, as the representatives of current wisdom, speak in order of age. While slightly different approaches to Job's problems are evident within the cycles, the speeches are somewhat repetitive and will not be traced in detail here.

Starting with the premise that God protects the lot of the righteous (4:1–6), Eliphaz and then Bildad and Zophar develop the inference that since Job is unprotected from adversity, he must be unrighteous. Within the first round the friends skirt the point at issue, which is the magnitude of Job's sufferings, and urge Job to come to terms with his hidden but unconfessed sin. From this position they never retreat, thus advocating an ironclad doctrine of retribution which, in its firmest presentation (see Bildad in 8:1–7), binds God to his world, leaving him no room to move.

Job, for his part, claims in this first round no more than that his sufferings are incommensurate with whatever fault may lie behind them (chaps. 6–7, 9–10, 12–14). He himself does not claim blamelessness (as Zophar asserts in 11:4), and by the end of the second round of speeches (chap. 21) Job has reached a position which categorically denies the position of his friends on retribution. The facts of the case, Job maintains, do not support the friends' cause, and he pushes the illogic of their attitude to its ridiculous conclusion.

Job asks only that his friends understand his plight. He agrees that an individual is accountable for conscious sins, but he is not aware of having sinned (6:24–25). In a poignant parody of Psalm 8 Job asserts that God has become his enemy, evoking the need for a personal audience with God (Job 7:11–21). No notion of a lawsuit to bring God to the bar is developed in these chapters, not even in Job's response to Bildad in the controversial chapter 9. Job is concerned as to how he might be vindicated, for he is certain that if he had the opportunity to confront God, he would be cleared. At the very least he would find out why he has been afflicted (9:16). What is at issue in this densely packed chapter is an understanding of the nature of a right relationship with God. Once that is understood, the difficulties of life will vanish, for they will be understood also. Of God's power and God's goodness he is convinced. He would be content if only God would tell him why he is suffering (see Job 7:20–21). The lawsuit issue is raised in Job 9 (see vv. 1–4) only to be dismissed by Job in this long speech (chaps. 9–10) which is a reiteration of his basic confidence in God as a faithful Creator. Yet in his longing for death (10:18–22) he has not moved from his position of chapter 3.

In his final speech of the first round, Job asserts that though God were to slay him, yet would he trust (13:15, KJV, NIV), affirming in this way not only his basic commitment, but also his acceptance of the underlying goodness of God. Job is thus all the more puzzled as to why God has acted as he has (vv. 24–25). Job 14 is a reflection upon the brevity of life and its purposelessness outside of the possibility of a life beyond this human dilemma. The primary theme in his second round of speeches (chaps. 16–17, 19, 21) is not hostility to God (16:6–17), but what seems to be the reverse! Job remains confident of final vindication (16:18–17:16), for he has a heavenly mediator (16:19) and does not rely upon the favor of his friends. He can understand neither why God has forsaken him (19:7–22) nor the attack of his friends (vv. 2–6). In the famous passage Job 19:23–29, he contemplates death, confident that after death there will be the possibility of contact with God, the experience that he has sought.

In the last round of the speeches, Job's arguments are longer (chaps. 23–24, 26), while those of the friends are curtailed, an indication of the direction in which the narrator is moving. Job still wishes to come before God (23:1–7), but God is inaccessible (vv. 8–17). Only Eliphaz in this round offers an effective speech (chap. 22). Bildad has virtually nothing to add (chap. 25), while Zophar does not even enter the ring. Clearly the friends' arguments have been totally rejected by the author. Job 26 is Job's final response to the three. After a short reply to Bildad (vv. 2–4), the chapter paints a magnificent picture of God, which anticipates the theophany of chapters 38–41.

Job never denies that he is a sinner. He affirms only that he cannot see any particular sin which has brought on this present crisis in his affairs. He never retracts from his position of absolute trust (Job 2:10), though he is tormented by the strange posture which God has evidently adopted toward him. The friends are inflexible in maintaining that Job's hidden faults are responsible for his present plight. Only occasionally throughout the dialogs do these representatives of traditional wisdom address the real issues. (See, e.g., the suggestion by Eliphaz in 5:17–27, which will be taken further by Elihu, that suffering is pedagogic.) We have reached the end of the dialogs, convinced that some personal encounter between God and Job is required.

Vindication of Job's Integrity (Job 27–28)

Job insists upon his personal integrity and hands over his case to God, asking for vindication in the face of his friends, who must in terms of their doctrine be subject to the fate of the wicked which Job so graphically depicts in 27:13–23. The ensuing magnificent poem on wisdom clearly reveals his impeccable orthodoxy. In Job 28 he meditates upon the illusory search for wisdom (vv. 1–11) and its inaccessibility (vv. 12–19). It is known only to God, who alone can reveal it (vv. 20–27). It is extremely significant that the fear of Yahweh, which is the beginning of wisdom (and indeed the traditional formulation of theological wisdom), is characteristic of Job (28:28; cf. 1:1). Such fear is the sole context in which a knowledge of God can be developed. The use of the divine name *Adonai* in verse 28, its only occurrence in the Book of Job, may underscore Job's uprightness and link him with orthodox wisdom.

Job's Dilemma and Elihu's Speeches (Job 29–37)

Job 29–31 reviews, as a final speech from Job, his past, acknowledging the great blessings he has received (chap. 29). These favors have all been lost, however, and he is now mocked by his friends (chap. 30). In his dilemma Job utters a great oath of innocence and places his case before God (chap. 31). We are now ready for the theophany of chapters 38–41, which is, however, preceded by the speeches of Elihu in chapters 32–37.

There is a wide range of opinion on the speeches of Elihu. Some judge their style to be pedestrian; others see it as artistic. Some regard them as mindless repetition of previous arguments; others think they offer the final solution to the problem. It is generally agreed, however, that their tone of command is a human anticipation of the imperative judgments to be delivered by the divine speeches which follow. They appear to be the author's last presentation of the attempt of secular wisdom to refute Job, a final human judgment preceding the divine.

Only in the fourth speech (chaps. 36–37) is new ground broken, as this speech functions to direct us to the divine speeches which follow. God's dealings with human beings are not simply in terms of rewards and punishments. They are also remedial and pedagogic (a position which Eliphaz earlier anticipated—5:17–27). Calamity in life brings its opportunity for trust, and thus the full answer to Job's problem cannot be found in the appeal to justice. The argument moves from the wisdom of God to his power, and thus to the astonishing control of God over a universe from which, for Elihu, he is somewhat detached, and in which humankind is only a passive spectator of divine events. Elihu is right to emphasize that men and women should stop to ponder the works of God. But Job has done that (chap. 26). What he needs now is the encouragement which can be given only by personal confrontation with the Creator!

God's Solution (Job 38–41)

God now reveals himself in a storm, reminding us of the beginning of Job's difficulties (Job 1:13–19) and thus providing a hint that this appearance will lead to their resolution. In the magnificent assertion of creative power which follows, God says indirectly that he does not choose that human beings should know all the factors which are operating in this present world. We may see the results of God's handiwork, but we do not know his purposes. There is no hint in these speeches that Job is being treated as a sinner; rather he is being treated as one whose horizons need to be expanded. God has now appeared in answer to Job's appeal. Thus at the end of chapter 39 Job is challenged to respond. His response to this first divine speech is subdued. He confesses ignorance, but not sin (40:3–5). As Yahweh had spoken twice in the prolog, a second divine speech now ensues (40:6–41:34). Moral issues are now much more prominent. Job can no more pronounce judgment in the moral realm (40:10–14) than he could control the natural realm, the subject of the previous speech. He must, therefore, be content to leave his life and its issues with God. He dare not provoke God any more than he would provoke Behemoth (40:15–24) or Leviathan (chap. 41), denizens of land and sea! (Most identify Behemoth as the hippopotamus and Leviathan as the crocodile; some suggest that mythical monsters are in view.)

Job's Response (Job 42:1–6)

The limits of traditional wisdom have been explored by the dialogs, the addresses of Elihu, and the divine speeches. In the last of these a solution has been pronounced. Job has received assurance that divine justice and power are established over all creation. He is now content and says so in 42:1–6, though specific answers to his questions have not been given. He has seen that human events are part of a larger whole, while his friends have argued within the tight contours of a cause-and-effect chain of sin and punishment. Throughout the whole of his ordeal, Job has maintained his integrity, and thus the divine evaluation of him in the prolog has now been justified.

The Book of Job has not solved for us the problem of human suffering. Indeed, that is not its intent. Rather, it has demonstrated the intimate connection of God with his world and his careful and detailed superintendence of it. It has dispelled all mechanical views of God and thus liberated the doctrine of God's sovereignty. God gives life, and God withdraws it. Meaning in life cannot be understood within its human compass, but only within the framework of a vision of God which looks for justification of the present puzzles of human existence in a life which is yet to come. This is the message that the book so eloquently delivers.

27

Proverbs

The Book of Proverbs concentrates upon everyday life. Most of the salvation-history motifs (exodus, conquest, covenant, etc.) are absent from the book. It focuses on the usual, the regular, rather than on the unique. There are hardly any national references beyond the material which may refer to the king or to the court.

Proverbs is a book about wisdom and its application to human life. The Hebrew word ḥokmâ, "wisdom," refers broadly to some skill or expertise, a natural endowment that one may possess, intelligence of a most general kind. It seems, moreover, to be used more technically in the Book of Proverbs for what can be acquired by instruction (see 21:11) or by observation of one's world (see 6:6–8). We will consider the definition further after surveying the contents of the book. For the time being we will define wisdom as the theory of knowledge which equipped individuals in the Old Testament to understand themselves and their world. The notions of both technical excellence and moral competence are included in the Proverbs usage. Wisdom thus not only offers philosophic insights into one's world, but also is basic to scientific method. Wisdom is and always has been, however, the gift of God (cf. Deut. 4:6).

The Book of Proverbs conforms to the genre of instructional literature prevalent in the ancient world, particularly the Egyptian *seboyet,* which included three elements: (1) a title, (2) an introduction (either prose or poetry) setting out the basis upon which instruction would proceed, and (3) the basic contents, admonitions and sayings linked together in a way which highlighted their interdependence (Waltke 1979, 221–38). This pattern is clearly reflected in the structure of the Book of Proverbs: (1) the title (1:1); (2) an introduction containing the rationale for the whole book (1:2–7); and (3) instructional material, which begins with the praise of wisdom (1:8–9:18). No detailed arrangement seems to prevail in the material after Proverbs 9. Sometimes collections are evident, and sometimes a catchword provides a framework of order. The last section on the virtuous wife (31:10–31), however, clearly balances the earlier warning contained in chapters 1–9 against "the loose woman" and is an obvious epilog, the more so since the woman of 31:30 is one "who fears the LORD" (Blocher 1977, 5). These details and the fact that Proverbs 10:1–22:16 contains 375 lines (the numerical value, in Hebrew, of the name *Solomon*) point to the book as a very careful editorial compilation. The outline of the Book of Proverbs is as follows:

1:1	Title
1:2–7	Introduction; purpose of the book
1:8–9:18	Admonitions and addresses
10:1–22:16	The proverbs of Solomon
22:17–24:34	Sayings of the wise
25–29	Further Solomonic proverbs
30:1–14	Sayings of Agur
30:15–33	A numerical poem
31:1–9	Sayings of Lemuel
31:10–31	In praise of the virtuous woman

Purpose and Theme of Proverbs (Prov. 1:2–7)

A series of key terms is densely packed in Proverbs 1:2–6, all of which contribute to our understanding the purpose of the book even before its theme is explicitly stated in verse 7: "The fear of the LORD is the beginning of knowledge." The precise arrangement of key terms in verses 2–4 indicates the purpose of the instructional material to follow, while verses 5–6 indicate the effect upon the wise. Verse 7 sketches the general context in which this process must operate.

Wisdom, *ḥokmâ* (1:2a), is linked with the series of terms which follow (Nel 1982, 109). Verse 2 lists *mûsār,* "instruction" or "correction" (see 1:8; 3:11; 4:13), and then *bînâ,* "understanding," a term that in Proverbs carries the sense of a basic insight into life and the ability to respond properly to life's experiences (see 1:5; 2:2; 3:19; 4:5, etc.). A collection of three interrelated terms follows in verse 3b: *ṣedeq,* "righteousness," which in Proverbs seems to mean the ideal order and harmony to be appropriated and expressed by the wise (8:8; 12:17); *mišpāṭ,* "justice," or the action by which *ṣedeq* is expressed, mainly by judicial means (2:8; 24:23; 29:4); and *mêšārîm,* "equity," a subjective term indicating here the personal stance to the ideal order which *ṣedeq* connotes (8:6; 23:16). These three terms imply a defined order to be brought into being and expressed by official and personal action. One who is untutored—the "simple" *(pĕtî)* of verse 4—may thereby deal "prudently" *('ormâ)* on the basis of knowledge now available to him. To the uninstructed *(na'ar,* "youth," parallel in v. 4 to *pĕtî)* "knowledge" *(da'at,* used seventy times in Prov.) and "discretion" *(mĕzimmâ)* are now both available. This knowledge involves an objective content, a subjective reception thereof, and a decision to act upon the content received (Nel 1982, 110–15). There is a close relationship between "knowledge of God" and "the fear of Yahweh" (see 1:7, 29; 2:5; 9:10), while "discretion" indicates the pursuit and demonstration of what is good (2:11; 8:12).

Attention to the implication of these terms assures the wise man of an increase in basic understanding (1:5). One who is insightful will now be able to reconcile the tortuous problems of life and to understand the material which the remainder of the book presents (v. 6). It takes the simple facts of life and puts them in the form of proverbs (*māšāl,* v. 6). Compared or contrasted with other facts or experiences, these aphorisms, models, or paradigms have an incisive effect. (The word *mĕlîṣâ* in v. 6, "figure," a parallel to *māšāl,* indicates a cutting word that can penetrate by the starkness of its presentation.)

The introduction leads to the key statement in the book: "The fear of the LORD is the beginning of wisdom." This statement appears in 1:7 (with "knowledge" for "wisdom") and 9:10, thus forming a frame for the determinative first section of the book (see also 15:33; 22:4; 23:17). "The fear of the LORD" illuminates the intelligence and thus makes wisdom possible (note the parallel with "knowledge of the Holy One" in 9:10); it provides the context within which wisdom can operate. A range of meanings is possible for *rē'šît* ("beginning"), but the word most probably means "what necessarily comes first in a sequence." In Proverbs it is best translated "principle" or "essence" (Blocher 1977, 15). Since "fear" is the proper attitude to be taken before God as he reveals himself (Deut. 5:29), the total phrase conveys the idea that wisdom, which is the theme of the Book of Proverbs, is not merely a set of maxims to control human behavior, but rather a world-view, a rule of life which brings us into contact with the principles of order which control reality.

The Message of Proverbs 1–9

This key section comprises ten admonitions (1:8–19; chap. 2; 3:1–12, 21–35; 4:1–9, 10–19, 20–27; chap. 5; 6:20–35; chap. 7) as well as other material, including a wisdom poem (3:13–20), addresses by wisdom (1:20–33; chap. 8; 9:1–6, 13–18), and maxims (6:1–19; 9:7–12). Wisdom metaphors are fivefold: evangelist (1:20–33; 8:1–21), tree of life (3:18), a way (4:10–19), a craftsman (8:22–31), and Dame Wisdom (chap. 9). A common thread in all of these metaphors is the fact that choice is an essential component of life; this fact is best embodied in the notion of two ways, taken up in detail in 4:10–19.

After the first instruction, a warning against seduction by sinners (1:8–19), wisdom as evangelist stands at the head of the streets and calls (vv. 20–33). Proverbs 2 provides an instructional introduction to the series of discourses which extends to 7:27. Wisdom must be desired (2:1–4), but it is the gift of God (vv. 5–8). Therefore it will protect against adversity (vv. 9–11), though opposition will come from men of perverse speech (vv. 12–15). Verses 16–19 present the image of the seductive woman, which is probably to be related to fertility-cult practices and the sexual overtones associated with them. This image is balanced in verses 20–22 by the reward for fidelity, inhabitation of the ideal land. Chapter 3 presents the way to get true wisdom, which is devotion to Yahweh (vv. 1–12). Wisdom's blessing is life (vv. 13–18), since it provides harmony with the purposes of creation (vv. 19–20) and thus affords protection and confidence (vv. 21–35). Proverbs 4:1–9 offers the father's (i.e., teacher's) advice for life: Get wisdom! Verses 10–27 introduce the celebrated motif of two ways: the way of wisdom (vv. 10–13, 18) and the way of folly (vv. 14–17, 19). The way of wisdom, which is clear and straight and leads to life, is the way of righteousness. By contrast the way of folly is darkened with obstacles, and those who tread it live in darkness.

This theme of two ways continues virtually throughout the remaining addresses, as does the pattern of introducing each of the ten addresses with the words "my son." The eighth discourse (chap. 5) is a warning against adultery and the "loose woman," a message which is reinforced in the next discourse (6:20–35), while the tenth concludes the series on the note of the call of the adulteress herself, who has occupied a central position in four of the instructions (chaps. 2; 5; 6:20–35; and now chap. 7). She also features in the didactic poem of contrasts in Proverbs 9. She seems to personify the fertility practices so common in Israel. A love cultivated for Dame Wisdom, however, will keep the disciple from her seductions (7:4–5).

The theme of the two ways is designed to underline the compelling worth of choosing wisdom, a matter of emphasis also in the poetic and proverbial material which links or expands the ten instructions. Dame Wisdom protects her traveling companion from being preyed upon by the strange woman who entices with inviting speech (5:1–4), but whose feet travel the path leading straight to Sheol (5:5–8). The actual author of this protection is Yahweh, who works through wisdom, the true source of knowledge (3:21–26). Ultimate deliverance from the loose woman (2:16–19) and rescue from all false paths which threaten covenant fidelity thus rest with him.

Proverbs 8 addresses the question of how the meaning which is implicit in the ordered world can impress itself onto the mind of human beings. The chapter serves to integrate the instructional material which has preceded. The relationship between wisdom and Yahweh has been clear since 2:1–6, where a search for wisdom is in fact a search for Yahweh, not for wisdom as an end in itself. Thus this search leads to a knowledge of God, by which the world may be rightly ordered. In 3:19–20 we learned that wisdom was Yahweh's instrument in ordering creation. Proverbs 8 takes us further in this direction, discussing this key to ordered reality. On the one hand, wisdom provides us with an understanding of the nature of reality and is in its essence the provision of a right world-view, while on the other hand, wisdom and the knowledge she provides always remain elusive and mysterious.

The address of 8:1–21, which contains wisdom's summons, is striking for its first-person tenor. It is potentially able to be heard by all, since it is issued in the most public of places—the town entrance (v. 3). Wisdom calls the audience to live, in effect, in harmony with the order of creation. But there is more mystery here, for in verses 22–31 wisdom speaks of her preexistence, of her relationship to Yahweh as his master workman *('āmôn)* and his delight in the production of the world (v. 30). In verses 32–36 we reflect back on the beginning of the chapter, and summons now becomes ultimatum, a demand for such commitment as will produce a knowledge of what wisdom really is.

Finally, in Proverbs 9, where the first part of the book is summed up, Dame Wisdom and Dame Folly are pitted as two rivals. Both sit at the highest point in the city and call out to the simple. While wisdom's invitation leads to life, that of folly leads to death. Two alternative religious stances, two basic ways of looking at existence, are being contrasted here.

The Message of Proverbs 10–31

The remainder of the book is given over to admonitions in which parallelism of various sorts is employed. Typically, an imperatival note in the first line of a two-line couplet is complemented by a motivation offered in the second line. While the imperatival note demands orderly conduct, the motivation appended advances an argument from human experience. Put otherwise, while the admonitions speak of adhering to the order of creation, the motivation presents this appeal as reasonable. The basic framework of these admonitions has been provided by the exposition of the nature of wisdom in chapters 1–9. The starting point of these admonitions is the recognition of evil as a breach of the created order, a breach which can be repaired only by the apprehension of and insight into the higher principle of wisdom, to which the Book of Proverbs is directing our attention.

There is little discernible structure in the collections, though chapters 10–15 tend to be pragmatic, and 16:1–22:16 religious. Nor does any particular social setting dominate (Nel 1982, 76–82). A court setting occurs on a few occasions, a wisdom-school background is suggested by many of the traditional topics discussed, and there is some interrelationship with cultic interests. We cannot determine a *Sitz im Leben* from the form of the admonitions themselves. They do presuppose a structured society, but more than that we are unable to say.

Proverbs 22:17–24:34 consists of "sayings of the wise" given over to, among other things, instructions for administrators and admonitions to industry and sincerity. Chapters 25–29 provide the second miscellaneous Solomonic collection. (A good case has been made that the approximately 130 lines in this section reflect the numerical value of the name of their collector—King Hezekiah.) Proverbs 30:1–14 stresses the limitations of wisdom, and verses 15–33 provide a numerical poem. The sayings of Lemuel's mother (31:1–9) condemn lust, drunkenness, and oppression, and prepare us for the artistic close of the book, an acrostic poem on the theme of the "good wife" (vv. 10–31), perhaps a counterpoint to the "loose woman" of chapters 1–9.

Right living is the theme of the Book of Proverbs. True wisdom depends upon an understanding of God's purposes in creation, which have been particularized, as we know, in salvation history. (Whereas prophecy reflected upon and responded to salvation history, the wisdom movement directed its attention to what creation itself implied for human conduct.) In this sense creation (understood as God's providential government of the world) intersects with salvation history (i.e., his special relationship to Israel). Law, the subject of prophetic reflection, came to be seen as the revelation of the divine will in the most general terms and was thus able to coalesce with wisdom—not as demand, but as an explication of the right attitude to be adopted to divine revelation—once it became clear that ethical responses derive their rationale from the understanding that human beings must live as subordinate creatures in a world in which Yahweh intends harmony and order to prevail.

This world can be understood only within a framework of dependence upon Yahweh, who through wisdom brought it into being. This is the message which Proverbs proclaims. Any act directed against this divine order of creation is an evil act. The wise person will thus shun evil, while, on the contrary, the fool is rash and presumptuous (14:16).

We cannot be satisfied, however, with a view which converts wisdom into a mere search for order, for such a view makes the concept mechanistic and depersonalized. In the final analysis, wisdom is a gift, but it cannot be limited to the subjective apprehension of the gift. As gift, wisdom is potentially available to all within the domain of creation. Thus it is not merely God's order in this world, but it is a knowledge of divine order and the implications of such a knowledge. It is a word about the world, an objective truth which, as gift, may be subjectively grasped. Such a word is, however, available only to those who are willing to sit before it and submit to it. The fear of Yahweh, a world-view which puts Yahweh at the center, provides the context in which wisdom, as the revealed knowledge of God subjectively believed, will operate. The christological movement of the New Testament which links wisdom and Word is therefore not only understandable but demanded.

28

Ruth

The Book of Ruth is found within the Hebrew canon in the Writings, probably because of its liturgical use at the Feast of Pentecost. Its position between Judges and Samuel in the Greek Old Testament was doubtless dictated by its content. That position seems appropriate, however, for the book is probably a product of the early monarchy, displaying the interests of that period. The question of its dating is contested; for example, the argument from the use of Aramaic forms is two-edged, just as easily providing evidence for an early dating as for a late dating. Its title is perhaps a misnomer, since the book is about Naomi's family.

The book exhibits a fivefold division (chaps. 1; 2; 3; 4:1–17a; and then the concluding genealogy of David in 4:17b–22). The message is a simple one. A family calamity is gradually reversed by a series of remarkable divine interventions which are quite behind the scenes and whose nature must be inferred. The addition of the genealogy at the end makes it clear that the book is a demonstration of the mysterious way in which God works through the processes of history, bringing fulness of life out of seeming hopelessness (a major theme of the book) and controlling the destiny of Naomi's family. The story runs its own course with inter-vention by the narrator only in 1:6 and 4:13. The book also displays the unobtrusive but active piety of the believer of the judges period; the divine name is prominent, occurring most frequently in the prayers (1:8–9; 2:12, 20; 3:10; 4:11–12, 14; cf. 2:4).

On the simplest level, Ruth concerns redemption of the plot of land which apparently still belonged to Naomi but had fallen into the hands of others after her departure for Moab. On a deeper level, the commence-ment of the book, which underscores the famine in the land, is to be con-trasted with the conclusion of the book and the Davidic genealogy there. Such a contrast indicates that the book points in more general terms to Yahweh's covenantal *hesed* ("loyal love, kindness") as it serves to provide background for the later career of King David. Ruth is, then, the typical believer to whom rest in the land will be granted; at this level she symbolizes Yahweh's wider attitude to Israel. The book is structured as follows:

1	Famine to harvest
2	Gleaning in Boaz's field
3	Rest for Ruth and Naomi
4:1–17a	Resolution at the town gate
4:17b–22	Davidic genealogy

From Famine to Harvest (Ruth 1)

The general movement within the first chapter is from famine to har-vest, from abandonment of the land to return. Verses 1–7 recount the migration to Moab and the decision to return to Judah. The unfortunate circumstances and the double catastrophe which prompted the return are described. In four dialogs (1:8–10, 11–14, 15–17, 1:19c–21) Naomi takes the issue forward, raising in 1:8–9 the key themes of the book, namely, a home, a husband, and kindness, which are to be provided for Ruth. The troubles of this chapter—the emptiness encountered in the famine and in the deaths of Naomi's husband and sons (vv. 3–5)—are countered by the note of hope on which the chapter ends. While Naomi remains the point of reference in the chapter, the confession of Ruth at verses 16–17 is central. The mention of Naomi's return in verse 22 underscores Ruth's ethnic background and thus her conversion.

Gleaning in Boaz's Field (Ruth 2)

The dialogic pattern of Ruth 2—Ruth and Naomi (vv. 2–3), Boaz and the reapers (vv. 4–7), Boaz and Ruth (vv. 8–15a), Boaz and the reapers

(vv. 15b–16), and Naomi and Ruth (vv. 19–22; see Prinsloo 1980, 334)—
places the exchange between Ruth and Boaz at the center. In this chapter
about gleaning in Boaz's field, chance seems to play its part (2:3), but this
is simply the narrator's manner of indicating that no human intervention had thrown Boaz and Ruth together. Chapter 2 closes with the end
of the harvest period and thus the end of the connection between Ruth
and Boaz, with the connection between Ruth and Naomi now resumed.

Yet the dialog between Boaz and Ruth demands that the narrative be
taken further. In the presence of Naomi's kinsman, Ruth in exodus
terms has declared herself to be a "foreigner" (2:10). Boaz then proceeds
to define her position in Abrahamic terms (but with reference also to
1:15–18): she has left family and land (2:11). His benediction upon Ruth
(v. 12) begins the process of fulfilment, which is taken further in verse
20, where Naomi sees Boaz's action as a demonstration of divine ḥesed.
This kindness (cf. 1:8–9) will eventually issue in the rest to be provided
under David (4:17b–22).

Rest for Ruth and Naomi (Ruth 3)

Home, husband, and rest remain to be provided for Ruth, but the processes of ḥesed have begun! Naomi once again takes the initiative in
dialog (vv. 1–6). Her words both begin and end the chapter (vv. 16–18),
but the center of attention is the encounter between Boaz and Ruth
(vv. 7–15). The close correlation of chapters 2 and 3 is shown by the comparable formats. In both, Ruth is put into contact with Boaz by Naomi
(in an opening scene); in both, Boaz as kinsman is the provider (gleanings
only in 2:18, but in 3:17 a very substantial provision of food as a gift); and
both end with Naomi's comment upon the implication of the meeting
which has formed the center of each chapter.

While Ruth 2 deals with the establishment of the relationship with
Boaz (note that his name frames the chapter—vv. 1, 23), Ruth 3 identifies
him as the one who will provide rest for Ruth (cf. vv. 1 and 18; in the
latter, Ruth is simply to wait until the matter is resolved). Ruth's redemption is now assured, either by Boaz or by a nearer kinsman (v. 13).

Resolution at the Town Gate (Ruth 4)

The town-council setting in Ruth 4 is fascinating. The meeting between Boaz, the kinsman, and the elders in verses 1–8 concerns Naomi's
right to sell land, a unique reference in the Old Testament. However, the
right of inheritance accorded to the daughters of Zelophehad, who died
without male issue (Num. 27:1–11), may provide some parallel. Ruth

4:5 is puzzling, but the use of "buy" *(qānâ)* in reference to Ruth could mean "acquire by marriage" (E. F. Campbell 1975, 147). There are clear differences between the use of the levirate law in Ruth 4 and the remainder of the Old Testament; verse 5 may therefore indicate a local application of a more general law. Perhaps the notions of redemption and marriage are to be separated, for Boaz takes up the matter of redemption in the presence of the elders (vv. 2–4), but the matter of marriage before all the people as well (vv. 9–10; see Davies 1983, 231). The theme of emptiness and fertility is carried forward into the marriage between Boaz and Ruth by the blessing called upon the marriage in 4:11, where Rachel and Leah provide examples of barrenness followed by fertility.

As the orchestrator of all these events (4:13), Yahweh has made his own name famous in Israel (though v. 14 may also ambiguously refer to the child born to Ruth). The child is the real redeemer of Naomi and in this sense her son (v. 17). He (Obed) will also build Ruth's house, which will be definitively established by David. The Book of Ruth thus operates as a counterpoint to the Book of Judges, indicating the type of kingship which was to operate as a result of covenantal fidelity, and the tranquility that a true faith communicates, as opposed to the general disorder of the period of the judges.

The events of Ruth happened "in the days when the judges ruled" (1:1), that is, when the covenant was placed in considerable risk by Israel. Ruth indicates how Israel's future will be preserved, namely, by the extraordinary initiatives taken throughout her history by Yahweh. The book points to him as Israel's Redeemer, great in *ḥesed* (Exod. 34:6). Undoubtedly the genealogy at the end of the book reflects its intent—to record the divine intervention which protected the family of Naomi. At a time when the covenant was threatened, Yahweh's *ḥesed,* seen in this book as establishing and preserving personal relationships, was in fact establishing Israel's history, a history which would be consummated by the birth of David, the establisher of Israel's rest and the bearer of a famous name (Ruth 4:14; cf. 2 Sam. 7:9).

29

Song of Songs

Early disputes about the canonicity of the Song of Songs were virtually settled by the pronouncement of Rabbi Akiba that "the whole world is not worth the day on which the Song of Songs was given to Israel; all the writings are holy, and the Song of Songs is the holy of holies" (Mishnah Yadayim 3:5). Contrary to Akiba, however, the prevailing interpretation of this vexed book is literalistic, seeing it as a collection of love lyrics bound together by interrelated themes, refrains, and repetitions into a dramatic expression of love's experiences. Recent attempts to find precise structural patterns in the Song, for example, chiastic devices, overlook the natural divisions within the Song itself and have not proved convincing.

Largely discredited today is the allegorical interpretation of the Song of Songs. To avoid the difficulties which the Song poses, Jewish and Christian expositors had viewed it as an allegory of Yahweh and Israel or of Christ and the church. Such allegorical approaches, however, tend to be impositions upon the material and not expositions of it. The cultic-mythological approaches, popular earlier this century, which saw the

Song as based upon fertility-cult parallels, are also not appealing. The parallels cited are tenuous and fanciful, and what is alleged to be the principal point of connection (the motif of a dying and rising God) is nowhere to be found in the Song. The wedding-week theory, which makes the book a cycle of seven descriptive love songs (Arabic *wasfs*) in praise of the physical features of the partners, each song to be sung on a particular day of the wedding week, founders on the fact that we cannot discern seven clear sections into which the Song is divided. In addition, there is a time gap between such relatively modern customs and the biblical period. The once-accepted dramatic theory, popular in the last century, presupposes the use of a form unknown to Israel in the biblical period.

The best approach views the Song of Songs as a collection of lyrics linked by interrelated themes and characterized by repetition of motifs, a lack of progression, and abundant symbolism. Erotic images are commonly employed. While we must recognize Israel's restraints upon premarital sex and adultery, the sheer unabashed nature of the book indicates that the whole subject of human love could well be presented biblically with a freshness and an absence of inhibition that are uncharacteristic of modern presentations. The Solomonic associations may suggest the line of interpretation to be followed as we try to understand this book, namely, that it belongs to the reflective literature of Israel's wisdom movement, which laid claim to Solomon's name and which was committed to the investigation of what constituted an ordered life. The assignment of the book to Solomon, moreover, presents no insuperable difficulties. The linguistic objections based upon the occasional Persian or Greek word can be countered, while the association of the content with earlier Egyptian love lyrics might well indicate that the book is as old as the era of Solomon.

Structure of the Song

Chapter 1:1 is the title, while verses 2–4 (despite the internal change of person, which may be a stylistic feature) are in praise of the lover. Verses 5–6 present the beauty of the beloved as seductive, but withdrawn and unconventional. The extremes contrasted in these two verses—country and city, simplicity and sophistication—typify much of the ambiguity and poetic fancy which are so characteristic of this book (Landy 1983, 144–48). Whatever the reason, the beloved is the subject of rejection by her family; she has been forced into a controlled environment apart from her "own vineyard." Verses 7–8 project a rendezvous between the two lovers, whose different status in the world (as king and shepherdess?) separates them and threatens them. Verses 9–11 imaginatively liken the beloved to a royal mare, that is, to a beautifully adorned member of the king's entourage; in response she likens their love to fragrance experienced (vv. 12–14). Verses 15–17 express the mutual admiration of lover and beloved, illuminating their relationship by reference to appropriate natural images.

In the garden imagery of 2:1–7, the beloved is presented as a chaste lily, and the lover as an apple tree, protective and yet desirable, under which the beloved shelters and feasts. Verses 8–17 are bound together by the arrival and the departure of the lover and speak of the springtime of love. Next, 3:1–4 is a dreamlike sequence referring to the beloved's search for her lover. Verse 5 is a refrain, and verses 6–11 a celebration of the Solomonic wedding. Song of Songs 4:1–7 praises the physical features of the beloved. Verses 8–11 are unified by the mention of Lebanon (vv. 8, 11), which represents an image of inaccessibility and yet of great beauty and charm, not precisely demarcated as the garden is. Chapters 4:12–5:1 return us to the garden imagery. The beloved is the symbol of the garden (4:12–14), a well of life (v. 15), with the lover an outsider seeking entrance and finding it (4:16–5:1). In 5:2–7 the lover is lost and the beloved humiliated. A refrain and question follow (vv. 8–9), which introduce a section describing the lover (vv. 10–16) and balancing his loss reported in verses 2–7. The question put by the daughters of Jerusalem to the beloved (6:1) is then answered by her in a section dealing with a descent that the pair make to the idyllic garden separated from the complex world outside, so that love may be recaptured (vv. 2–12). Chapters 6:13–7:6 offer a detailed personal description of the beloved, supplemented by the further metaphors in 7:7–9 comparing her to a date palm, heavy with fruit, attractive and enticing.

In 7:10–13 the beloved issues an invitation to the lover to greet the spring. Then 8:1–7 introduces a round of deeply intimate encounters where the lover is both brother and outsider (v. 1), and led into the chamber of the beloved's mother (vv. 2–3). There follows an injunction to the daughters of Jerusalem (the city is a conventional foil for the rustic beloved in the Song) to help preserve the moment (v. 4). The beloved returns from the desolate land on the arm of her lover, restored by the recollection of the apple tree (a symbol of the generative principle) where love had been encountered (v. 5). The theme of the book—love is as strong as death—then follows (vv. 6–7).

Finally, 8:8–14 returns us to the scenario of 1:1–2:7. The beloved is restored to the family relationship, protected and unassailable, attractive and now to be defended. The beloved then speaks of herself in these terms (v. 10), confessing that she has found peace in her surrender. The metaphor of the vineyard of 1:5–6 resurfaces at 8:11. Perhaps the vineyard of 8:11 is Solomon's kingdom (or harem? see Falk 1982, 133), with the "keepers" his officials into whose care the beloved was committed. But now, in verse 12, she has her own vineyard, worth indeed a kingdom ("you, O Solomon, may have the thousand").

This imaginative collection appropriately closes with the reappearance of the garden theme. But now companions occupy it, and the beloved sings of it, giving it meaning and tangibility (Landy 1983, 206–10). Love stronger than death will return us to Eden, or near to it, as we hear this diffuse, but thematically related collection of lyrics evocatively present idealized love, the highest of all human relationships.

Thematic Considerations of the Song

Successive chapters are locked together by common themes and motifs such as the vineyard, particularly the garden, flowers, trees, blossoms, and fruit. The significant garden imagery is most developed in the central poem of the book (4:12–5:1) and in 6:2–12, both describing the beloved, although such imagery abounds throughout and is the note upon which the book closes (8:13). The predominance of this cluster of motifs takes us back to Genesis 2 and to the theme of perfect love, which finds its most heightened expression in this idealistic situation. That the message of the garden dominates the opening and closing sequences of the book (1:2–2:7 and 8:8–14) indicates the degree to which the tone of Song of Songs is set by this imagery.

The basic message of the book appears in the major statement of 8:6–7 ("love is strong as death") and speaks for the preeminence of love and of its intensity and perhaps ultimate agony. We are thus dealing in the book with an imaginative meditation upon the relative perfection which is human love. The experiences described introduce the lovers to a new-found paradise in which love surpasses all that riches can convey and for which Solomonic splendor and even a kingdom can be cast aside. The garden imagery identifies the experience as the summit of human joy (2:3, 13; 4:3, 13–14; 6:7; 7:2, 8; 8:5), while the imagery drawn from flora (2:1, 16; 4:5; 5:13; 6:11; 7:2, etc.) and fauna (2:12, 14; 4:5; 6:9; 7:3, with fawn and dove being the principal symbolism for the two lovers) appeals to the harmony of orders and the integration of nature and experience of which Genesis 2 and Eden speak.

Such human experiences virtually serve to reverse the effects of the fall (note how 7:10 reverses the language of Gen. 3:16), providing in this garden encounter a fountain of life (cf. 4:15). Yet the rapture of this human experience is inevitably balanced by the restlessness which is characteristic of all human relationships and ever threatens their dissolution.

Thus the Song has as its goal the human ideal "the twain shall be one flesh." The book therefore serves as an idealization and commendation of human marriage, even though marriage is fraught with problems and ever under stress. The frank character of its language echoes the somewhat similar language used by Israel's prophets in describing the covenant relationship. We may fairly conclude that the marriage relationship is being depicted as a microcosm of what the covenant was intended to produce within the people of God as a whole.

But love is possible only within the limits that the enclosed garden imposes and within the presuppositions that the Eden image conjures up—namely, within the framework of a complete commitment of the partners to each other, united by the bonds of a common faith. Thus in our real world the garden motifs of the Song are necessarily mingled with threats to the garden, a motif which the book variously represents as wild growth, wilderness, hostile irruptions, drought, and the like. Only in the garden—an Eden ideal which is often interpreted in terms of the partners as well as in terms of their experience (see 4:12–5:1 and 6:1–12, where the loss of the beloved turns the thoughts of the lover to the garden, and a descent into it recaptures love)—only in this idealized circle of personal relationships can human love reach the depths of intensity of strength and commitment for which this book speaks.

Since the Song of Songs is a symbolic representation of the course of ideal love, persons or figures cannot be pressed for extreme literal meaning (e.g., Solomon or the daughters of Jerusalem). Such a view does not lessen the significance of the message of the Song. Indeed, proper evaluation of the type of language within a book is a necessary judgment which must precede its interpretation. Of course, there is a pronounced element of subjectivity in this, but we agree with those who suggest that a too literal approach to the Song (or an endeavor to find precise relationships between episodes) would rob the book of its evocative and yet haunting effect.

The appeal of the book has remained undimmed. It will continue to remind us of what God expects in the conduct of the most intimate of human relationships. As poetry and, indeed, as the poetry of allusion, it will continue to provoke and perhaps to baffle. Probably some recent approaches to the book have been oversophisticated, yet the artistry of the book, in which structural links and associated motifs abound, invites more than a superficial attempt to come to grips with its meaning. The theme "love stronger than death" reminds us of the perfect love which undergirds the whole of human structures. Thus, while the interpretation of the book as an analogy of Christ and the church fails to deal adequately with its contents, the Song of Songs as an idyll of perfect love is clearly pointing in this ultimate direction.

30

Ecclesiastes

The dating and the structure of Ecclesiastes and the difficulty in reconciling some of its material with traditional biblical teaching have provided the main areas of discussion which have arisen over the book. The title (1:1) and the epilog (12:9–14), however, provide clues to its purpose. On the question of dating, the consensus that the book is late need not necessarily be accepted. The linguistic and stylistic evidence may be differently interpreted. The breakdown of certain Hebrew syntactical constructions, as well as the use of language, could put the book either early, thus giving credence to its assertion of Solomonic connections, or late. The contents of Ecclesiastes may be summarized as follows:

1:1	Title
1:2	The message summarized
1:3–11	The search for purpose in life
1:12–2:26	The futility of human wisdom
3	What does it profit?
4:1–5:9	The trials of life

240

Prolog and Epilog (Eccles. 1:1–2; 12:9–14)

There are clear connections between 1:1 and 12:9–14 (the person of the Preacher is discussed by the book's editor, who also intervenes at 7:27) and between 1:2 and 12:8 (the Preacher's message), while the introduction to the book (1:3–11) corresponds to the tone of the postscript (11:7–12:8). The general introduction precedes the theme of the book in 1:2 ("vanity of vanities"), just as a repetition of the theme in 12:8 precedes a development of the significance of the book (12:9–14). Thus the end returns us to the beginning, a not unexpected twist in a book whose contents are very largely given over to underscoring the endless repetition of the elements within human experience.

We may thus discuss in detail 12:9–14 in order to have the purpose of the author well in mind as we pursue through the book the theme of vanity raised by 1:2 and 12:8. The claim is made that Qohelet's work (this name may mean "assembler" or "collector") belongs to the mainstream Old Testament wisdom movement, offers a proper framework for faith (he "taught the people knowledge" [12:9]), and represents a very careful evaluation of and reflection upon the subject matter which he presents. The "proverbs" (měšālîm) referred to in verse 9 are clearly the "words" of verse 10, that is, the total substance of his presentation, which has taken the form of grouped poetical sayings which find their significance only within the world view (12:8) which 12:9–14 presupposes. What has been written, it is asserted in verse 10, conforms to the norms of mainstream theological tradition, a point which is emphasized by the use of yōšer, "uprightness" (i.e., what conforms to a standard), and 'ĕmet, "truth."

What has been put forward is meant to stimulate to reflection (12:11), as does the thought of the whole wisdom movement. We notice the use of "goads" for the individual pronouncements, "nails" for the collected whole. The words of the wise are provocative, like the jabs of a shepherd's goad (Fox 1977, 103), and yet even wisdom teaching of this character must defer to the demand to fear God and keep his commandments (vv. 13–14). Moreover, beyond the limits of life to which Qohelet has referred in his teaching, there lies the fact of judgment to be encountered (v. 14).

The introduction (v. 1) as well as the defense of the book (for its content is clearly controversial) in 12:9–14 is supported by an appeal to the thematic considerations which the book will treat (1:2, which is repeated in 12:8 just before the defense). The thesis of the Preacher is that the totality of human experience is "vanity." This word is not necessarily pejorative in its meaning. Hebrew *hebel* ("vanity") refers to something insubstantial, temporary, and ephemeral, something which may be whisked away, leaving behind no remainder. In this book, though, *hebel* appears to underline somewhat negatively the limits of human achievement. The point is that the empirical investigation of life on which the work is about to embark will indicate the unprofitability of an approach to life which rests simply on this plane. The Preacher's painstaking confrontation with life has led him into an endless series of dead ends. In itself, of course, this carries with it the negative overtones which the material immediately following the opening of the book then proceeds to develop.

The Introduction and Conclusion (Eccles. 1:3–11; 11:7–12:8)

Prompted by the search for human significance, the Preacher in 1:3–11 develops the theme that nothing final results from toil. This conclusion is then illustrated by the endless repetition in the world of nature. Toil is futile because of the finiteness of man and the limitations imposed by his environment. Emphasis on and the implications of these limitations which life imposes are returned to in 11:7–12:8 and will be considered again in our overall review. In view of the epilog (12:9–14), the implications to be drawn are obvious: humankind must operate within these limits because they cannot be changed. People must therefore come to terms with themselves and with their world.

Qohelet's Personal Experience: The Futility of Human Wisdom (Eccles. 1:12–2:26)

This section, which pursues the worthlessness of human wisdom, begins with a statement of Qohelet's intention to investigate the round of human experience (1:12–15). This study leads him to deprecate as a worthless end the pursuit of human reflection on life (vv. 16–18). The pendulum then swings, and a negative verdict upon pleasure and material gain as pursuits is offered (2:1–11). An assessment of the relative merits of wisdom or the lack of it then follows (vv. 12–17), before we are brought to the theme of death as the negation of all human endeavor (vv. 18–23). This fact forces us to the conclusion that we must live for the moment, accepting what God, this somewhat remote figure, gives, since nothing can be done apart from him and since he disposes as he pleases (vv. 24–26).

What Does It Profit? (Eccles. 3)

Ecclesiastes 3:1–9 illustrates what has preceded by a review of the significant moments which come into each life. In each recurring event an individual is helpless, and the search for security is meaningless, given the unpredictable way in which life unfolds. Only God knows how events interact and have meaning; humans can appreciate this truth only as a doctrine, not as a fact of experience (vv. 10–11). We are forced to conclude, therefore, that we can enjoy life only under the conviction that God has given us a vision of the future, that he has put eternity into our mind (vv. 12–15).

There is, then, a natural movement in this demonstration of human futility, as Qohelet surveys the presence of injustice within human structures. Justice cannot always prevail (3:16), given the inhumanity of men and women. The theory of divinely meted justice is nevertheless advanced in verse 17 as an article of faith, since its operation is not always seen in life. Yet humankind is, like the animal world, mortal (vv. 18–20). Who knows, however, whether death is the end (v. 21)? Though death faces us, let us live our present life (v. 22), making the most of current opportunities.

This section thus answers the question of what remains, raised in 3:9 as the summary of a review of life's moments. Nothing remains! Thus the search for relative advantage (in toil, wisdom, etc.) which characterized chapters 1–3 has been consistently negated by the intrusion of death into our world and the basic unpredictability of life (see 2:14–16). All we can do is take the present as God-given (3:22).

The Trials of Life (Eccles. 4:1–5:9)

From chapter 4 onward Ecclesiastes assumes a more impersonal note. The theme of social injustice is taken up in 4:1–3. In verses 4–6 we hear that honest toil has value relative to slothfulness, but that human rivalry thwarts ambition. Labor and loneliness are then drawn together as themes in verses 7–12, where the creation of relationships is urged and is contrasted with the type of success which isolates, a motif illustrated by the example of rulers who are abandoned by fickle public opinion (vv. 13–16). The connecting thread in 4:1–12 is that the difficulties of life are made a little easier if there are others who can share the common burden (Ogden 1984, 452). The advice to listen carefully rather than to participate thoughtlessly is illustrated with reference to the cult (5:1–2).

Loose talk is likened to an unwholesome dream or fantasy (v. 3), and this general theme of discreet silence as opposed to rash vows (vv. 4–7) is then extended to the injunction to keep one's counsel in the face of obvious injustices which cannot be remedied (vv. 8–9).

The Perils of Wealth (Eccles. 5:10–6:9)

The emptiness of an acquisitive life is a theme generally pursued in 5:10–6:9. Wealth brings its own problems (5:10–12), is easily lost (vv. 13–14), must be surrendered at death (vv. 15–16), and breeds anxiety (v. 17). Ecclesiastes 5:18–20 then advances the same summary conclusions as have been previously offered (cf. 2:24–26). We are to accept what God has given. If that be wealth, then let us view it as a gift, not as the result of human achievement. Reflections upon the same theme continue until 6:9. Human wealth and the toil which produces it lead merely to impermanent consequences, for in the face of death, which mocks all desires, all gains must be handed over (6:1–6). In view of our insatiable appetites, let us enjoy the moment rather than long after a future fulfilment (vv. 7–9).

What Is Good for Humankind?
(Eccles. 6:10–8:17)

Ecclesiastes 6:10–12 sounds once again a common note: If all things are predestined, what can one do in view of one's ignorance? These verses begin a new section but hardly, as some have claimed, divide the book, since the prominent theme of the second half of the book, the inability to find out, is clearly evident in 2:19; 3:21–22; and 5:1. Chapters 7–8 then emphasize our inability to discover what is good (Ogden 1979, 348). There is no discernible order in a world which we must just accept. The theme "who knows what is good for man?" dominates the poem of 7:1–14. Typical Qohelet contrasts are made—death is better than life, wisdom better than folly, the end better than the beginning, and wisdom better than wealth. Attached to these statements, however, are counterpositions which negate the relative advantage of wisdom. The poem concludes with a question relating to God's creation: Can we make straight what we see in life as crooked (cf. 1:15)?

As the theme of the search for the good continues, Ecclesiastes 7:15–18 dismisses the customary opinion that piety and longevity are to be yoked. Verses 19–22 assert that there is a real advantage in wisdom, but the question is then raised, Where can wisdom of this character be found (vv. 23–24)? A meditation on this search for wisdom as opposed to folly continues in verses 25–29 and is illustrated by the traditional topic of the "strange woman" (i.e., folly) to be avoided. Human beings are indeed created uncomplicated, but they make life difficult as they continually contrive clever plans ("many devices," v. 29).

Chapter 8 continues with this search for wisdom, which certainly is a good. In the face of this search, who is truly wise (8:1)? Yet wisdom does have a role to play in tempering conduct to the circumstances. Thus submission to royal authority, autocratic in its display, is reviewed (vv. 2–4). The king must be obeyed, for we live in his time and we are generally powerless (vv. 5–9). This saying is illustrated by the admonition that though wickedness may temporarily flourish and thus provide stimulation for others to follow its lead, they should resist (v. 10). The theoretical statement is then made that judgment will finally come (vv. 11–13). But life is a puzzle, and we cannot count on retribution (v. 14). We must, it is concluded again, therefore enjoy our present life (v. 15). Life is a predetermined set of events, and an individual placed "under the sun" is simply exposed to its caprices (vv. 16–17).

The Value and Limitations of Wisdom (Eccles. 9:1–11:6)

Ecclesiastes 9:1–16 presents humankind as confronting life and facing the inevitable end—death. Life is predestined (vv. 1–2), and death is the lot of all (v. 3); the relative advantage of life simply serves to throw into relief the finality of death (vv. 4–6). Again the conclusion is: let us enjoy the life which we have (vv. 7–10). We cannot know the timing of God's events, and we must operate within our limitations (vv. 11–12). Wisdom is important, however, and if recognized, it can serve a valuable social function (vv. 13–16).

Next, 9:17–10:20 stresses the profitability but vulnerability of wisdom (Ogden 1980, 37). According to 9:17–18, wise words are better than the intemperate outburst of a ruler, though a little folly may destroy wisdom's input (10:1). On the other hand, the conduct of a fool proclaims his insensitivity (vv. 2–3). Turning again to the place of wisdom, the passage teaches that the wrath of a ruler can be deflected by wise action overcoming folly (10:4). Verses 5–7 both advocate that authority be dispensed by the wise and recognize that mistakes may lead to drastic consequences. The place of wisdom as an aid in life is considered (vv. 8–11). It can help but is exposed to the insidious influences (the bite of the serpent) which can bring it down. Wisdom controls the future, but the fool is unaware that this knowledge is hidden (vv. 12–15). Verses 16–20 return us to the caution of 9:17, as they speak of the danger of folly and the value of wisdom.

Finally, 11:1–6 is a call to adventurous living in the context of what may be experienced in our world notwithstanding the limitations of what can be known (Ogden 1983, 229). This section thus operates as a corrective to the overcaution of 9:17–10:20 (note that Ecclesiastes is a book of balance). We must not let caution rule our life; rather, we must continue with what life has called upon us to do, remembering, however, that we are not in control of events!

A Concluding Postscript: "Enjoy Life, but Be a Realist!" (Eccles. 11:7–12:8)

Life itself is a wonder (11:7)! In Ecclesiastes 11:8a the theme of enjoyment is raised and is then expanded in verses 9–10, while verse 8b broaches the theme of death. This latter theme is taken up in 12:1–8 (Loader 1979, 108). The enjoyment of life is a pattern of thought which should be set in youth and then control the way life is lived (11:8–10). God as Creator (12:1) and Sustainer (the giver of "spirit," v. 7) is the determiner of life's outcomes. The interpretation of 12:1–8 is contested. The verses are a description of the ebbing of human vitality, whether in old age or in death. Finally, the human structure collapses, and the person goes to the everlasting darkness of death. From the perspective of human thought under the sun, the book proper closes with its insistence upon the fleeting character of life's purposes (12:8).

Qohelet has aimed at describing the popular conceptions of how life is controlled and the search for wisdom, which is advocated to keep such immoderate views of life in check. Thus there is the constant struggle in this book to equate the facts of life with the precepts by which life must be regulated. Life has to be lived within the limits that our lack of knowledge imposes and in the recognition that death is the great threat that must be faced (see 2:18–23; 3:18–20; 5:13–17; 6:1–6; 7:1–4, 15–18; 8:15–17; 9:1–12).

Qohelet sees no discernible moral order available to humankind in this world, and his doctrine of limits accounts for the strange series of ambivalences and contrasts which mark his work. But in taking this approach Qohelet is not reacting against the need for piety and its expression. He, like Job, is merely taking the wisdom movement of his own day to task for its overemphasis upon a cause-and-effect nexus between act and consequence. Traditional conclusions of popular wisdom are therefore pilloried throughout the book.

The consequent emphasis of the book has been upon the transcendence of God, upon his detachment, aloofness, removal from, and yet sovereignty over the human scene. This last item is necessarily emphasized since the real danger which Qohelet is combating is the human attempt to control the world, for such effort is essentially an attack upon divine sovereignty and inscrutability.

A doctrine of creation, however, underlies the Preacher's thinking (see 3:11, 14, 20; 7:14; 8:17; 11:5; 12:7). We are inevitably, therefore, reminded in this book of our creatureliness. We live an existence which the book broadly defines as "under the sun." Thus no key to the meaning of life can be found within our closed circle of existence (3:10–11; 7:14; 8:17). Qohelet exhibits a polarity and tension of experience in all his presentation. He also strongly affirms the transcendence of God but links it with constant admonitions throughout the book to find the purpose for life in acceptance of what God gives and in the reminder that we stand under his judgment. We are thus to live in the knowledge that God is the determiner of what happens (1:15; 5:8; 9:1–2).

In the final analysis, events do not come to us haphazardly, for there is a higher cause prevailing than that by which life is customarily directed. Thus the first half of the book stresses the theme that enjoyment is what profits (2:24; 3:13, 22; 5:18; 8:15), for this attitude takes life as it is, given from the hand of God. Traditional wisdom is transitory and is summed up by the many references to vanity throughout the book, since it so easily succumbs to the pressures of life.

By any standard, Ecclesiastes is a fascinating book, not easily interpreted in detail (the attempts at schematic analysis of its contents are legion), and probably only loosely structured. But the message is clear—the fear of God leads to life. Since the book ends on that note, Qohelet's teaching is commended, albeit with some reservations, by the editor. Conventional wisdom, which stands implicitly condemned for having ignored this divine truth, is rejected. This fear of God, as we have noted in the case of Proverbs, is fidelity to divine revelation and thus ultimately fidelity to the covenant relationship. From all this there flows axiomatically the further injunction enjoined on us as the book closes, to keep God's commandments.

31

Lamentations

Five poems compose the Book of Lamentations. The first four are acrostics (i.e., each verse begins with a sequential letter of the Hebrew alphabet). The authorship of the book, conventionally ascribed to Jeremiah (on the basis of 2 Chron. 35:25), is unknown. The fivefold structure of the book shows little or no progression, but offers a repetitive analysis (as the use of the acrostic device suggests) of the passions that the fall of Jerusalem aroused and the significance of this fall for the history of Israel. The book centers particularly on a reflective analysis of the place of Judah within the history of salvation, a matter which had now been called into question. Chapters 1 and 2 are related, since each has twenty-two verses of three lines. Chapter 4 is an acrostic of two lines per alphabetic letter. That chapter 5 is not an acrostic serves to give it emphasis. The general structure of the acrostic pattern is preserved in chapter 5 to the degree that it also has twenty-two verses. Chapter 3 seems the climax of the acrostic structure, with three verses for each letter of the alphabet and thus sixty-six verses in all. The book can be summarized:

Zion, the Forsaken Widow (Lam. 1)

The theme of the first poem is the desolation of the holy city; the refrain "there is none to comfort her" is repeated five times (1:2, 9, 16, 17, 21). We gather that it was the divine intention that there should be no comfort, that the destruction of the city and the temple should raise a question mark over the place of Judah within the purposes intended for the people of God. The whole book in fact makes this point under repetitive emphasis. Zion is spoken of in the third person in the first half of the chapter, thus setting the tone for the book (vv. 1–11, 17). Elect Zion has now been reduced to desolate widowhood (v. 1)! That is, the divine covenant with her from Sinai through David now seems to have been broken, and the marriage dissolved. A powerful personification of Zion as a deserted and a degraded woman begins the chapter, as present and past are contrasted (vv. 1–3). Her function as the city of God has ceased with the fall of Jerusalem, for none now come to her solemn assemblies (v. 4a). People and city grieve because of this severe affliction (vv. 4b–7). The reason for this condition is the depth of her rebellion (vv. 8–9). She has therefore been delivered to the adversary, the temple profaned, and its treasures pillaged (v. 10). The height of despair is depicted by reference to the famine, with which the first half ends (v. 11).

Zion herself speaks in 1:12–22, punctuated by an authorial comment in verse 17. The turning point in the chapter is a plea for pity from Yahweh (v. 11b) and from passersby (v. 12), for she has been demeaned by God (vv. 13–14) and her young men have been consumed (vv. 15–16). Verse 18 is the heart of her self-examination. Covenant involves obligation. Yahweh has been faithful, Jerusalem has not. Foreign alliances have been her undoing (v. 19). The confessional strain continues with a plea to Yahweh to witness her sufferings (vv. 20–21a), a plea which gives way to a call to Yahweh to requite her enemies on their day (vv. 21b–22). Thus what happened came from God's hand and was justified, but the hope is faintly expressed that it will not be the end, that God in due time will requite her enemies.

God, the Destroyer of Zion (Lam. 2)

God is depicted as having sacked the city (2:1–9a); all relationships have been broken, for lines of communication through the leaders have ceased (vv. 9b–10). The Divine Warrior has turned his hand against his own city (vv. 4–7), cutting off all that seemed to identify Judah as the people of God (temple, kingdom, festivals, and cult). The speaker now empathetically enters into Zion's grief and is moved to tears by the distress which, as in chapter 1, culminates in famine (vv. 11–12). The second half of the chapter is his first-person meditation on a sorrow for which he can find no comparison (v. 13). But a word is required from him, for prophetic counsel has been false (v. 14). Zion's fall from her position as the world's center has been mocked by enemies (vv. 15–16; cf. v. 15 with Ps. 48:2). Yet Yahweh himself has been the author of the tragedy (Lam. 2:17), as the fall of Jerusalem is presented in terms similar to those predicted of Babylon in Isaiah 14:12–21. So what has happened has been the outworking of the covenant curses (Lam. 2:17). Zion is now called upon to articulate her grief (vv. 18–19), and she responds in the lament of verses 20–22, the theme of which—the affliction of the day—returns to the thesis of verses 1–2 (Johnson 1985, 64).

Patience Through Suffering (Lam. 3)

The tone of this poem is heavily personalized, moving from a first-person-singular depiction of the suffering endured, where the speaker laments over the distress of Zion that has been divinely induced (3:1–18), to a contemplation of the bitterness of affliction (vv. 19–20). A central middle section of the poem runs from verses 21 to 42 (Johnson 1985, 66). This section, the exact middle of the book, gives the theological solution to the riddle of the disaster. The steadfast daily mercies of the Lord engender hope (v. 23), and the thought is born that punishment is not a final rejection but has rehabilitation in view (vv. 31–33). God stands behind the whole course of events (vv. 37–39). Out of evil good will now come (v. 38), and Zion's inhabitants may now lift up their hands to heaven (v. 41). With verses 42–51 analysis of the reasons for the disaster begins again, which must move the Lord finally to pity (v. 50). In the closing section of the chapter, the individual lament resumes with the description of the persecution at the hands of the enemy (vv. 52–54). God, however, takes up Israel's cause, having heard the plea of distress (vv. 55–57). This knowledge emboldens the speaker to call directly and confidently for the requital of Zion's enemies (vv. 58–60). In typical lament fashion, verses 61–66 close this strong chapter of self-awareness and affirmation by drawing attention to the attitude of Zion's enemies, to whom Yahweh will appropriately respond.

The Guilt of Zion's Leadership (Lam. 4)

Third-person address is used in 4:1–16, followed by a description in the first person. As in chapters 1–2, the distress of Jerusalem is climaxed in the horrors of famine and even cannibalism (v. 10). The unthinkable has happened—Jerusalem has fallen! The course of the tragedy is further reviewed in the second half of the chapter (vv. 12–22). Nobles, priests, prophets, and the search for foreign alliances have all contributed to Jerusalem's fall. This disaster has occurred despite a declared doctrine of Zion's inviolability (v. 12)! Davidic kingship—the divine representative who incarnates life (cf. 4:20 and Gen. 2:7), the tree of life itself (Lam. 4:20)—has been brought to an end by the capture of its last representative! Enemies (typified by Edom) may triumph for a moment, but the day of their punishment will come (vv. 21–22).

Hope for the Future (Lam. 5)

The last poem seems a chorus piece in the first-person plural, a prayer of the community. The Promised Land is gone (5:1–5) because of a dependence upon foreign alliances (vv. 6–7). The review of present troubles continues through verse 18: lack of law and order, famine, atrocities, and the sufferings of the people. The turning point comes in verse 19, which affirms God's eternal kingship. The book concludes with a direct call to Yahweh to forgive, though his people are undeserving (vv. 20–22).

Lamentations is a powerful attempt, through careful arrangement of stylistic devices, to come to terms with the reality of the destruction of Jerusalem in 587/586 B.C. All that stood for Israel outwardly—Davidic kingship, priesthood, cult, prophecy, temple, and even the land itself—is gone. What will now become of the doctrine of Israel's election? This sustained lament over Zion's present position takes its rise from the hopes that had been bound up in her. But to live as a chosen people meant acceptance of covenant responsibility, and the doctrine of election confronts in Lamentations the theme of curse for covenant breach (see 1:3, 5, 9; 2:20; 3:45; 4:10, 16; 5:12, all of which reflect the theology of Deut. 28). Covenant requirements had been progressively jettisoned by Israel, and thus the loss of the land, the extreme penalty for covenant default, had been imposed.

Lamentations 3 forms the theological center of the book. The review moves, as we have noted, from suffering to conviction to hope. Such a frank admission of guilt was the platform upon which a theology of history could be built during the exile. Reliance upon the externals of the faith had brought Israel to ruin. It would be the daunting task of exile to perceive that the election of Israel preceded all externals. Yahweh, who had selected her, would continue with her if he chose.

32

Esther

The rationale for the Book of Esther is found in 9:20–32, where the institution of the Feast of Purim is narrated, a festival which celebrates the vindication of the Jews over a concerted attempt during the Persian period to eliminate them. Esther is the only Old Testament book not represented at Qumran, and Talmudic disputes occurred over doubts about its canonical authority because (1), as the rabbis noted, the name of God does not occur in its 167 verses though the name of the Persian king is mentioned often, and (2) no cognizance is taken of Jewish customs, law, or history. We would be very much the poorer for its absence, however, since its rich theology of allusion to God's shaping history (even though he himself might be hidden) is of ongoing Christian significance. The contents of Esther are as follows:

1	The rejection of Queen Vashti
2	The choice of Esther as queen
3	Haman's plot
4–7	Esther's intervention and Haman's fall

Narrative Details of Esther

The setting is the Persian court during the reign of Ahasuerus (probably Xerxes I, who ruled from 485 to 465 B.C.). Though questions have been raised as to the historicity of the book, Esther exhibits a detailed knowledge of the Persian court, and it is clear from other sources that Jews did rise to positions of authority at Xerxes' court. The book opens with a lavish banquet to which Xerxes' queen Vashti is summoned. Her refusal to appear leads to her being replaced by Esther (her court name— her Jewish name was Hadassah). Ironically, Esther controls the king more completely than did her determined predecessor. We are then introduced to Mordecai, whose ancestors were carried from Jerusalem in the deportation of 597 B.C. Mordecai is a "son of Kish," reminding us of the earlier Saul, as Haman, an Agagite (3:1), is connected by the Talmud with the Amalekites, Saul's opponents in 1 Samuel 15. Esther, doubtless involving some compromise on her part (with a tolerance of foreign customs, like the stance of Dan. 2–6), was ordered by Mordecai to conceal her Jewish background (Esther 2:10). By chance, Mordecai overhears a plot to assassinate the king (vv. 19–23) and is able through Esther to make the matter known.

Chapter 3 introduces us to Haman and to Mordecai's refusal to bow before him (vv. 1–6). Haman then seeks to eliminate the Jews as a result of this decision by Mordecai. Haman, with whom the ascendancy remains until chapter 5, obtains by payment the right to put his proposal into practice throughout the empire (3:7–15). The fate of the Jews is sealed for the day before the celebration of the Passover, or the thirteenth day of Adar (v. 13). Esther is pressed by Mordecai to approach the king (chap. 4), and the key verse 14 points to her fateful role. For this purpose and for this time she has come to power, a statement that clearly alludes to God's hidden control. Though not bidden by the king, Esther approaches Ahasuerus, is remarkably received, and is able to persuade both the king and his prime minister, Haman, to accept her invitation to two successive banquets (5:1–8).

Haman, elated by recent events, now resolves to hang Mordecai (5:9–14). A further chance happening intervenes, as the king, unable to sleep, discovers in the royal records his indebtedness to Mordecai (6:1–9). Haman is forced to honor Mordecai with the honors he ironically thought intended for himself (vv. 10–14). By the second banquet the initiative is with the queen (chap. 7). She is able to plead for her people, identify Ha-

man as the enemy, and, after his pleas for his life are ironically misconstrued by the king, have him hanged upon the gallows constructed for
Mordecai. The relationship of Mordecai to Esther is made clear to the
king (chap. 8), the decree of Haman for the destruction of the Jews is reversed, and Mordecai, robed from now on as a king, moves freely in royal
circles (8:15; note how 2:5 has previously hinted at his royal descent).
Armed with the king's command, the Jews rise against their opponents,
executing Haman's sons as well (9:1–19). Esther 9:20–32 tells of the institution of the Feast of Purim in two accounts (vv. 20–28 and 29–32;
note also the earlier anticipation in vv. 16–19), recalling the slaying and
hanging of Haman's sons on two successive days (vv. 10–15), the deliverance from whose father the feast perpetuates. Esther 10:1–3 brings to
mind the opening details of chapter 1, taking us back to the wealth,
power, and courtly pomp of kingship with which note we began (Jones
1978, 36–43).

Theological Motifs of Esther

The absence of coincidence in history (see Esther 4:13–14) is the major theme struck by this book, despite the lack of any direct reference to
God throughout. History is divinely directed, and God will intervene for
Israel as he has done in the past. This theme makes understandable the
recurring allusions to the history of salvation, principally to the exodus
and the Joseph narrative. Like Moses, Esther occupies a key position at a
foreign court. Esther and Mordecai may provide parallels to Moses and
Aaron. Mordecai and Haman clash, as Moses and Pharaoh did. In both
cases the Jews are in the hands of a tyrant and are delivered. Several dangerous meetings with each king are necessary, and the prestige of the
leader is enhanced by them. The exodus events culminate in Passover,
those of Esther's period in Purim, which recalls Passover. Both Exodus
and Esther present narratives of a great deliverance accomplished
through a complex combination of improbabilities. Of course there are
differences (see Berg 1979, 31–35). Moses works not through but against
the administration; the analogies between Esther and Moses and between Mordecai and Aaron cannot be consistently maintained; the Jews
do not leave Persia. Nevertheless, the cumulative evidence favors the
drawing of general comparisons (Loader 1978, 418).

As he is in the Joseph narrative, Yahweh remains basically concealed.
There are other points of comparison, particularly the influence of a
well-placed person (cf. Daniel and Judith) at a time of great difficulty for
the Jewish people, together with the skill, wisdom, and decorum of that
individual. Esther is also like Ruth in its concern with the way in which
the hidden purposes of God order the future. The evidence of Yahweh's

operation throughout Esther is available for the discerning, the faithful. Here the remarkable series of coincidences in the book may be noted: Mordecai chances to hear the plot against the king; Ahasuerus at a critical time has insomnia, and Mordecai is thus saved; Haman enters the court at a moment when the king is pondering a suitable reward; the king returns to the fateful second banquet just when Haman has fallen on Esther's couch in supplication.

Thus, though God saved the Jews through a series of natural events, the undercurrent of the account makes it clear that Jewish obedience to this higher power is the factor to which history bends. Perhaps the absence of direct mention of the Deity heightens the emphasis upon human responsibility that the book appears to bring. But Esther is the account of a great reversal of fortunes, seemingly occurring through a conjunction of fickle circumstances—hence the feast name *Purim*, "lots," commemorating both the "chance" which the book underscores and the historical casting of lots by Haman for the destruction of the Jews (9:24).

At the same time the narrative is one of high artistry, making its message deliberate and not incidental. Eating and drinking motifs provide a structural link for key passages. There is a strong parallel between the relationship of Mordecai and Haman and that of the Jews and their oppressors. The book begins and ends with the account of a feast (1:3, 5; 9:17–18). Two feasts occur at the center of the book, given by Esther for Haman and the king, with the point of transition in the book coming between the two. In each case the feast leads to rejection and elevation: Ahasuerus's involves Vashti and Esther, Esther's concerns Haman and Mordecai, and Purim affects the enemies and the Jews (Berg 1979, 31–35).

The tale is thus an entertaining one which may be read on several levels. But though it may look like a story of human initiative and success, we who read it well know that the help which it presents could have come only "from another quarter" (4:14).

33

Daniel

The inclusion of Daniel in the Writings of the Hebrew canon does not necessarily mean that by the time of its production the prophetic canon had closed. Nor does Daniel's place in the canon necessarily mean that it must be dated in a Greek or even Maccabean period. It simply points to the book's use of another genre of biblical literature, apocalyptic, making its contents other than prophetic in the accepted sense of the word. Beginning with Daniel, the term *apocalyptic* is applied to material bearing the general character and features of that book. It is not our purpose to argue here that the origins of Hebrew apocalyptic are basically rooted in Old Testament prophecy, with certain affinities as well to the wisdom movement, nor to insist that foreign influences featured little in the development of the medium. Although such arguments can be sustained, we are concerned to offer some background explaining the very different theological outlook which is characteristic of Daniel and which separates the book from the Old Testament prophetic traditions. The subject matter of Daniel is as follows:

The apocalyptic movement arose in Israel in response to a defined need, the catastrophe of 587/586 B.C. It was thus a form of literature raised up to meet the crisis of the end of the nation and to deal with an exilic situation where foreign powers exercised mastery and the people of God were in retreat under persecution. What course would the history of salvation, expressed to that point through the nation of Israel, now take in these changed circumstances? Apocalyptic basically involves the uncovering of the shape of this future by a series of divine disclosures, usually through supernormal means such as dreams and visions. God promises to respond to the crisis which has afflicted his faithful (no longer the people as a whole) in history. Salvation is now the promise held out to the faithful; since nationalism vanishes on this level, universality, a world-encompassing judgment from which the kingdom of God will emerge, is an emphasis of the literature. History is now seen to bear a cosmic significance, to be the interplay of principalities and powers, with the decisions which control it being taken within the heavenly session in which Israel's God presides. The nature of the kingdom of God as coming by divine and remarkable intervention is disclosed, as is the nature of the heavenly being who as world ruler (note "one like a son of man" in Dan. 7:13) will implement the shape of the end. The apocalyptic literature thus offers the reassurance to Israel that God has not abandoned history; his control over it is being exerted, despite other impressions which its course may suggest. No longer in this medium is national Israel the center of revelatory attention. Now it is the faithful and the wicked, the godly and the apostate. Appropriately, since the judgment of individuals is reserved for beyond time, a doctrine of resurrection also emerges in literature of this type (see Dan. 12). But since the development of apocalyptic has its roots deep in Israel's past and beyond, older traditional motifs are also featured in Daniel and in this literature generally.

Daniel, an extremely undervalued and sophisticated book, brings the message of the Old Testament to fruition. Its dating is often disputed, and it is regularly suggested that its extreme attention to detail in the matter of the Seleucid wars with Egypt (chap. 11) places this book in the early Maccabean period. This detail, however, is not so precise as is often alleged, and it is doubtful whether this feature of the book diminishes the probability of dating it in the Persian period. But the issue of dating and the complexity of historical references and cultural allusions within the book are not simply resolved. There is now a greater disposition to conclude that the material from chapters 1–6 (the so-called court tales) stems from the Persian period, even if (as the recent arguments go) it was revised in other interests during the Maccabean period!

The Two Halves of the Book of Daniel

The book falls into two clear halves, chapters 1–6 and 7–12. Such a division, however, ignores the major exegetical problem of the book, namely, the use of two languages—Hebrew in 1:1–2:4a and chapters 8–12, and Aramaic in 2:4b–7:28. No analysis of the book is satisfactory which does not come to terms with the peculiarity of the two languages and the probability that the Hebrew interprets the content of the Aramaic. (Dan. 1 is introductory, and Dan. 8–12 depends upon chap. 7.) The Aramaic sections appear to offer a sequence which is relatively self-contained and complete: chapter 2 corresponds to chapter 7, 3 corresponds to 6, and chapters 4 and 5 are interrelated. To put it another way, we have in these chapters a sequence of authority and deliverance (see fig. 3).

Figure 3 **The Sequence of Daniel 2–7**

Daniel 2 Authority
Daniel 3 Deliverance
Daniel 4 Authority
Daniel 5 Authority
Daniel 6 Deliverance
Daniel 7 Authority

The provision of Hebrew in Daniel 1 may have been required for canonical purposes, and we may say the same for chapters 8–12. Since, however, chapters 8–12 apply to the particular Israelite situation under review there the more universal truths conveyed by Daniel 7, the use of Hebrew from this point of view is highly appropriate. The use of Aramaic, the lingua franca of the Persian period, intrinsically carries with it a note of universality and puts us in touch with the major purpose of the book, which is to survey the course of human history from the advent of the "times of the Gentiles" until the ushering in of the kingdom of God. In summary, we may see Daniel 1 as introductory and the Aramaic sections as self-contained, with their implications for Israel being drawn out in chapters 8–12.

Daniel's Exile (Dan. 1)

Daniel 1 introduces us to the Jewish captives, taken in a siege of Jerusalem in about 603 B.C., sixteen years before the fall of the city. The first two verses of the book are the only place where the name of a Jewish king appears, and there is little interest thereafter in a concept of national Israel. The unthinkable has happened—the Jerusalem temple has been profaned and the temple vessels taken. Nebuchadnezzar no doubt viewed them as deity symbols and their capture as a demonstration that his gods were mightier than the God of Israel.

Babylon is interestingly designated in verse 2 by the rarely occurring term "land of Shinar." This phrase occurs only four times in the Old Testament, three of them in remarkable contexts (Gen. 10:10 is a geographical reference of no significance for our purposes). In Zechariah 5:11 sin in the form of a woman in a measuring basket is consigned to the "land of Shinar," where fittingly a "house," that is, a temple is built for it. Babylon is, then, the place where sin is deified. The other major reference is in Genesis 11:2, where the "land of Shinar" became the center for realizing what has been the persistent humanistic dream of one world, one common set of social values, and one language. This attempt to order the world without reference to the Creator, this misplaced search for the center, was then rejected. And now in the "land of Shinar" (Dan. 1:2) we find this common set of unities (one language, one social policy, one common bond of education, etc.) consciously revived as a tool of empire by Nebuchadnezzar. Since there is a remarkable degree of allusion in these early chapters of Daniel to the material of Genesis 1–11, we have probably in Daniel 1:2 a deliberate reference to the Babel incident and to Nebuchadnezzar as the humanistic reviver of those policies. Daniel, in spite of all this, exhibits a faith which survives when every form of institutionalism has been removed. The laconic conclusion of the chapter (1:21) reports that Daniel outlives the Babylonian Empire and sees the ushering in of the Persian period. He has exhibited the uncompromising characteristics of the man of faith, whose life is able to sustain the effects of a changed world. He is thus the exemplary figure of the period.

Nebuchadnezzar's Dream (Dan. 2)

The highly significant Aramaic section begins at 2:4a. The chapter is devoted to the dream of Nebuchadnezzar and its interpretation. The paradox of this chapter is that through the unlikely medium of a bizarre dream God communicates reality to Nebuchadnezzar. Neither the empire over which he presides nor the decisions that he takes provide reality for Nebuchadnezzar. The element of reality is the contact which the dream permits him with the controller of history. Now he needs someone to interpret the nature of reality, to put the wild shapes of the night into proper perspective. Daniel, as Joseph did before him in Genesis, can put the pieces of the puzzle together. (There is a marked similarity between the presentations of Daniel and Joseph. Both were captives at the royal court, both succeeded where the professionals failed, both were promoted as a result, and most important, both operated in an Israel that stood before an exodus, a major impending change.) In short, only Israel, only the community of faith, has the answer as to the direction history will take.

The interpretation of the dream as involving progression but deterioration within four successive kingdoms is characterized by the strange blend of sequence and yet simultaneity. Thus, on the one hand, the empires give way in a sequence of decreasing splendor though increasing strength (gold to silver to brass to iron); yet, on the other hand, the image which they compose is destroyed as one whole. Perhaps the four kingdoms are a picture of the totality of human government, representative of the human power structure, of the human image. Clearly the historical sequence of kingdoms which is presented is simply various fine-tunings of the anti-God human power structure. Progressive human government will inevitably exhibit the same innate tendencies to search for its center within itself. But whatever changes may be introduced, there is no substitute for the ideal kingdom of God's rule. This kingdom will be brought in, the interpretation explains, with decisive suddenness. The image of a stone cut without hands which then fills the whole earth seems to have Zion overtones (cf. Zion as a stone in Isa. 28:16), perhaps pointing obliquely to the familiar prophetic eschatology involving the establishment of Jerusalem as the ideal-world center.

Defiance and Deliverance (Dan. 3–6)

While Daniel 2 presents a clash of authorities, the kingdom of God confronted by human power, Daniel 3 takes up the notion of dominion as displayed through the counter–image of man (cf. Gen. 1:26) which

Nebuchadnezzar constructs on the plain of Dura for his world to see. The image in this chapter is clearly a symbol of his worldwide dominion, and this tremendous assertion of sole power by Nebuchadnezzar cannot go unchallenged. The remainder of the chapter deals with a counterdemonstration of divine power. The three Jewish captives who refuse to submit are rescued from the furnace, in which a fourth "man" appears. Finally, Nebuchadnezzar acknowledges the power of their God to deliver.

The challenge to divine authority implicitly posed by Nebuchadnezzar in Daniel 3 is the theme with which chapter 4 proceeds. The chapter has a tripartite outline of dream (vv. 1–18), interpretation (vv. 19–27), and realization (vv. 28–33). Again the king has a perplexing dream, and again Daniel presents its meaning. The king is called upon to repent and remember his creatureliness. The great tree of the dream, stretching from earth into the heavens, under which all find shade and food, is clearly the counter–tree of life, the world tree, the Babylonian Empire under whose aegis all may find security and sustenance. It is an assertion of Nebuchadnezzar's Babylon as the New Eden. The claim that to be related to this tree is to be related to the source of life (v. 12) is contemptuously denied by the detail of the chapter. Nebuchadnezzar, because of his pride, is reduced to the creatureliness which he has spurned, when twelve months subsequent to the dream he is dismissed from his kingdom (vv. 29–33). Later he is restored on the basis of genuine repentance and acknowledgment of the true place of the kingdom of God (v. 34).

In Daniel 5 Belshazzar, the eldest son of the usurper Nabonidus, is king. (His reign is disputed, but Nabonidus was resident for much of the period immediately preceding the fall of Babylon in 539 at Teima in Arabia. If not king, Belshazzar was probably regent.) The place of the temple vessels is important in this chapter. Their use in a Babylonian orgy by a ruler who had not profited from Nebuchadnezzar's experiences would have been the climactic affront for the Jew. We feel, inevitably, that the end of Babylon for such hubris is near. This presumption must draw punishment, and the mysterious handwriting on the wall announces the demise of the Babylonian power.

Deliverance of the captives is the theme of Daniel 6, as it had been in chapter 3. There is again an unreasonable royal command involving a religious practice, and again the pious Jew (this time, Daniel) refuses to obey. The conspirators implicate Daniel in chapter 6, as they had implicated his companions in chapter 3. Daniel is remarkably rescued from the lions' den, as the Jewish youths had been from the furnace.

Judgment for the Saints (Dan. 7)

Chapter 7 falls into two halves (vv. 1–14 and 15–28). In the first half the visionary emphasis dominates. Four beasts arise out of the inimical, primeval foe, the sea. Probably the number four suggests the totality of the threat from the forces of chaos, though in the later application of the material the beasts are historicized in terms of four empires (as in chap. 2). Total opposition to the kingdom of God is thus represented in this bestial, semihuman form. From the fourth beast, to which special attention is paid, there arises a little horn (7:8). It is tempting to identify the little horn of 8:9 with this horn, though the former may be a historicization of this more general concept.

Clearly the vision is not interested in strict chronology, since the fourth beast is destroyed before the remaining three lose their dominion (7:12). We may note also that the underlying imagery of the vision appears to lean heavily upon the old yet still widely current mythology of the triumph of the hero deity over the forces of chaos (the creatures from the sea in chap. 7). The judgment scene unfolds in verse 9 as the heavenly council convenes; the opening of the books of destiny (v. 10) appears to make this judgment the final universal human event.

There now comes one who is with designed ambiguity described as "one like a son of man" (7:13), a typically vague apocalyptic description of what appears to be in this context a heavenly being who comes on clouds (literally, it would seem), the attendants of deity in the Old Testament. If the underlying mythology is pressed, some triumph over the forces of chaos might seem indicated, but it is doubtful whether such neat parallels may be drawn.

We should note that the presence of the "one like a son of man" is generally to be associated with judgment, since his appearance in the heavenly sphere is virtually coincident with judgment's having been pronounced. Dominion (i.e., what had been promised to humankind originally), glory, and an everlasting kingdom are then given to this figure. To this apparently divine man, the manifested image, power is given. All things are summed up by his appearing. His coming ushers in the age of everlasting dominion.

In the second half of the chapter this Son of man does not appear. We do find there, however, the saints of the Most High (vv. 18, 22, 25, 27), who do not figure in the first half of the chapter. There is no need to see the Son of man as other than representative for the saints. We are not required to identify the saints with him or to presume that he suffers with them. Indeed, the second half of the chapter seems obviously a historical application of the first half. Nor are the saints of the second half of the chapter heavenly beings, as some have argued (in the Old Testament, "holy ones" encompasses both divine and human beings). The message of the second half of the chapter seems directed at the suffering faithful of any age. In Daniel's era and subsequently they are to take comfort from the fact that the issues affecting the history of their day, for which they suffer, have already been determined. The die has been cast in their favor, the high court has convened, and judgment has been pronounced. All that is now required is to make individual application of this judgment.

Vision and Interpretation (Dan. 8–12)

Chapters 8–12 work out these details. The sequences of vision and interpretation which Daniel 7 has advanced are continued in these chapters. Chapter 8 seems to concentrate upon the second and third figures of the vision of Daniel 7. Greece's replacement of the Persian power and then the emergence of Alexander's successors (Ptolemy in Egypt, Philip in Macedonia, Seleucus in Syria and Babylon, and Antigonus in Asia Minor) provide the historical background. There is a concentration upon the Seleucid kingdom and upon the little horn (8:9), Antiochus IV Epiphanes. His hubris reaches to an assault upon heaven and God himself (vv. 10–11). This passage might be a foreshadowing of Antiochus's possession of the Jerusalem sanctuary from 167 to 164 B.C. Or perhaps, as some suggest, there has been a blurring of the boundaries in 8:1–12: Israel and the host of heaven attacked by Antiochus have become mixed or fused (see v. 24).

Daniel 9 begins with Daniel's prayer. The detail of verse 1 continues to puzzle, but "Darius the son of Ahasuerus, by birth a Mede" may be a royal title. He may have been Gubaru, the general who conquered Babylon, or he may be identical with Cyrus. Israel's offenses against the covenant are confessed in this prayer, touched off by Daniel's meditation upon the seventy years of exile of Jeremiah 25:11–14 and 29:10. It is now realized that the exile has become open-ended. Israel can only hope for God's forgiveness (Dan. 9:9), and Daniel finally prays that the holy city and sanctuary will be rebuilt (vv. 17–19).

The answer comes from Gabriel in 9:20–27. The particular details in verses 24–27 operate between two poles: (1) the people and their sins and (2) the future of Jerusalem. These concerns are alternately addressed in the verse structure which follows. The question of a precise approach to these verses has drawn three major responses:

1. The numbers are to be symbolically interpreted: history from Daniel's time to the second advent is being generally presented.

2. The calculations end with the desecration of the temple by Antiochus IV Epiphanes.
3. The message is to be referred to the advent and the crucifixion.

Of these three options, the first is to be preferred, since any attempt to establish a precise timetable leads to difficulty. The use of symbolic number in apocalyptic is in any case expected.

Daniel 10–11 is also tied together by the device of vision and interpretation. Beside the Tigris, Daniel receives yet another vision (10:1–11:1). This sets the stage for the account of the Hellenistic wars which follows. In Daniel 10 we are taken behind the scenes, and it is indicated that the real conflict is even now being fought by principalities and powers in the heavenly places. Angels representing both Persia and Greece (10:13, 20) are contending with Michael. In the explanation which begins in 11:2 Persia is quickly disposed of, and the remainder of the chapter turns to the fortunes of the Seleucids and the Ptolemies. Verses 6–20 deal with the wars between these two dynasties; verses 21–45 detail the fortunes of Antiochus Epiphanes (175–164 B.C.). This latter account merges into an antichrist presentation in 11:36, where Antiochus comes into direct conflict with God himself.

In Daniel 12:1 Michael the protector of Israel intervenes. The distress which is described before his intervention is the familiar one of apocalyptic woes which precede the inbreaking of the final kingdom. This seems to be confirmed by the mention of the resurrection in verse 2. The interpretation of this verse is not easy, but the probable exegesis confines those resurrected to the righteous only; that is, it is a resurrection of the faithful which is being described. The righteous who rise shine as stars in the firmament, a reference to their heavenly character, and they are, in view of the terminology used (*maśkîlîm*, "wise," in v. 3), to be related to Daniel himself (cf. 1:4, 17). And in view of Isaiah 52:13, where the Servant's activity has been characterized by the use of *śkl*, the related verb, they are to be seen as a servantlike community of the faithful, that is, a community of saints. The prophecy is then sealed until the appropriate period (Dan. 12:4).

The epilog (12:5–13) is a revelation to Daniel himself of the time involved. How long, he asks (vv. 6–7), shall it be to the end of these wonders? That is, how long will the distress of the end time last? This has no reference to Antiochus Epiphanes, since the events of the end time as they are described in 11:40–45 do not tally with what we know of his career and his death. The three-and-one-half times of 12:7 has in view the period from the beginning of the end to the end itself. In verses 11–12 yet another period is alluded to, namely, the desolation of the sanctuary by Antiochus Epiphanes (in 167–164 B.C.), which has been referred to in 8:13–14.

The Book of Daniel has moved from the saints in chains to the saints triumphant. Its theme has been the survival and vindication of the people of God in the face of mounting world opposition. In this great struggle between the two imperia involved, the kingdom of God will prevail. History is firmly under divine control; and if it seems not to be, we are to take heart from what we know to be the case from this revelation from behind the scenes. God is working all things out, the Son of man will come, dominion will be given to him, and he will reign forever and ever. Of course we recognize that in the ministry of Jesus the advent of that Son of man indicated the beginning of the end, with judgment announced by the very fact of his coming. The world and its structures have been judged by his ministry and by his death, but his resurrection has assured us that his second coming to enter into dominion will sum up history and ensure our final salvation.

34

Ezra-Nehemiah

The books of Ezra and Nehemiah may be treated together, since their common authorship is generally accepted, though the question of their relationship to the Books of Chronicles is a matter of some dispute. The view that Chronicles was the product of an authorship different from Ezra-Nehemiah has become more widely adopted. The absolute dating of Ezra-Nehemiah is contested, as is the relative order of the return of the two reformers. The difficulty is occasioned by the fact that there were two Persian kings of the period who bore the name Artaxerxes (see Ezra 7:1; Neh. 2:1), namely Artaxerxes I (Longimanus, ruled 465–424 B.C.) and Artaxerxes II (Mnemon, ruled 404–359 B.C.). On the grounds of probability and content we shall adhere to the traditional dating of Ezra's return at 458 B.C. and Nehemiah's at 445 B.C., noting, however, that the question of dating or order does not materially affect the interpretation of the books. It is more likely that Chronicles was written after the close of the Ezra-Nehemiah period, and that it reflects upon the period of the two reformers, as we shall argue later. In our judgment, little hangs upon the formerly argued close association of Ezra-Nehemiah and Chronicles. We may approach the Book of Ezra thus:

Rebuilding the Temple (Ezra 1–6)

It is noteworthy that Ezra begins and Nehemiah ends with detail relating to the temple. Indeed, it is not too much to claim that such a temple orientation, which is sustained throughout the two books, gives to them their inner consistency. This unity clearly prevails in the case of Ezra, which is almost entirely devoted to temple matters. The first six chapters of Ezra do not concern the reformer, but because of their temple orientation can be conveniently grouped under his name. These chapters are taken up with a temple-rebuilding program and ostensibly do not prepare us for Ezra's coming nor for the issues which he will confront. But we see how connections between Ezra 1–6 and 7–10 may be forged. When Ezra does come, he too is concerned with the regulation of worship in Jerusalem and with the rightful function of the temple. He thus continues the emphasis struck in chapters 1–6.

The Book of Ezra commences with the decree of Cyrus (538 B.C.) permitting the Jews to return to rebuild the temple in Jerusalem (1:1–4). An Aramaic form of this Hebrew decree is repeated in an official context in Ezra 6; thus the first six chapters, separated in time from the remaining four by almost a century, begin and end with this temple motif. The language of Ezra 1 is more theologically reflective and echoes the close of 2 Chronicles, while Ezra 6 is an official record. The language of Ezra 1:1–4 (as we shall note later when dealing with the similar 2 Chron. 36:22–23) sustains the second-exodus expectations built by Isaiah 40–55 around Cyrus. Cyrus was to be the architect of the second exodus and in effect the restorer of the city of God, preparing in this way for the fulfilment of the prophetic eschatology of the exilic period, which held that Jerusalem, restored, reintegrated by covenant, and the center of a cleansed land, would become the world center to which all nations would rally in pilgrimage.

Stirred up by the decree are the key tribes of Judah, Benjamin, and Levi (Ezra 1:5), which assume an important role in the genealogies of 1 Chronicles 1–9. It is pointedly noted that Cyrus returns the temple vessels which Nebuchadnezzar had taken, thus indicating that the exile had historically ended (Ezra 1:7).

Ezra 2 is a difficult chapter. Various hypotheses to interpret this long list of returnees have been advanced. Perhaps the suggestion which most commends itself, in view of the controversy arising over the rebuilding of the temple, is that the chapter is basically a list validating the builders of the second temple and furnished to the Persian governor during the disputes of the Haggai-Zechariah period. We may note that the Cyrus decree had laid on the returnees the responsibility for building the temple (1:3).

Ezra 3:1–6 probably refers to the rededication of the altar (and nothing more) shortly after the first return (Williamson 1983, 23). There is a clear attempt, in the interests of continuity, to duplicate the dedication of Solomon's temple, since the rededication of Ezra 3 takes place at the Feast of Tabernacles (vv. 4–6), the period at which the first temple was dedicated. But this new beginning was only tentative, for the foundation stone was not yet laid. The next phase of building operations (3:7–4:3) occurs at the instigation of the returned prophets Haggai and Zechariah at the beginning of the reign of Darius I (520 B.C.). This second temple was five years in the building (4:24 and 6:15); and thus the total work, begun in earnest after an initial tentative period of two years (3:7–8), took seven years, as the first temple had (Williamson 1983, 25). Ezra 3 seems thus a typological account of the building of the second temple, juxtaposing for this purpose events in the reigns of Cyrus (vv. 1–6) and Darius (vv. 7–13).

In Ezra 4:1–3 we learn that "the adversaries of Judah and Benjamin" opposed rebuilding in the Zerubbabel-Joshua period. The opposition during the entire period of Cyrus and Darius is summed up in verse 4 as coming from "the people of the land." (Ezra 4:4–5 seems to summarize the difficulties of the period; see Talmon 1976, 323.) "People of the land" is a common Old Testament phrase which has no unitary meaning but must be interpreted in the light of particular contexts. In view of this context of opposition, the term here may best be referred to the population of Palestine who had not gone into exile (perhaps they were non-Jewish and included the Samaria nobility). They appealed to a continuity of sacrifice at the temple site since their transmigration to Palestine in the time of the Assyrian king Esarhaddon (681–669 B.C.). Nothing is known of such a movement, but it would have been consistent with Assyrian policy. Certainly the later Samaritans cannot be meant by the reference, since that sect did not come into being until well after the close of the Ezra-Nehemiah period, was impeccably orthodox, and would not have appealed to such a syncretistic background. Whoever the adversaries were, the returnees saw themselves committed as a group to the rebuilding of the temple. (In v. 3 note the word yaḥad, "together," which here may mean "congregation"; see Talmon 1953, 133.)

Ezra 4:6–23 (with v. 24 an editorial link introducing the detail of chaps. 5–6) then proceeds to document the community difficulties from the time of Darius I to Nehemiah. Chapters 5–6 return to the matter of the rebuilding of the temple under Haggai and Zechariah. The first half of the Book of Ezra concludes with the temple rebuilt; thus the theme of rebuilding has provided the continuity for these six chapters.

Return of Ezra (Ezra 7–10; Neh. 8–10)

Ezra 7 presents the return of Ezra himself, who gives his name to the whole book. Ezra 1–6 has established the theocratic basis of the new community, and Ezra 7–10, together with the rest of Ezra's memoirs in Nehemiah 8–10, continues with an emphasis upon the person of the reformer.

It is now clear that we may dismiss the traditional picture of Ezra as the father of Judaism, the beginner of a new movement which substituted a Judaism of obedience to the law for the older biblical picture of the nation of Israel. It is equally clear that the identification of Ezra as the imposer of the law who brought back the canonical Pentateuch is no longer a satisfying one. Both of these proposals of older research have undergone considerable modification in recent presentations. Certainly Ezra's prominence in Ezra 7 is hardly based upon any innovative restoration of law to the community, since the role of law in Ezra 7 is arguably subordinated to temple and cultic concerns. To take this point a little further, while it is true that Ezra is presented as "a scribe skilled in the law of Moses" (7:6), this is a reference to a law whose components are presupposed by the writer to have been in active use by the immediate postexilic community (see 6:18). Although the law was relatively unknown to the popular community (a common enough situation in the Old Testament), there does appear to have been an upper stratum who knew it and also were encouraged to communicate it (7:25). The fact that the law was read by Ezra at the Feast of Tabernacles in 444 B.C. in connection with covenant renewal (Neh. 8:1) suggests that the writer had a return to older paths in mind in Ezra 7 (cf. Deut. 31:10–13). Indeed the law may have been read regularly following Ezra's return in 458. (Eybers 1976, 20, suggests every seven years.) Certainly the reading of the law in Nehemiah 8 was designed at that stage to operate analogously to the reading of the law in earlier periods, such as under Josiah (2 Kings 22–23).

All of this accords well with the range of prophetic concerns which Ezra (and Nehemiah) displays in an Israelite state dominated by priestly influence. The reading of the law was probably designed to stir the populace at large to covenant renewal rather than to provide for community regulation in itself. Such a renewal movement does take place later in Nehemiah 9–10. Even the alleged concentration upon precise legal observance in Ezra 9–10, as well as the action taken against intermarriages between Jews and aliens, was not an end in itself. For it also involved a second-exodus motif (as did the processional character of the return in Ezra 7–8, strikingly reminiscent of the prophetic expectations of Isa. 52:7–12), namely, the cleansing of the Promised Land from defilement (cf. Lev. 18:24–30; Ezek. 36:16–36; see Koch 1974, 184–89), and it instanced the operation of covenant law at work in the returned community. Thus the sequence of temple cleansing or restoration of proper worship, the reading of the law, reform measures, and the conclusion of a covenant in Ezra 7–10 and in Nehemiah 8–10 takes up concerns similar to those which the reforming kings of the Books of Chronicles espoused. Platforms of this character were always within the mainstream of the concerns of the Old Testament reformers.

Furthermore, one must not lose sight of the all-Israelite character of Ezra's activities. The point has been made that within the narratives concerning Ezra personally, the term *Israel* is used more than twenty times, while "Judah" occurs only four times (7:14; 9:9; 10:7, 9, all geographical references). Ezra is sent, as the terms of his commission make clear, to "all the people in the province Beyond the River" (7:25), that is, to virtually the entire population of the older Cisjordanian boundaries of the Davidic empire. This all-Israel tone in Ezra (and Nehemiah) sustains prophetic concerns and cautions us from construing action taken during this period as anti-Samaritan. This emphasis upon the purpose of Ezra's return follows hard upon earlier material bearing upon the unsuccessful character of the first return under Sheshbazzar, Zerubbabel, and Joshua in chapters 1–6. It may have been designed, therefore, to present a contrast between what was respectively achieved under the leadership of these two returns. We are probably being encouraged by this all-Israelitism to view the results of the Ezra mission as more determinative for the final shape of the community than were those which had been achieved in earlier measures taken after 537 B.C.

Important in the Ezra materials in this connection is the covenant renewal ceremony of Nehemiah 8–10. Ezra's reading of the law is followed by Levitical exposition (8:7–8); it is the Levites who draw out the implications of this covenant renewal in terms of the salvation history reviewed in the long prayer of 9:5–37. The emphasis in this prayer is upon the gift of the land as the fulfilment of the promise to the fathers, while the concluding verses rhetorically indicate the position in which the people of God, now returned to the land, find themselves: they are slaves. That is to say, they are conscious that the real exodus of prophetic concerns still awaits them, and for its blessings they pray. Striking in this covenant renewal of chapters 8–10 is the absence of general priestly support. Priests are not associated in the reading of the law, and their support for the reform movement seems to have been only perfunctory.

Return, Rebuilding, and Reform (Neh. 1–13)

The prophetic concerns of Ezra to which we have pointed are echoed in Nehemiah. The contents of this book are as follows:

1	Nehemiah's call and prayer
2	Nehemiah's return
3	The rebuilding of the walls
4	The opposition to the rebuilding
5	Economic reforms
6	Nehemiah's opponents
7, 11–12	The completion of the task
8–10	Ezra's reading of the law; covenant renewal
13	Nehemiah's second term

We should note the quasi-prophetic manner in which the Book of Nehemiah opens. True, God does not speak to him in a typical prophetic consultation, but the divine will is clearly indicated, and Nehemiah is equally clearly charged to implement it (chap. 1; see Ackroyd 1970, 30). As the rebuilder of the city walls (chaps. 2–3), he is also cast into the traditional leadership role of the ancient world (Smith 1971, 129–30). As the facilitator of political stability and the resolute upholder of the law (as the book presents him to be), Nehemiah in his mission evinces not only prophetic traits but also royal ones. He is thus a religious reformer who can be cast into the very best traditions of a Josiah or a Hezekiah. Though he is a formidable figure whom a consortium of local rulers cannot daunt (chap. 4), he is not indifferent to the social plight of the common people. The economic measures which he takes in Nehemiah 5 are designed to win popular support and thus broaden the reform base as much as they are to check the power of the Samaria-based opposition (chap. 6). Popular measures of this character were apparently intended to clear the way for the very significant steps which Nehemiah would take after the preliminary tasks of rebuilding the Jerusalem walls and repopulating the city had been completed (chaps. 7 and 11–12).

Nehemiah took these steps after his return to Jerusalem at an unspecified time subsequent to his recall by the Persian king in 433/432 B.C. (Neh. 13:6). Some have supposed that the character of Nehemiah's political pretensions aiming at kingship led to the recall (see 6:7). Doubtless, however, such assertions were ploys of his opponents. The impact of the reforms in 13:4–22 clearly struck at priestly privilege.

Once again in the history of Israel an eminent layman, prompted by a divine call, directed his attention in a prophetic manner to cultic abuse (Smith 1971, 133). Perhaps the period immediately after these measures was the high-water mark of the reform movement. Nevertheless, that divisions within the community had been exacerbated by Nehemiah's reforms is evident from his bold measure expelling from Jerusalem the son-in-law of Sanballat, governor of Samaria. This son-in-law was also the grandson of the ruling high priest of the period, Eliashib (13:28).

This sustained attack on priestly privilege by these reformers was not to prevail. After 400 B.C., that is, after the close of the Ezra-Nehemiah period, the power of the Jerusalem priesthood gradually became dominant, and the theology which had prompted the Ezra-Nehemiah movement became one of popular hope, being taken up about 150 B.C. in the rise of the Pharisaic movement.

The Ezra-Nehemiah complex covers a period of some 140 years. It begins by offering, in the Cyrus edict, encouragement for the Jewish community to return and to rebuild its theocratic institutions and thus to prepare for the eschatological "shaking of the nations" for which Haggai and Zechariah looked. At the conclusion to the Book of Nehemiah, the period ends upon a note of profound disappointment, with the community wracked by divisions between the priesthood and the laity. The Nehemiah party is opposed by a Jerusalem officialdom supported in turn by a powerful Samaria faction whose Persian sympathies, we know from extrabiblical sources, are pronounced. Although the Ezra-Nehemiah period began with the high hopes attached to the Cyrus edict, it ends with a frank admission by the author of Nehemiah of the failure of an experiment and with the community divided.

The pendulum was poised to swing against the reforms. With the advent around 400 B.C. of direct Persian government, a Jewish state emerged that was dominated by the priesthood. This government would endure, with all its tight bureaucratic authority, until the Maccabean revolt. Against the background of this failure and the despair in pious circles that it engendered, the Books of Chronicles, as we shall argue, were probably written. But with Ezra-Nehemiah the stirring of new and important lay movements within Judaism had begun. The political wielding of entrenched priestly power prevented the initiatives of the period from bearing fruit, however. Subsequent to the Maccabean revolt the Pharisees countered this priestly power, but it took the greatest of all lay reformers, Jesus of Nazareth, to put this power finally to rest and to introduce the measures whereby divine government, a hope which had inspired Ezra and Nehemiah, could operate.

35

Chronicles

In the Hebrew Bible, Chronicles ends the Old Testament canon. Since the Books of Chronicles probably represent the latest composition within the Old Testament, this placement may be justified on historical grounds alone. Yet the shape of the canon seems to have been theologically ordered, and the similarity between Genesis and Chronicles has often been commented upon. Like Genesis, Chronicles begins with creation, tracing the human race from Adam before narrowing the divine choice at the beginning of the second chapter down to Jacob (Israel). Both Genesis and Chronicles end with a prospect of redemption and a prophecy of a return to the land. Moreover, Chronicles neatly summarizes the theology of the canon, ending its account at the exile but maintaining an open-ended attitude to the future.

The closing verses of 2 Chronicles (36:22–23) inform us that the end of the exile as prophesied by Jeremiah (Jer. 25:12) occurred in the first year of the Persian king Cyrus. Yahweh stirred up the spirit of Cyrus, who then made a proclamation throughout his kingdom, thereby putting his own realm into the context of a general world rule by Yahweh.

The decree, which is stated in terms of a commission given to Cyrus by Yahweh, directed the exiled Jews to return to Jerusalem to rebuild the temple of Yahweh. As we have seen, these closing verses of Chronicles appear as Ezra 1:1–3. This linkage suggests the continuity of the two works, a position held as axiomatic until perhaps the last two decades. On such an assumption the Books of Chronicles were theologically preparatory for the work of Ezra-Nehemiah which followed. Thus the purpose of Chronicles was traditionally assumed to be support for the community reforms which Ezra and Nehemiah endeavored to implement.

The balance of scholarship now seems to favor separation of the two works. The theological differences in stance, however, which are often appealed to, are not compelling. Our survey of Ezra-Nehemiah has indicated that these books deal with the formation of an ideal worshiping unit, Israel, centered around the present purified temple. These theological considerations are in fact shared by the Chronicler, who goes, however, somewhat beyond Ezra-Nehemiah in the pronounced eschatological note that characterizes his work.

Despite theories that much of the books existed as a first draft in the Haggai-Zechariah period (expansions then occurring by adding the genealogies of 1 Chron. 1–9, etc.), any attempt to date the books must come to terms with the material in 1 Chronicles 3:17–24, which seems to take the Davidic dynasty down to about 400 B.C. This majority opinion for the dating of the books between 400 and 350 B.C. may be sustained by an understanding of their purpose, a task which we now undertake. We may outline Chronicles as follows:

1 Chron.	**1–9**	Genealogies
	10	Saul
	11–29	David
2 Chron.	**1–9**	Solomon
	10–36	The history of the south: Rehoboam to the exile

Genealogies and the Purpose of Chronicles (1 Chron. 1–9)

The genealogies in 1 Chronicles 1–9 provide clues to the purpose of the books. These genealogies are concerned with God's design for all Israel (as the concentration of interest indicates), but with special attention being given to Judah and Levi. The first chapter moves from the broad base of creation, tracing the links through Abraham and Isaac. Chapter 2 then begins with Jacob, concentrating thus upon the holy line of Israel as it will be displayed through the twelve tribes. In short, the

Chronicler is keen to assert that the purposes of God in creation are realized through Israel in the Old Testament. Indeed, the unity of all Israel as a covenant people determined by divine election is emphasized throughout the two books. It has been noted that Jacob is consistently called Israel in these early chapters (1:34; 2:1; 5:1; 6:38; 7:29). There is a brief genealogical attention to all tribes except Dan and Zebulun (both situated in the extreme north), but the major focus of interest is upon Judah and Levi, or, put otherwise, upon the dual structure of prince and priest which was fundamental to the thinking of the postexilic community, a pattern of thought dependent upon Ezekiel 40–48.

This emphasis upon the nature of the true Israel and its leadership is brought to a climax in 1 Chronicles 9, which names some of those who participated in the reestablishment of Israel after the exile. As many have noted, all of this reflects the Chronicler's stress on "all Israel." (This phrase is a favorite one of the books, occurring more than thirty times.)

The Reigns of Saul and David (1 Chron. 10–29)

The Chronicler begins his account of the monarchical period with the reign of Saul, showing how this disastrous kingship left the state bereft and exposed to the Philistines. Thus the author puts before his audience the catastrophe which resulted from Saul's rule. In chapters 11–16 the ark is the major topic; the capture of Jerusalem and the anointing of David are subordinated here to the primary concern of bringing the ark to Jerusalem. It is pointedly remarked that Saul had neglected the ark (13:3).

Chapters 17–29 discuss the Davidic preparations for the building of the temple. A prime indication of purpose is given by the Chronicler in chapter 17, especially verse 14, where the settlement of kingship on Solomon is bound up with the more primary matters of the temple and the kingdom of God. David's reign, which is to be extended through Solomon, is highly commended. God has taken the kingdom away from Saul and given it to David, who has been chosen to build the temple, for which there were plans in writing from the hand of the Lord (28:19). Solomon's function is to build "a house of rest" for Yahweh (v. 2). Thus the construction of the temple serves to underscore the theocratic note of kingdom. This link between temple building and the kingdom of God finds its theological conclusion in Cyrus's edict to restore the temple, recorded at the end of 2 Chronicles. In passing we might note that the Chronicler does not appear to have been interested in the person of David in terms of any messianic expectations, nor does he glorify Solomon later individually. The concentration of interest upon these two personalities in Chronicles is in connection with their roles as temple builders.

The Chronicler does not hesitate to use material which is discreditable to David. The census and ensuing plague in 1 Chronicles 21 (cf. 2 Sam. 24), for which David was responsible, are reported in detail because they contribute to the narratives concerning temple erection. The remainder of 1 Chronicles concerns the temple personnel and various administrative measures preparatory to the building of the actual Solomonic temple—matters of great importance to the community of the fourth century B.C.

The Reign of Solomon (2 Chron. 1–9)

Solomon is viewed merely as the builder of the temple and not, as some have suggested, the perpetuator of the Davidic dynasty. He is portrayed as the builder of a house of rest for Yahweh (1 Chron. 28:2), indicating again the concern of the writer with theocracy and not with messianism. Congruent with this emphasis is the manner in which 2 Chronicles 1 presents Yahweh's donation of wisdom to Solomon. While in 1 Kings 3 Solomon's receipt of wisdom is connected with the theme of his good government, in 2 Chronicles 1 the donation occurs in close conjunction with the account dealing with the transfer of cultic interest from the great high place of Gibeon to Jerusalem. Solomon is presented in these chapters as a zealous patron of the cult and the builder of the temple, surpassing even David. Almost the whole of chapters 2–8 narrates the building of the temple, while the fact that the commencement of his reign is placed at Gibeon serves to emphasize how Solomon led all Israel in procession from Gibeon to the true shrine. The most significant event of his reign is the dedication of the temple, and the major moments connected with it—the transfer of the ark (chap. 5) and Solomon's prayer of dedication (7:1–3)—are both marked by divine epiphanies. As he does with David, the Chronicler in his presentation of Solomon ignores almost everything which is noncultic.

It is consistent with the emphasis in Chronicles on the kingdom of God that the reign of Solomon ends with the pilgrimage of the queen of Sheba to the wisdom and splendor of the Solomonic court. This court is a symbol pointing beyond itself to a higher reality. Thus the Sabean queen comes as the representative of her world (cf. 2 Chron. 9:23). All the indications of a Gentile pilgrimage to the divine city are there, and we may therefore understand why earlier in Solomon's reign the Gentile Hiram of Tyre confessed that God had given the kingdom to David's son to build a house for the Lord (2:12).

History of the Southern Kingdom
(2 Chron. 10–36)

In keeping with the theocratic interest to which we have pointed, 2 Chronicles 10–36 emphasizes the prophetic direction to which the southern kingdom was subject after the building of the temple. Direction of the kingdom through prophecy had always been a characterizing feature of the period of the united monarchy. As a result of the focus in Chronicles on "all Israel," we might expect that in the period of the divided kingdom a good deal of attention would be paid by the writer to the fortunes and future of the north. But since the southern kingdom is the visible carrier of the Israel concept, 2 Chronicles, unlike the Books of Kings, concentrates almost exclusively on the southern kings. Good kings such as Asa, Joash, Hezekiah, and Josiah either make appeals to the north or reform the temple or both. A Solomonic type of restoration occurs under Hezekiah, whose reforms to the temple are treated at great length. Both Hezekiah and the subsequent Josiah center their reforms on a missionary thrust to the north, with the aim of an Israel of twelve tribes united under a Davidic king. Hezekiah begins at the cultic center, cleansing the temple. Once again Israel, by this symbolic act of the cleansing of temple and land, together with the celebration of the Passover under Hezekiah, is restored to an exodus situation: the people of God are fitted for occupancy of the land. While Hezekiah becomes a second Solomon, Josiah is the promoter of a Davidic revival. The provisionality of the Solomonic temple is made clear by the profanation to which Josiah's successors subject it (2 Chron. 36:14) and of course by its ultimate destruction. Yahweh has warned north and south by his prophets, but such counsel has never been received (vv. 15–16). Consequently, the symbol of the theocracy, the temple, is finally destroyed, and its sacred vessels carried into captivity (vv. 17–18). These calamities fulfil Jeremiah's prophecy of seventy years of exile (v. 21), a situation which the Cyrus edict is designed to reverse (vv. 22–23).

Older expositors saw Chronicles as motivated by an anti-Samaritan polemic, with its "all Israel" theology providing the counter. But it is clear that to regard the Chronicler merely as a southern sectarian is to misread the plain facts of his work, since for him there is only one Israel. The writer is interested in the construction in his own day of an ideal worshiping unit, Israel, centered in a purified temple.

The view that the Chronicler is a proponent of Davidic-Solomonic messianism (with David and Solomon related as promise and fulfilment) still enjoys popularity. Of course, the Davidic-Solomonic emphasis of the Books of Chronicles is not in dispute. There is a concentration upon the eternal dynasty of David, and David and Solomon are presented as promise and fulfilment. The function of the Solomonic account is to assure us that the eternal character of the dynasty has been secured. We must not, however, place too much emphasis upon this dynastic hypothesis. Rather, we must read the ideal presentations of David and Solomon in Chronicles against the frequent indications that David was not without his faults (cf. 1 Chron. 13 with 15:11, 13; see also chap. 21; 22:7–8; 28:3). All this is quite apart from the common traditions of Samuel and Kings, which were certainly available to the Chronicler and which reflect so adversely upon the character of these two kings. It makes more sense, then, to suppose that the function of the Davidic-Solomonic narratives in Chronicles is theocratic, emphasizing the kingdom of God more than the dynasty. In the exilic and postexilic writings there is an absence of any particularly messianic emphasis other than what is supposedly found in Chronicles. The restoration prophecies of Isaiah 40–55 contain virtually no mention of any Davidic hope, nor does the Book of Ezekiel, which emphasizes God's kingship (e.g., Ezek. 20:33). No Davidic presence in the new temple is described in Ezekiel 40–48. True, Ezekiel 17:22 affirms that God has not forgotten his Davidic promises, but that passage may be only remotely messianic, while the review in Ezekiel 19 of Judean kingship from 609 B.C. onward ends on a note of lament and thus without prospect for the Davidic house.

Nor can Haggai and Zechariah be drawn into this debate with any real conviction. Zerubbabel is admittedly a replacement for Jehoiachin in Haggai 2:23, since that verse has Jeremiah 22:24 in view, but he is addressed in that section as governor of Judah (Hag. 2:21). He is probably therefore operating as no more than a continuity figure, only a very general reminder of God's fidelity to the promises to David. The evidence for messianism from Zechariah is likewise very slender. Of course Zerubbabel, who is venerated in both Haggai and Zechariah, is the temple builder, and in that sense he continues the hopes expressed in the Davidic promises. But on the whole there seems to be little real interest in messianism.

The edict of Cyrus at the end of 2 Chronicles raises for us the particular question of purpose and the eschatological direction of the Books of Chronicles. The language of 2 Chronicles 36:22–23 sustains for the generation of the Chronicler the projections of a new exodus that were set by Isaiah 40–55. (The return to the land, the renewal of the covenant, and the building of the temple are all implied or articulated by this theme.) This focus is clearly congruent with the second-exodus emphasis of

Ezra-Nehemiah. The message of Chronicles, then, is that the kingdom of God will come, the second exodus will occur. Jerusalem will be the world center to which Gentile kings will come. If the Books of Chronicles were written to introduce the Ezra-Nehemiah reforms, then we might see this work as setting the tone for the second-exodus theology of those books, whose reform movement eventually failed. But if, as is more likely, Chronicles is to be separated from Ezra-Nehemiah, then the Cyrus edict is used as a conclusion in order to indicate that the failed Ezra-Nehemiah reforms had set directions which were to be maintained. The temple-centered society of the postexilic period had set a model of divine government. Thus the tenor of traditional prophetic eschatology (Isa. 2:2–4; Mic. 4:1–5) has been preserved.

Between 400 and 350 B.C. the Chronicler looked back to the program of Isaiah 40–55, to which the decree of Cyrus had called attention. That program had not been implemented, though the exile had historically ended. But this did not mean that the second exodus would not occur. Indeed, the recent efforts of the Ezra-Nehemiah period were attempts to implement the program. Chronicles injects a note of hope into a tired community. Yes, the physical exile has ended, and the future is now open-ended. The theology of Isaiah and the measures taken by Ezra-Nehemiah point toward the future. The Books of Chronicles refer to ideal, eschatological Israel. The notion of an ideal Israel under a theocracy, the model kingdom by which the world will be drawn, is thus presented by the Chronicler in a basic restatement of the older prophetic positions. God will not withdraw from his commitment to the world, a commitment given at creation and then affirmed through the call of Israel. Accordingly, the disappointments of the present, argues the Chronicler, must spawn a theology of hope.

Bibliography

Ackroyd, P. R. 1968. *Exile and Restoration*. Philadelphia: Westminster.
———. 1970. *The Age of the Chronicler*. Selwyn Lectures for 1970. Supplement to *Colloquium: The Australia and New Zealand Theological Review*.
———. 1978. "Isaiah 1–12: Presentation of a Prophet." VTSup 29:16–48.
Andersen, F. I. 1958. "Who Built the Second Temple?" *ABR* 6:1–35.
———. 1976. *Job: An Introduction and Commentary*. Downers Grove, Ill.: Inter-Varsity.
Andersen, F. I., and D. N. Freedman. 1980. *Hosea: A New Translation, with Introduction and Commentary*. Garden City, N.Y.: Doubleday.
Barton, J. 1980. *Amos's Oracles Against the Nations: A Study of Amos 1:3–2:5*. Cambridge: Cambridge University Press.
Berg, S. B. 1979. *The Book of Esther*. Missoula, Mont.: Scholars.
Beuken, W. A. M. 1967. *Haggai-Sacharja 1–8*. Assen: Van Gorcum.
———. 1972. "Mišpāṭ, the First Servant Song in Its Context." *VT* 22:1–30.
Bird, P. 1981. "'Male and Female He Created Them': Gen. 1:27b in the Context of the Priestly Account of Creation." *HTR* 74:129–59.

Blocher, H. 1977. "The Fear of the Lord as the 'Principle' of Wisdom."
  TynB 28:3–28.
Brueggemann, W. 1969. "Amos' Intercessory Formula." *VT* 19:385–99.
———. 1972. "Life and Death in Tenth-Century Israel." *JAAR* 40:96–
  109.
Campbell, A. F. 1975. *The Ark Narrative.* Missoula, Mont.: Scholars.
Campbell, E. F. 1975. *Ruth.* Anchor Bible. New York: Doubleday.
Carlson, R. A. 1964. *David the Chosen King.* Stockholm: Almqvist and
  Wiksell.
Childs, B. S. 1978. "The Exegetical Significance of Canon for the Study of
  the Old Testament." VTSup 29:66–80.
———. 1979. *Introduction to the Old Testament as Scripture.* Philadel-
  phia: Fortress.
Clark, W. M. 1969. "A Legal Background to the Yahwist's Use of 'Good
  and Evil' in Genesis 2–3." *JBL* 88:266–78.
Cohn, G. C. 1969. *Das Buch Jona im Lichte der biblischen Erzählkunst.*
  Assen: Van Gorcum.
Collins, J. J. 1977. *The Apocalyptic Vision of the Book of Daniel.* Mis-
  soula, Mont.: Scholars.
Davies, E. W. 1983. "Ruth IV 5 and the Duties of the Gō'ēl." *VT* 33:231–
  34.
De Vaux, R. 1970. "The Revelation of the Divine Name YHWH." In *Proc-
  lamation and Presence: Old Testament Essays in Honour of G. H.
  Davies,* ed. J. I. Durham and J. R. Porter, 48–75. London: SCM.
De Waard, J. 1977. "The Chiastic Spirit of Amos 5:1–17." *VT* 27:170–77.
Duhm, B. 1892. *Das Buch Jesaia übersetzt und erklärt.* Göttingen:
  Vandenhoeck and Ruprecht.
Dumbrell, W. J. 1974. "Spirit and Kingdom in the Old Testament." *RTR*
  33:1–10.
———. 1977. "Some Observations on the Political Origins of Israel's Es-
  chatology." *RTR* 36:33–41.
Erlandsson, S. 1970. *The Burden of Babylon.* ConBibOT 4. Lund:
  Gleerup.
Eybers, I. H. 1976. "Chronological Problems in Ezra-Nehemiah."
  OTWSA 19:10–29.
Falk, M. 1982. *Love Lyrics from the Bible.* Sheffield: Almond.
Fishbane, M. 1975. "Composition and Structure in the Jacob Cycle
  (Gen. 25:19–35:22)." *JJS* 26:15–38.
———. 1979. *Text and Texture.* New York: Schocken.
Fokkelman, J. P. 1975. *Narrative Art in Genesis.* Assen: Van Gorcum.
Fox, M. V. 1977. "Frame-Narrative and Composition in the Book of
  Qohelet." *HUCA* 48:83–106.
Fretheim, T. E. 1978. "Jonah and Theodicy." *ZAW* 90:227–37.

Gitay, Y. 1980. "A Study of Amos's Art of Speech: A Rhetorical Analysis of Amos 3:1–15." *CBQ* 42:293–309.

Greenberg, M. 1972. "The Plagues of Egypt." In *EJ* 13:604–13.

———. 1983. *Ezekiel 1–20*. Anchor Bible. New York: Doubleday.

Halpern, B. 1974. "Sectionalism and the Schism." *JBL* 93:519–32.

———. 1978. "The Ritual Background of Zechariah's Temple Song." *CBQ* 40:167–90.

Hanson, P. D. 1975. *The Dawn of Apocalyptic*. Philadelphia: Fortress.

Haran, M. 1978. *Temples and Temple-Service in Ancient Israel*. Oxford: Clarendon.

Holladay, W. L. 1974. *Jeremiah: Spokesman Out of Time*. Philadelphia: Pilgrim.

Houser, M. K. 1978. "Holiness in the Book of Leviticus." Master's thesis, Regent College.

Hunter, A. V. 1980. *Seek the Lord! A Study of the Meaning and Function of the Exhortation in Amos, Hosea, Isaiah, Micah, and Zephaniah*. Baltimore: St. Mary's Seminary and University.

Janzen, J. G. 1982. "Eschatological Symbol and Existence in Habakkuk." *CBQ* 44:394–414.

———. 1983. "Samuel Opened the Doors of the House of YHWH." *JSOT* 26:89–96.

Jensen, J. 1979. "The Age of Immanuel." *CBQ* 41:220–39.

Johnson, B. 1985. "Form and Message in Lamentations." *ZAW* 97:58–73.

Jones, B. W. 1978. "The So-Called Appendix to the Book of Esther." *Semitics* 6:36–43.

Kaiser, W. C., Jr. 1974. "The Blessing of David: The Charter for Humanity." In *The Law and the Prophets: Old Testament Studies in Honor of O. T. Allis*, ed. J. H. Skilton, 298–318. Nutley, N.J.: Presbyterian and Reformed.

Kiesow, K. 1979. *Exodustexte im Jesajabuch*. Göttingen: Vandenhoeck and Ruprecht.

Knierim, R. 1968. "The Messianic Concept in the First Book of Samuel." In *Jesus and the Historian*, ed. F. T. Trotter. Philadelphia: Westminster.

Koch, K. 1974. "Ezra and the Origins of Judaism." *JSS* 19:173–97.

Kooy, V. H. 1975. "The Fear and Love of God in Deuteronomy." In *Grace upon Grace: Essays in Honor of L. J. Kuyper*, ed. J. I. Cook, 106–16. Grand Rapids: Eerdmans.

Kraus, H.-J. 1966. *Worship in Israel*. Oxford: Blackwell.

Landy, F. 1983. *Paradoxes of Paradise: Identity and Difference in the Song of Songs*. Sheffield: Almond.

Levenson, J. D. 1976. *The Theology of the Program of Restoration of Ezekiel 40–48*. Missoula, Mont.: Scholars.

Loader, J. A. 1978. "Esther as a Novel with Different Levels of Meaning." *ZAW* 90:417–21.

———. 1979. *Polar Structures in the Book of Qohelet*. Berlin: De Gruyter.

Lohfink, N. 1969. *Christian Meaning of the Old Testament*. London: Burns and Oates.

Lundbom, J. R. 1975. *Jeremiah—A Study in Ancient Hebrew Rhetoric*. Missoula, Mont.: Scholars.

McCarter, P. K. 1980. "The Apology of David." *JBL* 99:489–504.

McConville, J. G. 1979. "God's 'Name' and God's 'Glory.'" *TynB* 30:149–63.

———. 1984. *Law and Theology*. Sheffield: Sheffield University Press.

McKenzie, S. L., and H. N. Wallace. 1983. "Covenant Themes in Malachi." *CBQ* 45:549–63.

Magonet, J. 1983. *Form and Meaning: Studies in Literary Techniques in the Book of Jonah*. Sheffield: Almond.

Malamat, A. 1968. "The Last Kings of Judah and the Fall of Jerusalem." *IEJ* 18:137–56.

———. 1976. "Charismatic Leadership in the Book of Judges." In *Magnalia Dei: The Mighty Acts of God—Essays on the Bible and Archaeology in Memory of G. Ernest Wright*, ed. F. M. Cross et al., 152–68. Garden City, N.Y.: Doubleday.

Mettinger, T. N. D. 1976. *King and Messiah*. ConBibOT 8. Lund: Gleerup.

Milgrom, J. 1975. "The Priestly Doctrine of Repentance." *RB* 82:186–205.

Millar, W. 1976. *Isaiah 24–27 and the Origin of Apocalyptic*. Missoula, Mont.: Scholars.

Miller, P. D. 1969. "The Gift of God: The Deuteronomic Theology of the Land." *Int* 23:451–65.

Nel, P. 1982. *Structure and Ethos of the Wisdom Admonitions in Proverbs*. Berlin: De Gruyter.

Niditch, S. 1986. "Ezekiel 40–48 in a Visionary Context." *CBQ* 48:208–24.

Ogden, G. S. 1979. "Qoheleth's Use of the 'Nothing Is Better' Form." *JBL* 98:339–50.

———. 1980. "Qoheleth 9:17–10:20: Variations on the Theme of Wisdom's Strength and Vulnerability." *VT* 30:27–37.

———. 1983. "Qoheleth 11:1–6." *VT* 33:222–30.

———. 1984. "The Mathematics of Wisdom: Qoheleth 4:1–12." *VT* 34:446–53.

Olson, D. 1985. *The Death of the Old and the Birth of the New: The*

Framework of the Book of Numbers and the Pentateuch. Chico, Calif.: Scholars.

Parunak, H. V. 1979. "Structural Studies in Ezekiel." Ph.D. diss., Harvard University.

———. 1980. "The Literary Architecture of Ezekiel's *MAR'ÔT 'ĔLŌHÎM*." *JBL* 99:61–74.

Paul, S. M. 1970. *Studies in the Book of the Covenant in the Light of Cuneiform and Biblical Law*. VTSup 18.

———. 1971. "Amos 1:3–2:3: A Concatenous Literary Pattern." *JBL* 90:397–403.

———. 1972. "Prophets and Prophecy." In *EJ* 13:1150–75.

Petersen, D. L. 1977. *Late Israelite Prophecy*. Missoula, Mont.: Scholars.

Porten, B. 1967. "The Structure and Theme of the Solomon Narrative (1 Kings 3–11)." *HUCA* 38:93–128.

Prinsloo, W. S. 1980. "The Theology of the Book of Ruth." *VT* 30:330–41.

———. 1985. *The Theology of the Book of Joel*. Hawthorne, N.Y.: De Gruyter.

Rainey, A. F. 1970. "The Order of Sacrifices in the Old Testament Ritual Texts." *Bib* 51:485–98.

Robinson, G. 1980. "The Idea of Rest in the Old Testament and the Search for the Basic Character of Sabbath." *ZAW* 92:32–42.

Sakenfeld, K. 1975. "The Problem of Divine Forgiveness in Numbers 14." *CBQ* 37:317–30.

Schmidt, W. H. 1973. *Die Schöpfungsgeschichte der Priesterschrift*. 3d ed. Neukirchen-Vluyn: Neukirchener.

Smith, M. H. 1971. *Palestinian Parties and Politics That Shaped the Old Testament*. New York: Columbia University Press.

Talmon, S. 1953. "The Sectarian *yaḥad*—A Biblical Noun." *VT* 3:133–40.

———. 1976. "Ezra and Nehemiah." In *IDBSup*, 317–28.

Thompson, J. A. 1980. *The Book of Jeremiah*. Grand Rapids: Eerdmans.

Toombs, L. E. 1965. "Love and Justice in Deuteronomy: A Third Approach to the Law." *Int* 19:339–411.

van der Woude, A. S. 1969. "Micah in Dispute with the Pseudo-Prophets." *VT* 19:244–60.

Vannoy, J. R. 1978. *Covenant Renewal at Gilgal*. Cherry Hill, N.J.: Mack.

von Waldow, H. E. 1974. "Israel and Her Land: Some Theological Considerations." In *A Light unto My Path: Old Testament Studies in Honor of J. M. Myers*, ed. H. N. Bream et al., 493–508. Philadelphia: Temple University Press.

Walsh, J. T. 1977. "Genesis 2:4b–3:24: A Synchronic Approach." *JBL* 96:161–77.

———. 1982. "Jonah 2:3–10: A Rhetorical Critical Study." *Bib* 63:219–29.

Waltke, B. K. 1979. "The Book of Proverbs and Ancient Wisdom Literature." *BibSac* 136:221–38.

Weinfeld, M. 1972. *Deuteronomy and the Deuteronomic School*. Oxford: Oxford University Press.

Wenham, G. J. 1971. "The Deuteronomic Theology of the Book of Joshua." *JBL* 90:140–48.

———. 1979. *The Book of Leviticus*. NICOT 13. Grand Rapids: Eerdmans.

Williamson, H. G. M. 1983. "The Composition of Ezra 1–6." *JTS* 34:1–29.

Willis, J. T. 1969. "The Structure of the Book of Micah." *SEÅ* 34:5–42.

Wilson, G. H. 1985. *The Editing of the Hebrew Psalter*. Chico, Calif.: Scholars.

Wilson, R. R. 1972. "The Interpretation of Ezekiel's Dumbness." *VT* 22:91–104.

Zimmerli, W. 1979. *Ezekiel I: A Commentary upon the Book of the Prophet Ezekiel, Chapters 1–24*. Philadelphia: Fortress.

———. 1982. *I Am Yahweh*. Atlanta: John Knox.